Blood, Sweat, and Mahjong

To Estelle
with affection!
Ellen

A volume in the series

Anthropology of Contemporary Issues

EDITED BY ROGER SANJEK

A full list of titles in the series appears at the end of the book.

Blood, Sweat, and Mahjong

FAMILY AND ENTERPRISE IN AN OVERSEAS CHINESE COMMUNITY

Ellen Oxfeld

Cornell University Press

Ithaca and London

First published 1993 by Cornell University Press.

Library of Congress Cataloging-in-Publication Data

Oxfeld, Ellen, 1953–
   Blood, sweat, and mahjong : family and enterprise in an overseas Chinese community / Ellen Oxfeld.
       p.   cm. — (Anthropology of contemporary issues)
   Includes bibliographical references and index.
   ISBN 0-8014-2593-X (cloth : alk. paper). — ISBN 0-8014-9908-9 (paper : alk. paper)
       1. Chinese—India—Calcutta.   2. India—Ethnic relations.   I. Title.
II. Series.
DS432.C5094   1993
954′.147004951—dc20   92-56779

Printed in the United States of America

For my parents

Contents

Preface

This book is about individuals and families in movement, their harmonious and conflicting relationships with one another and with those they consider outsiders, and their steadfast convictions as well as their ambivalent and contradictory beliefs and attitudes. I focus on these issues through an examination of the family dynamics, ethnic role, and ideological orientations of members of a diaspora Chinese community located in Calcutta, India. Tracing the pathways of community members across time and space, I include within my purview both their initial emigration from China to India and their subsequent immigration to North America.

As with many projects, the beginnings of this one are not easy to identify definitively. My interests in the cultures and histories of East and South Asia go back to high school days and deepened during my years at Williams College. After graduation from college, I was the fortunate recipient of a Thomas J. Watson Foundation Fellowship, which enabled me to study Chinese in Taiwan and Hong Kong and also to travel through Thailand and India. It was on this trip that I became aware that Calcutta was home to a rather fascinating overseas Chinese community. I returned to the United States to study social and cultural anthropology at Harvard University, and when the time came for me to choose a site for fieldwork, I decided that an investigation of the Calcutta Chinese community could combine my interests in Chinese culture, Indian society, and the dilemmas and difficulties faced by ethnic minorities.

I was especially fortunate in that the members of the Calcutta Chi-

[ix]

nese community generously extended their hospitality and opened their lives to me. It is to them, therefore, that I owe the greatest debt of gratitude. So many community members came to my assistance that it would be impossible to thank each one individually. I would, however, like to thank in particular Lee Chiu Fong, Chen Kuin Fong, and their respective families. Both were more than generous hosts, and Lee Chiu Fong, who had an instinctive sense of the kinds of issues I was interested in, was (and still is) an endless source of information and insight.

I also thank the Anthropological Survey of India in Calcutta, with which I was affiliated during my research from 1980 to 1982. Hirendra K. Rakshit, who served as its director at that time, guided me in the intricacies of obtaining necessary official approval for my research. Jyoti Sen, who was my adviser at the Survey, provided many hours of stimulating ideas and advice. My fieldwork in 1980–81 was funded by the American Institute of Indian Studies (AIIS), and in 1981–82 I received financial support from a National Resource Fellowship. During both of these years, Tarun Mitra, the director of the AIIS office in Calcutta, was of invaluable assistance in both the logistical and bureaucratic aspects of my research. Purnendu Bose, reknowned for his camera work in Indian films, and his family in Calcutta were also a source of friendship, technical support, and intellectual stimulation, as were the members of the Basu family of Kalyani and Calcutta.

Summer research in Toronto in 1986 and a trip to Calcutta in 1989 were partially funded by the Middlebury College professional development fund, and the completion of this book was made possible by an academic leave from Middlebury College during the 1990–91 school year. While I was in Toronto, both Dee and Peter Thompson and C. C. Chen were particularly helpful.

During the writing of this book I profited immensely from the acumen and discernment of many distinguished scholars within and outside of Middlebury College. In particular, I thank Rubie Watson, Hill Gates, Stevan Harrell, Arthur Kleinman, Susan Brownell, Jean Burfoot, Lynel Long, Claudia Strauss, David Nugent, Jan Albers, Paul Monod, Shank Gilkeson, Susan Gray, and Burke Rochford for their insightful comments on portions of the manuscript. Thanks also go to Nur Yalman, Sally Falk Moore, Ezra Vogel, and Myron Cohen, who read much of this material in earlier incarnations and who gave many invaluable recommendations. In that regard, I also mention the late Judith Strauch, who served as one of my advisers at Harvard. Although she did not live to see the completion of my project, her work on overseas Chinese and on ethnicity served as a model for me, and her supportive guidance and friendship will always be remembered.

I am also grateful to both an anonymous reviewer for Cornell University Press and Roger Sanjek, the editor of the Anthropology of Contemporary Issues series at Cornell. Their suggestions and criticisms helped me to create a more focused theoretical discussion and a greater degree of ethnographic depth in the final version of the manuscript.

Finally, a special thanks goes to my parents, Edith and Emil Oxfeld. In addition to their everpresent moral support, they were tireless proofreaders. Reading and rereading numerous drafts and ferreting out countless awkward phrasings, they applied themselves to the task with unfailing patience and abiding good humor.

Earlier versions of three chapters appeared in the following journals: Chapter 4 as "Profit, Loss, and Fate: The Entrepreneurial Ethic and the Practice of Gambling in an Overseas Chinese Community," *Modern China* 17(2) (1991):227–259; Chapter 6 as "The Sexual Division of Labor and the Organization of the Family and Firm in an Overseas Chinese Community," *American Ethnologist* 18(4) (1991): 700–718; and Chapter 8 as "Individualism, Holism, and the Market Mentality: Notes on the Recollections of a Chinese Entrepreneur," *Cultural Anthropology* 8(3) (1992):267–300. I thank Sage Publications,publisher of *Modern China,* and the American Anthropological Association, publisher of *American Ethnologist* and *Cultural Anthropology,* for permission to reprint (not for sale or further reproduction).

ELLEN OXFELD

Middlebury, Vermont

A Note on Chinese
Romanization and Names

Because most of the interviews I conducted in Chinese were in Mandarin rather than Hakka, all Chinese expressions in this book have been romanized in Mandarin. With the exception of Chinese words included in direct quotations from other sources, these expressions are romanized according to the pinyin system. In quotations where Chinese words are spelled according to different systems of romanization, and where these spellings differ markedly from the pinyin versions, I have added the pinyin romanizations in brackets. Chinese names are spelled with the surnames first when they come from a Chinese source, when they refer to members of the Calcutta Chinese community, or when they refer to a well-known person whose name is conventionally spelled with the surname first (such as Mao Zedong). Chinese names are spelled with the surname last when they refer to authors of essays or books in English. The names used to refer to members of the Hakka Chinese community, both in Calcutta and in Toronto, are pseudonyms.

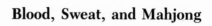

Blood, Sweat, and Mahjong

[1]

Family Trajectories and
Pariah Enterprise: Hakka
Chinese Tanners of Calcutta

It is a warm August morning in Scarborough, an eastern suburb of Toronto. As I walk along the quiet empty streets lined with rows of two-story brick houses, my thoughts shift from the setting before me to the energetic and densely inhabited streets of Calcutta, where I lived between 1980 and 1982.

Calcutta is a pulsating city, a mosaic of different ethnic, caste, and religious groups. The worldwide fame of Mother Teresa, and other individuals who work with Calcutta's poor, has created a popular image of Calcutta as a sea of poverty and destitution. But while the poor are indeed present in Calcutta, the city is also the commercial, industrial, and intellectual center of northeast India. It is a city of many faces. As the journalist William Stevens wrote: "For a city long pictured as the ultimate urban disaster area, a place of putrefying decay and absolute human misery, Calcutta rises awfully early, works awfully hard and radiates an astonishing amount of energy" (1983).

Chinese Tanners of Calcutta—Remembering the Setting

During the years 1980–82, and again in the summers of 1985 and 1989, I conducted fieldwork in a community of Hakka Chinese who had found a profitable niche in Calcutta's leather industry. The Hakka are a distinctive speech group who live in certain regions of the southeastern Chinese provinces of Guangdong, Fujian and Jiangxi (see Map 1). It is thought, however, that they migrated to south China several

[1]

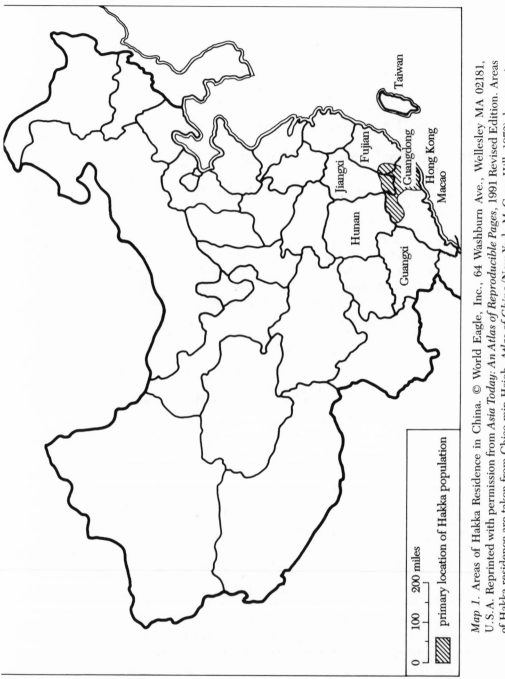

Map 1. Areas of Hakka Residence in China. © World Eagle, Inc., 64 Washburn Ave., Wellesley MA 02181, U.S.A. Reprinted with permission from *Asia Today: An Atlas of Reproducible Pages*, 1991 Revised Edition. Areas of Hakka residence are taken from Chiao-min Hsieh, *Atlas of China* (New York: McGraw-Hill, 1973), by permis-

Taiwan

Fujian

Jiangxi

Guangdong

Hong Kong

Macao

Hunan

Guangxi

0   100   200 miles

primary location of Hakka population

centuries ago from the north. Indeed, the word *hakka* means "guest people" in Cantonese, and the Hakka therefore received their name from speakers of the Cantonese language, who consider themselves to be the natives of Guangdong Province (Cohen 1968:247).

A small number of Hakka Chinese immigrants to Calcutta entered into the manufacture of leather during the World War I era. This occupation, considered to be polluting by high-caste Hindus and normally left to untouchables or Muslims, proved to be a lucrative source of income. Although the entire Chinese population of Calcutta consists of no more than eight thousand individuals, the Hakka Chinese now own and operate the vast majority of tanneries there, and their contribution to the Indian leather industry is far from negligible on a national scale. Calcutta is one of three major centers of the tanning industry in India, surpassed only by the cities of Madras in the south and Kanpur in the north.

The Hakka do not comprise Calcutta's entire Chinese population. Cantonese-speaking immigrants from Guangdong Province and immigrants from the central Chinese province of Hubei have also settled in Calcutta. The Cantonese are known primarily as carpenters, whereas the major business of the small Hubeinese community is the operation of dental clinics. In addition, the Hakka Chinese themselves are involved in other industries besides tanning. They own and operate shoe shops, hairdressing salons, and restaurants. But the tanning industry still engages the largest number of Calcutta's Hakka population, and the Hakka community itself is by far the largest of the three Chinese subgroups.[1]

The Chinese tanning area is situated on the eastern periphery of Calcutta in an area known as Dhapa (it is sometimes referred to as Tangra or Tapsia since it straddles two districts of those names). Approximately three hundred tanning businesses, the majority employing between five and fifty workers each, are found there. Housed in large concrete buildings of two and three stories, or small one-story

[1] Although the Calcutta census has never broken down the Chinese population on the basis of language, the numerical dominance of the Hakka can be gleaned from the following: there are two Chinese schools for Hakka students and only one for Cantonese students; furthermore, Hubeinese and Cantonese who live in Calcutta are frequently able to converse in Hakka, whereas few Hakka learn Cantonese or Hubeinese (Cantonese and Hubeinese informants assert that this is a result of the Hakka dominating Chinese life in Calcutta). The number of tanning businesses (approximately three hundred in 1980) clearly establishes tanning as the most important occupation of the Hakka. Only shoe shops come close (150 such shops in 1980).

[3]

structures with tile roofs, these factories are connected by a maze of unpaved, frequently muddy paths as well as open sewers through which the by-products of the tanning process flow. Yet the tanneries in this rust-colored industrial environment serve as both residences and factories for the Hakka Chinese who live and work there.

At the entrance to each factory stand large impressive wooden doors, above which the name of the enterprise is painted in Chinese characters. As you pass through these doors into the main manufacturing areas, you may notice decorative sheets of red paper with gold lettering pasted on the walls. These are popular Chinese proverbs, and most of them—such as *yi ben wan li*, which means that for each unit of currency invested, one should profit ten thousand times, and *huo ru lun zhuan*, the hope that one's goods will rotate like a wheel, in other words, be in high demand—express the desire for business success. Frequently, there is an altar at one end of the factory floor, on which sit such popular deities as Guanyin, the Buddhist goddess of mercy, and Guangong, a god of war, but perhaps more significant, a god of wealth and stores. Images of the spirits of happiness, wealth, and longevity, Fu, Lu, and Su, are also commonly displayed.

Once inside the tanneries, you may notice that in many of them kitchens and dining spaces are placed directly on the factory floors. Chinese women cook in areas adjacent to those where their Indian employees shave pieces of leather or throw rawhides into tanning solutions. Drying vegetables hang beside drying hides. Small children run about the factories, and elderly and middle-aged women often sit outside the large factory doors and gossip. In the early morning, you can see these women, dressed in Chinese pajamas, shopping for food in a market near the center of the district. Meanwhile, Indian laborers deliver rawhides to the tanneries, and the tannery employees themselves, mostly Chamars, an untouchable caste associated with leather work, arrive at the factories to begin their workday. Later in the day, these workers can be seen nailing semifinished pieces of leather to dry on boards under the hot sun.

The tanning area presents a mixed impression. The strong odor emitted by the tanning process, workers sweating under the hot sun, pushcarts, trucks, and machinery all suggest an industrial locale. The children running about while playing and buying snacks from vendors, and the groups of Chinese women, standing or sitting while gossiping in front of the big factory doors, suggest a residential area. The industrial waste, mud, and smell hardly make the outdoor areas a garden spot. Yet the residential quarters within the tanneries are often quite large and amply furnished.

In the living rooms, finely crafted woodwork is highlighted by Chinese wall hangings, usually delicately stitched embroidery pictures of birds, trees, and flowers. The latest rages in high-tech consumer gadgets may also be present (while I was there in 1982, videocassette recorders were just beginning to catch on). The one constant reminder of the community's occupational calling is that leather seems to be everywhere. Not only is leather used for covering chairs, but large pieces also cover the broad wooden beds, creating cool, comfortable platforms for sleeping—and for gossiping, taking tea, and for children's play.

Five Years Later—A Calcutta Chinese Family in Toronto

All the aforementioned images, and even my memories of the stench of tanning, pass through my mind on this particular August morning in Toronto in 1986. Perhaps it is because the Toronto street on which I walk, almost antiseptic in appearance, and without a soul passing by, is at such variance with the tanning area. And yet, the association in my mind is natural, for I am going to interview a man whom I knew from the Calcutta Chinese community.

With a prosperous tanning business back in Calcutta, and two married sons who attend to its daily operation, Mr. Kong now has both the economic wherewithal and the time to make fairly frequent trips abroad. This is especially the case during the monsoon season in India, when the tanning business is rather slow (since most tanners rely on steady sunshine rather than expensive automation to dry their semi-finished leather). Every few years, Mr. Kong, his wife, or sometimes both of them, visit their four other children, two married sons and two married daughters, who now live in Toronto.

Mr. Kong is known in the Calcutta community as an expansive talker. He likes to boast that he runs one of the most successful tanning enterprises in the community and to extol the merits of his youngest son, who has taken on a good portion of the responsibility for their business. He complains with equal animation about his eldest son, who he feels lacks talent, is lazy, and does nothing to further the fortunes of the enterprise.

During my initial fieldwork, verbose Mr. Kong naturally became

[5]

one of the first residents of the Calcutta Chinese community with whom I was able to talk at some length about their lives in India, particularly the histories of their families and businesses. I learned from Mr. Kong how his father and father's brother journeyed to India in the early 1920s, how they became involved in tanning, and how the business, which they started in a bamboo shed, grew and divided among their descendants into several separate factories.

Now, during the summer of 1986, I am conducting further research in Toronto, because a considerable number of Calcutta Chinese have immigrated there. Earlier in the week I telephoned Mr. Kong's son Stephen, whom I had never before met, and I was rather relieved to find out that his parents were visiting, thus saving me the problem of approaching him as a total stranger. I arranged for an interview with Stephen, at which time I also met with his brother and sisters in Toronto; after the interview, we all went out to a famous *dim sum* restaurant. But soon after this excursion, I realized I still had some questions for Mr. Kong himself; hence, the reason for my visit this August morning.

As I enter Stephen's house, I find in progress a small celebration in honor of his son's second birthday. Two lighted candles top a cake. Stephen's parents, wife, and two small children are present, as well as his wife's father and sister, his own sister, and her young son. After enjoying our cake and exchanging pleasantries, Mr. Kong looks at me. Not wishing to forget the purpose of my visit, he says, "Ou Xiaojie [literally, Miss Ou—Ou being my Chinese surname], why don't you ask your questions now?"

I sit down at the table and begin to ask questions, most of which pertain to family and kinship in the Calcutta Chinese community. As had been the case in Calcutta, Mr. Kong seems to enjoy holding court, speaking in Mandarin and sprinkling his remarks with four-character phrases, or aphorisms, which he writes down for my benefit. I have gotten onto the subject of marriage and marriage negotiations in Calcutta, and want to know why the services of a matchmaker are deemed so essential among Calcutta Chinese when people all know one another so well; as in many small communities, there are few strangers. Mr. Kong proceeds to discuss the difficulties and embarrassments that are avoided by not conducting face-to-face negotiations with the family of a potential bride or groom. Then he turns around toward his daughter Sheila, who is standing in the corner of the room, and exclaims emphatically, "She didn't have a matchmaker when she got married, and now look, they can't agree on anything!"

[6]

I try unsuccessfully to move the discussion away from his daughter's situation and back to more general considerations, but somehow Mr. Kong continues pointedly returning to his daughter and her marriage. For instance, after more discussion about the merits of having a third party to mediate in disputes, Mr. Kong remarks that in the Calcutta community, matchmakers sometimes intervene in clashes between spouses, helping them to come to amicable settlements. He notes that divorce is practically nonexistent there. "It's not like here," he states acidly, "people get in an argument and the next thing you know they're stirring up a divorce. . . . They start to talk, and before they talk reason [*daoli*], they talk law [*falu*]!"

At times, Sheila also interjects a comment. When I ask about Canada and whether matchmakers are used there, she remarks, "No, we don't use [them] here, it's like in Western countries." In fact, I later discover that this is not always the case, and that some members of the community in Toronto still use matchmakers. But Sheila's defensiveness this morning can easily be understood, for I soon learn that not only is she in the middle of a divorce, but she is also the first emigrant from her community to face such a prospect, and it is the cause of many of her father's pointed remarks this morning.

Much on this trip to Canada annoys Mr. Kong. His grandchildren misbehave wildly in front of him, whereas the presence of a grandfather in the Calcutta Chinese community is usually enough to put a damper on most children's rowdy horseplay. The same grandchildren pay no heed to their elders during mealtimes, simply digging into the food without waiting for a signal to begin from the most senior individual at the table. And now, Mr. Kong's youngest daughter is getting divorced!

Mr. Kong uses a phrase to describe divorce (*hen duibuqi de shiqing*), which roughly means that divorce is "a very rude affair" but really conveys much more. The word *duibuqi* can indicate not only that you have been unfair to someone, but more than that, that you have caused that person to lose face.[2] If you *duibuqi* a person, you've acted in very bad form, stepped on his or her toes. In a sense, Mr. Kong indicates

---

2 It is important here to make a distinction between two different words in Chinese that are both translated as "face" in English. *Lian* refers to one's character, whereas *mianzi* refers to one's social standing and prestige. To lose *lian* is much worse than to lose *mianzi*, because not all people have high status and social standing, but all would like to be respected as individuals who obey and act according to the basic moral norms of society. As Hsien Chin Hu puts it, "To be able to count on the confidence of his fellowmen even the poorest peasant or laborer will be anxious to preserve his *lien*

that by getting a divorce, the couple offend not only each other, but their family and community as well.

Indeed, the birthday party this morning symbolizes to me the changes that have occurred after immigration both in his family and among other community members. In Calcutta, birthdays are celebrated every ten years, beginning only when one turns sixty-one. These are large gatherings attended by hundreds of guests and are public testimonials to the standing or the status an individual and his family have achieved over long years in the community. This Canadian birthday party could not be at greater variance with those in Calcutta; it is held in honor of a two year old, and it is small, private, and modest.

Yet although he is dissatisfied because he believes his family in Toronto has abandoned some important principles of proper Chinese living, it is still important to Mr. Kong that at least some of his children settle in Canada. His family, like many others in the Calcutta community, is dispersed around the globe, just as his father and his brother, who left China to come to India, were part of an earlier process of dispersion and resettlement.

Families across Time and Space: Agency, Constraint, and Contradiction

What has prompted the emigration of Mr. Kong's children and other members of their community? To answer this question, we need to understand three conceptually separable, but in fact interrelated, processes: the internal dynamics within their families, their entrepreneurial ideology and practice, and their role as a pariah ethnic group in their host society of India. I focus in this book on the relationship between these three factors—family, entrepreneurship, and ethnic role—in an attempt to understand the dynamics of Chinese families in an overseas and entrepreneurial setting. Such an analysis must of necessity view the trajectories and strategies of families and family members across both time and space, and as such, while I concentrate

---

[*lian*]. He cannot achieve *mien-tzu* [*mianzi*], the reward for success in life, but he can conduct his life so that no blemish can be cast on his character" (Hu 1944:63).

The kind of "face" that is lost when a family member commits a morally offensive act is *lian*, since one loses not only social prestige but also basic moral standing.

my analysis on the Calcutta community, I also consider the lives of their predecessors who emigrated from China, and the dispersion of community members to North America, particularly to Toronto.

As I argue later in this chapter, studies of immigrant entrepreneurs, including the overseas Chinese, have paid insufficient attention to the connections between the internal dynamics of their families and the exigencies of their host societies. These internal family dynamics and external social structures work together in ways that both constrain and enable ethnic minority entrepreneurs in their particular economic roles. While the social, class, and ethnic composition of these host societies often structure the types of economic activities that such immigrant groups may pursue, members of these groups may also actively manipulate their kinship systems to gain economic advantages in those spheres of activity open to them. Moreover, kinship obligations may limit as well as open up economic possibilities, and family arrangements may themselves change in response to the exigencies of life in a particular host society.

Further, as I show in this study of the Calcutta Chinese and their relatives in Toronto, the underlying ideologies and motivations of such immigrant entrepreneurs are neither straightforward nor simple. First, family relationships often create ambivalence in regard to economic action. Does one work single-mindedly toward a profit or give a break to a relative? Moreover, the entrepreneurial ethic itself is often riddled with contradictory imperatives and evaluations, such as the notion that one can control one's fate through wise investment and decision, and the idea that economic outcomes are ultimately a matter of mere luck.

Indeed, the title of my book refers to just such a contradictory imperative. The reference to "blood and sweat" comes from a phrase that community members frequently quote about hard work. Mahjong, on the other hand, is a Chinese gambling game played frequently in Dhapa. While the Dhapa Chinese condemn all gambling as wasteful when done to excess, they also acknowledge that gambling ironically reenacts some of the central contradictions of the entrepreneurial ethic itself, such as the injunction to rely on one's skills and hard work versus the undeniable factor of luck in one's ultimate success or failure.

On a more general level, I hope through my analysis of Hakka Chinese families in India, their predecessors in China, and their family members in Toronto, to add a new emphasis to the understanding of

[9]

families in terms of both their spatial and their temporal dimensions. Of course, in any account of human agency or action, time is of paramount importance. As Jean-Paul Sartre observed, cultural behavior is "temporal." It is not simply "past determinations ruling men in the way a cause rules its effects." For "everything changes if one considers that society is presented to each man as a perspective of the future and that this future penetrates to the heart of each one as a real motivation for his behavior" (1963:96). Thus, "our roles are always future, they appear to each one as tasks to be performed, ambushes to be avoided, powers to be exercised, etc." (1963:107). In other words, people create agendas. That these agendas may themselves be the product of a distinctive cultural and social environment should not blind us to the fact that while people are indeed acted upon by outside forces, they respond to these forces with an array of individual, familial, and extrafamilial strategies, and these strategies are worked out over time.

The French sociologist Pierre Bourdieu, in a classic work based primarily on his fieldwork in Algeria, has called attention to the importance of time, strategy, and cultural aims in the study of kinship. Bourdieu emphasized the idea that kinship structures and rules, or kinship relations, are used strategically to fulfill "vital material and symbolic interests" (1977:38). Like Sartre, Bourdieu emphasizes the importance of time in the study of social forms; for strategy is nothing less than the playing out of aims and goals over time. Yet his conception of strategy does not ignore the very real fact that all strategies are pursued within existent social frameworks, and that the motivations themselves, the aims and goals which people strategically pursue, are culturally constructed.

This last point is critical. To say that people use their kinship systems in a strategic way does not necessarily imply that all people have the same strategy, or even the same goals. Some writers, Sylvia Yanagisako, for example, have criticized Bourdieu's approach for ignoring culture, reducing kinship to "rational utilitarian calculation" (Yanagisako 1985:13). Yet people can utilize their kinship systems in pursuit of a variety of goals. And Bourdieu clearly states that kinship fulfills not only "material" but also "symbolic" interests (1977:38).

Most analysts recognize time as an important aspect of social action; space, however, is often given less attention. In David Harvey's words, "Social theories . . . typically privilege time over space in their formulations. They broadly assume either the existence of some pre-existing spatial order within which temporal processes operate, or that spatial barriers have been so reduced as to render space a contingent rather

[10]

than fundamental aspect to human action" (1989:205). But, in fact, space both shapes and is shaped by human action.

As we will see in subsequent chapters, in the case of Hakka Chinese families like Mr. Kong's, the dispersal of family members over space is part of a strategy through which economic and political risks are contained. But, in addition, as their family histories have unfolded, the nature of space has itself been transformed. While populations have migrated to various parts of the globe throughout history, people have been able to communicate and move with relatively greater speed in recent years. This ability is one aspect of the phenomenon that David Harvey calls "time-space compression" (1989), a phenomenon that involves the breaking down of spatial impediments to more rapid movements of humans and capital.

The increased rapidity and ease with which populations can move around the globe, however, has led to some ironic results. Diverse peoples come into more frequent contact through both physical proximity and satellite communications. But at the same time, they are also able to maintain links more easily with their "home" territories. Thus, it cannot be assumed that movement and contact will lead to a blending of cultures or the loss of a sense of cultural distinctiveness by different groups of migrants. Rather, "time-space compression" may also help engender a sense of cultural distinctiveness. Indeed, the maintenance of distinct cultural identities may be a response to flux and movement itself. Thus, while the Hakka Chinese families who are the subject of this book have *used* space in their strategies, the changing nature of space itself has had implications in their continuing social relations, a topic I explore more deeply in the Epilogue.

In attempting to understand the organization and development of family and firm among Hakka Chinese tanners, therefore, we must think in terms of both temporal and spatial strategies, and in terms of both human agency and social and cultural constraints. Further, these strategies have evolved in the pursuit of goals that are often ambiguous and contradictory as well as clear-cut. I develop these themes further at the end of this chapter, but first I must turn to a brief summary of three more specific, but relevant, bodies of literature—theories about pariah capitalism and middleman minorities, work on the developmental cycle within the Chinese family, and studies of Chinese entrepreneurial ideology. Because some familiarity with all three areas is necessary to an understanding of the material that follows, I present their most relevant aspects here and also explain where the unanswered questions remain.

Pariah Capitalists and Middleman Minorities

When Stephen Kong decided to migrate from Calcutta to Toronto, one of his first considerations was political security. The Chinese of India have faced political insecurity ever since the Sino-Indian Conflict of 1962, which engendered very bitter feelings in India and therefore had severe repercussions for the small Chinese community. Although the Chinese were not physically attacked by members of the general populace, their Chinese ancestry was used as a basis for governmental restrictions and deprivations of rights. Many lost citizenship; others were interned or deported; still others lost their freedom of unmonitored movement. The experience created a feeling of insecurity among Indian Chinese, and many fear that it might reoccur, or that they might suffer even more dangerous retribution if the political situation between China and India becomes tense again. As Stephen stated, "We look at what happened to the Sikhs [referring to the period when Indira Gandhi was assassinated in 1984, and there were physical attacks and killings of Sikhs by angry and revengeful crowds], and we think we are just as noticeable. If China goes to war with India again, it could happen to us."

In their relative degree of commercial success, and their lack of political power, the Calcutta Chinese resemble a type of social group often referred to as "pariah capitalists" (Hamilton 1978) or "middleman minorities" (Bonacich and Modell 1980). The key characteristics of all such groups are a fair to high degree of economic success coupled with lack of political power and social status. The Chinese of Southeast Asia, the Jews of pre–World War II western Europe, and the Indians of East Africa have all been used by theorists as examples of pariah entrepreneurs. I turned first to literature about these groups in trying to understand the intricacies of the Calcutta Chinese social situation.

The term *pariah capitalist* was coined by Max Weber in the early 1920s, when he wanted to distinguish between a system of *rational capitalism*, which he described as having originated in the West, and the economic activities of alien groups, which he termed *pariah capitalism* (1983:131). For Weber, rational capitalism entailed several specific requirements including systematic accounting of profit and loss, a free market for both goods and labor, and a uniform code of law, uniformly applied (1983:110). Thus, capitalism, as opposed to the onetime pursuit of "booty," entails the operation of "continuing rational capitalistic enterprise: that is, for the constant *renewal* of profit, or *profitability*" (1978:333).

[12]

Pariahs, said Weber, are a "hereditary social group lacking autonomous political organization and characterized by internal prohibitions against commensality and intermarriage. . . . Two additional traits of pariah people are political and social disprivilege and a far-reaching distinctiveness in economic functioning" (1978:493). Because pariah groups were kept apart from the rest of civil society, said Weber, they could utilize different standards when dealing with outsiders and insiders (1983:131). Accordingly, Weber held that they were not responsible for the development of rational capitalist practice as he defined it, since it entailed uniformity and universality.

But many subsequent social theorists pointed out that it was precisely among alien populations that trade and entrepreneurship developed first. The economist Karl Polanyi, for instance, suggested that market activity as opposed to reciprocity was unlikely to occur in small solidary communities. Bargaining activity could more easily transpire between groups, rather than within them, because of the nature of the social relationships it entailed. As Polanyi pointed out, "Exchange at fluctuating prices aims at a gain that can be attained only by an attitude involving a destructive antagonistic relationship between the partners" (1957:255).

In many early civilizations, merchants and traders were outsiders, although they worked in the interests of native rulers, helping them to extract taxes from the populace. Most of the traders mentioned by Homer, for instance, were non-Greeks, just as the majority of those written about in the Bible were non-Jews (Jiang 1968:151). Indeed, rulers and merchants often had a relationship fraught with contradictions. Rulers were unwilling to do the "dirty work" entailed in the day-to-day contact with the masses in which merchants engaged. But at the same time, because of their wealth, merchants were a potential threat to ruling powers. When the merchant class was composed of aliens, however, they were easier to control. They lacked a native power base from which they could challenge rulers, and should their actions become menacing, they could be threatened by the rulers with deportation, or deprivations of political rights.

By utilizing a group of aliens as merchants, governments could also maintain greater control over the common folk among the native populace. In nineteenth-century Thailand, for instance, all male Thai freemen were bound by the requirements of corvée labor (Skinner 1957:96). But Chinese were exempt from corvée labor requirements, and unlike Thai agricultural freemen, who were bound to a patron, they could travel freely. This arrangement was most beneficial to the

[13]

Thai kings. As G. William Skinner points out, Chinese could serve as procurers, traders, and shippers of commercial agricultural products in Thailand, and in lieu of serving as corvée laborers, they were charged a tax high enough to add revenue but not so high as to discourage them from continuing to immigrate to Thailand (1957:97).

The Jews in Poland filled a niche similar to that of the Thai Chinese. When the Jews began to settle in Poland in the twelfth century, no native commercial class existed. In addition, the Polish aristocracy needed tax collectors. In order for Poles to perform these functions, it would have been necessary to liberate the serfs (Eitzen 1968:225). Thus, the Jews were at first welcomed by the Polish aristocracy, although as with most pariah minorities, their welcome did not last forever.

Gary Hamilton cogently defined the nature of pariah capitalism when he said, "The essence of pariah capitalism . . . is a structure of power asymmetry which enables an elite group to control and prey upon the wealth generated by a pariah group" (1978:4). The most extreme instance of this power asymmetry was that of the Jews in Christian Spain. The Jews were legally the property of the king, who was the sole grantor of Jewish rights and privileges (Hamilton 1978:4).

Of course, pariah capitalism was not the only form of relationship that existed between trading diasporas and host communities. Philip Curtin points out that trading communities, such as those established by the Europeans in Asia from the sixteenth through the eighteenth centuries, actually brought their "trade enclaves under their own military control." And ultimately, "toward the end of the eighteenth century, they had used force so effectively that at least the British East India Company in India and the Dutch East India Company on Java had stopped being militarized trade diasporas and became true territorial empires" (Curtin 1984:5).

Nevertheless, the development of colonialism and international marketing did not put an end to pariah capitalism as one form of relationship between traders and host society. Rather, the nature of connections between pariahs and ruling elites changed from personalized forms, such as that between the Jews and the king in medieval Spain, to contractual relationships between members of pariah groups, who acted as middlemen, and members of the elite. Indeed, as colonialism emerged, the elite who were served by these middlemen were frequently the colonial occupiers. In Indonesia, for instance, Chinese ventured into the interior and bought produce, which they would then sell to Dutch export firms (see Furnivall 1944; Purcell 1965).

Needless to say, such activities did not always endear the pariahs to the native populace, and they have frequently been the targets of mass hostility and resentment. Indeed, one of the difficulties often faced by such groups is that they, rather than the ruling groups which may profit from their activities, are viewed by the poor members of the native populace as their true agents of oppression.

Edna Bonacich has developed this concept further in her analysis of "middleman minorities" (Bonacich and Modell 1980; Bonacich 1973). For Bonacich, middleman minorities are groups that exhibit a number of common characteristics. First, they fill a "status gap" between elites and masses—a fitting example is that of the Chinese of Mississippi, described in a work by James Loewen (1971). The Mississippi Chinese owned and operated small retail stores in rural areas. They thereby engaged in daily and constant contact with blacks, something which white Mississippians were reluctant to do in a highly segregated society. At the same time, the white power structure had an interest in keeping the blacks themselves from entering business. Since the blacks were much more numerous than the Chinese, and had resided in Mississippi for so many generations, they could presumably utilize increased economic resources to threaten the whites politically—something which the small community of immigrant Chinese could not do.

Bonacich points out that middleman minorities often engage in activities that the host society considers to be impure, unholy, or degrading (1973:584). Christians, for instance, were not allowed to lend money, whereas the Jews were bound by no such restrictions. In Thailand, pigs were slaughtered and butchered by Chinese, since the Buddhist Thais regarded such activity as a violation of the Buddhist precept of nonviolence (Skinner 1957:217).

Middleman groups, says Bonacich, often have a "sojourner mentality" (1973:584); that is, they think they will not settle where they are living. They come to the host society to make money, and often "since they plan to return [to their country of origin] . . . have little reason to develop lasting relationships with members of the surrounding host society" (1973:286). This mentality results in a savings rather than a spending orientation and enables them to accumulate more capital which can be invested in other enterprises (1973:584). Of course, sojourner orientations are often the result of discrimination or persecution by the host society. As playwright and essayist Frank Chin has so powerfully argued:

> We [Chinese in the United States] did not make life bearable here with idealized notions of Chinese culture and a dream of going home rich until an honorable life in America was made impossible. We were fishermen, farmers, shoemakers, cigarmakers, laundrymen, miners all over the West wherever we could go, until we saw that America . . . was determined to wipe us out. The California laws against entry of Chinese women had been struck down in court, because the Constitution didn't allow states to mess with immigration; that was for Congress to do, and in 1924, Congress did (1972:62).

Bonacich does not deny that host hostility contributes to the sojourning orientation of middleman groups; what is important for her is that both host hostility and sojourning orientations help to establish another common characteristic of middleman minorities—a high degree of internal solidarity. Although middleman groups may be "riddled with division and conflict, based on regional, linguistic, political or religious differences found in the homeland," asserts Bonacich, these differences are put aside in the face of the host society (1973:586). In a work coauthored with John Modell, she goes on to state that while such solidarity may enable middlemen to cooperate efficiently economically, it also opens them up to even greater attack from host populations, who see them as clannish, disloyal, and as draining the host society of money (Bonacich and Modell 1980:20).

Bonacich's final points about middleman minorities concern the nature of their enterprises. It is the family firm, she says, that typifies the economic activity of middleman minorities. Furthermore, she insists that industrial entrepreneurship is rare among middlemen groups, since it requires a long-term investment in nonmovable assets, preventing such entrepreneurs from leaving their host society if circumstances demand it (1973:585).

Because of their involvement with industrial entrepreneurship, an activity which requires them to invest in a great deal of nonliquid wealth, the Calcutta Chinese deviate from the patterns delineated by Bonacich and others. Yet they retain many other characteristics of the groups described in this chapter. Like pariah capitalists, they lack political security and work in occupations denigrated by the host society; in this case, jobs associated with the lowest rungs of the Hindu caste system. And, like middleman minorities, they run family businesses and display ambivalence, even antagonism, toward their host society. Furthermore, although industrial entrepreneurship might be a barrier to geographical mobility in some cases, this has not been the situation with the Calcutta Chinese. As illustrated by Mr. Kong's family, this group has been able to achieve a high degree of movement and mobility through the use of ties to and assistance rendered by family and kin.

It is in this area, the analysis of kinship and family, that theories about pariah capitalism and middleman minorities tell us little. Bonacich, for example, emphasizes the fact that middleman businesses tend to be family businesses. But she gives no details about how differing kinship systems might influence either the organization of these businesses or the strategies used by group members in the host society. A kinship system in which only one heir inherits, for instance, would certainly have different implications for the organization of family firms than one in which all sons inherit equally. And yet, discussion of the effects of particular kinship structures on middleman minority firms has not been prevalent in the literature.[3]

Therefore, though I found middleman minority theory useful in explaining the status and position of a certain type of minority group, I had to look elsewhere for an analysis of how the microdynamics within families articulate with and affect the ethnic roles that middleman minorities play. One work that does address some of these problems is James L. Watson's study of a Chinese lineage village in Hong Kong and its emigrants in England (1975). Watson not only analyzes the effects of

[3] For example, analyses of overseas Chinese groups who can be categorized as middleman minorities often neglect this sort of examination of internal family dynamics and processes. Although numerous books and articles, particularly those on the Southeast Asian Chinese, discuss features of internal group organization among overseas Chinese, the relationship between kinship systems and business practice is not prominent among the themes considered. The most common topics investigated are the nature of overseas Chinese political organization (Skinner 1958, 1968; Wang 1981); social organization (Crissman 1967; Freedman 1960; Willmott 1960); value systems (Ryan 1961); changing status in the host society (Loewen 1971); acculturation and assimilation (Coughlin 1960; Skinner 1973a, 1973b); economic roles and activities (Cator 1936; Freedman 1959; Light 1972; Omohundro 1981; Wertheim 1964; Willmott 1960); and finally the changing relationships between overseas Chinese communities and those who hold political power (Coppel 1976; Skinner 1968, 1973a; Somers 1964).

Except for James L. Watson's analysis of the manner in which lineage ties were used by Hong Kong emigrants in the restaurant business in London (1975), and John Omohundro's study of Chinese business families in the Philippines (1981), the institutions investigated in greatest depth in most studies of overseas Chinese society tend to be those surrounding the family, rather than the family itself.

Chinese lineage organization on patterns of emigration to Britain but also examines the use of lineage ties in the villagers' new economic niche in England—the restaurant business. Watson's book, however, is concerned primarily with the effects of emigration on the home community. For at the time of his research, the majority of emigrants studied by Watson still intended to return to Hong Kong. The Chinese of Calcutta, on the other hand, dispensed with plans to return permanently to their home communities in China after the revolution of 1949. For whatever their political allegiances might be, most seem to agree that their standard of living is higher as overseas Chinese entrepreneurs than it is likely to be in China for the foreseeable future. Accordingly, I focus not on the communities of origin in an indigenous Chinese setting, but on the community in Calcutta, where the Chinese are an ethnic minority.

I also found fruitful sources in two works on American ethnicity. Carol Stack's *All Our Kin* (1974) and Micaela di Leonardo's *Varieties of Ethnic Experience* (1984) are especially pertinent to my endeavor, for they focus primarily on the relationship between ethnic role and kinship systems among specific ethnic minorities, although their subjects cannot be classified as middleman minorities or pariah capitalists. Di Leonardo demonstrates in her study of Italian-Americans that both the political economies of the regions from which Italians emigrated and to which they immigrated, as well as the developmental cycle within families, have important effects on ethnic and familial strategies and roles. As she states, "An Italian household . . . consisting of a young man and a pregnant woman differs markedly from that of a middle-aged couple, their coresident adult son, and the husband's elderly mother. Much work on ethnic families glides over these differences by exalting the 'extended family'" (1984:113).

Carol Stack's work on African-American families in the urban ghetto also provides an exemplary model of an analysis that connects family processes and ethnic roles. Through an intensive examination of how inner-city African-Americans define kin, how and why household composition changes, and which kin one can get help from and give assistance to, Stack demonstrates that what whites perceive as "broken" families among African-American ghetto residents are really dense webs of kinship, finely tuned to the demands of living as an economically oppressed racial minority in the American economy (1974).

Both Stack and di Leonardo demonstrate that a comprehension of internal family dynamics is highly relevant to an understanding of an

[18]

ethnic group's economic and social role. I certainly found such considerations paramount in my own analysis of the Calcutta Chinese. As I
attempt to show in this book, understanding the dynamics within
Calcutta Chinese families is absolutely critical to understanding both
the development of their businesses and the strategies adopted by
individuals and families in their host society. In Stephen Kong's case,
for instance, familial factors have been as important as political ones in
his decision to emigrate. In a family structure in which all brothers
inherit equally, there is always a chance that even a prosperous enterprise will be less lucrative when the business is split up among five or
more brothers. Some brothers may have to leave if the enterprise is to
provide any kind of a living for those who remain behind. Although
Stephen's family is prosperous, his emigration still lessens the economic risks of keeping all sons together in one business. And it does so
while also providing an overseas connection, a connection which other
family members can utilize if they later need to emigrate because of
changes in India's political climate.

In my attempts to understand the trajectories of Chinese families in
Calcutta, therefore, I realized that an analysis of both their ethnic role
and their family system was necessary. In the following section, I
briefly summarize those aspects of Chinese family organization that
are most pertinent to the analysis of Chinese families in Calcutta.

Family Cycles and Family Strategies

As the case of Mr. Kong's family illustrates, families are not static.
Obviously, even in the most homogeneous of societies the events of
birth, marriage, adoption, death, and migration can add to or deplete
family membership. Therefore, when describing the types of families
characteristic of a society or culture, one must at the very least do so in
the context of their developmental courses.

One of the most lucid explanations of the developmental cycle within the Chinese family, and of the relationship between changes in
family form and economic organization, can be found in the work of
Myron Cohen on Hakka Chinese families in rural Taiwan (1970, 1976).
Although he states clearly that there is not one set developmental
sequence, Cohen accepts the analytical categories of an earlier writer,
Olga Lang, and proposes that three basic family types—conjugal,
stem, and joint—encompass most of the conceivable variations in

Chinese family structure. In Lang's (and Cohen's) terminology, conjugal families are composed of a husband, wife or wives, and children. In stem families one of the sons is himself married and has children, and in joint families more than one son is married and has children (Cohen 1976:61). In fraternal joint families both parents are already deceased. In stem, joint, and fraternal joint families, family members share in a joint economy.

Referring to these family types, Cohen states, "Arranged from the simplest to the most complex, they define the limits within which changes in either direction may occur. At the same time, they describe the maximal developmental sequence, which goes from conjugal family to stem to joint to fraternal joint and back to conjugal" (Cohen 1976:68). Implicit in this scheme is the assumption that families divide—that a set of brothers, each of whom has an equal claim to the estate, will ultimately establish separate households, taking their share of an estate once held jointly by all of them. This process of dividing family assets among those who have a claim to them, usually all the sons, is called *fenjia*. Daughters, it should be pointed out, normally marry into their husband's families (the Dhapa Chinese use the words *chu jia*, which literally mean "to leave the house," when describing a daughter's marriage).[4] Although they may bring along a dowry, they have no official claims to a remaining share of their natal families' estates.

The question of when and if family division (*fenjia*) has occurred is therefore critical to the determination of family form. Utilizing Cohen's terminology to analyze Mr. Kong's family, for instance, one would categorize his family as a joint family, since he lives and shares a business with two married sons in Calcutta. His sons in Toronto might also be considered a part of this family if they still had a claim in the business, even if they did not take an active role in it. Hence, physical propinquity or the lack of it is less important in determining family

---

[4] "Major marriage," or the practice of an adult woman marrying into her husband's family, accompanied by a dowry, was long thought to be the dominant pattern in Chinese society. But recent research, particularly the studies of Arthur Wolf and Chieh-shan Huang (1980), has demonstrated that other forms of marriage, which were previously considered to be anomalous deviations, may actually have been much more common than originally thought. These include "minor marriage," in which an infant girl was adopted by her future husband's family and married to her "brother" only after they come of age; and "uxorilocal marriage," in which the husband resided with the wife's kin and might also agree that one or more of his offspring takes his wife's surname.

[20]

form than the question of who has claims to the family estate or property. Thus, if Mr. Kong's Toronto-based sons have already been compensated for their share of the business in cash or otherwise, and therefore have no remaining claim to it, then the family can be said to have divided (*fenjia*). In this case, Stephen, his wife, and sons can be said to comprise a conjugal family of their own. (Family segments that *do* live under one roof stop sharing meals and a stove when family division occurs.)

Although daughters are usually not a party to the division of the family estate (I discuss some exceptions in Chapter 7), it is inaccurate to describe Chinese families solely in terms of patrilineal and patrilocal structures. Several analysts have pointed out that in addition to agnatic ties, affinal connections are frequently utilized by Chinese family members. These affinal links are often given prominent expression in family rituals (Ahern 1975; Freedman 1970; Gallin 1960; Watson 1981, 1985; Wolf 1970). Moreover, Margery Wolf, in developing the notion of the "uterine family" (Wolf 1972:33), notes that the bonds between a mother and her children exist within a larger patrilineal unit and are often the longest-lasting and most emotionally crucial ties a woman experiences. Finally, recent studies of working women in Taiwan and Hong Kong indicate that unmarried daughters may now be of great "use" to their families: since working daughters remit the majority of their earnings to their families, they subsidize the educational and career advancement of their younger brothers (Greenhalgh 1985b; Kung 1984; Salaff 1981).

It should be emphasized here that it is not only family form itself that is significant, but also the manner in which family economy articulates with these forms. Cohen, for instance, compares family types in terms of who controls finances, how labor is divided within the family, how and when a family diversifies its economic activities, and how and when families divide.

One might legitimately ask, however, whether the agrarian and indigenous Chinese setting of Cohen's study, and the studies of other scholars who analyze Chinese kinship (see, e.g., Baker 1968; Gallin 1966; Levy 1949; Yang 1945), makes them inapplicable to families in overseas Chinese communities, which are urban and engaged in commercial or industrial pursuits. In their considerations of household form, Robert Netting, Richard Wilk, and Eric Arnould note that in many societies there is a "persistence of household norms and structures through time and over large areas . . . despite changing eco-

[21]

nomic and political situations" (1984:xxx). On the whole, I did find that among Chinese families in Calcutta, the trajectories of their developmental cycle bear great similarities to those of the rural Chinese families analyzed by Cohen and others. Conjugal, stem, and joint families are easily recognizable. So, too, are quarrels or creeping dissatisfactions among brothers and their respective families, and eventual divisions of joint families into several smaller conjugal ones. Calcutta Chinese families have also employed links with their affines and their married daughters for the purposes of business development and emigration.

As I illustrate in subsequent chapters, one reason for the maintenance of this family structure may be the ease with which it can be utilized in the organization of family business. This manipulation of traditional Chinese family relationships within contemporary Chinese businesses has been noted by Susan Greenhalgh in her work on family firms on Taiwan. As she points out, family members can be called on to "staff key positions" in networks, to "recruit labor, capital, and information," and in "strategies of spatial dispersal and economic diversification" (1988:231). Likewise, Siu-lun Wong, in a study of Shanghai industrialists in Hong Kong, indicates that the family "provides the impetus for innovation and the support for risk taking" (1988:170).

Furthermore, as in the rural settings described by Cohen and others, migration from the Calcutta Chinese community is partly a response to some of the limitations imposed by patrilineal, partible inheritance in particular families. Cohen mentions, for instance, that it was not uncommon for some sons in rural areas of China to leave home in order to pursue a trade or business in a town or city. Certainly, as in most cases of migration, a general lack of economic opportunity in the home community combined with the pull created by the opening up of labor markets and opportunities in other areas were crucial here.[5] But migration also helped resolve the difficulties of dividing a finite estate among many heirs. Through emigration, new sources of income could be found which would either add to a commonly shared purse or at least not drain the resources of those left behind.

Likewise, among the Calcutta Chinese, the number of brothers and

[5] See Eric Wolf's chapter "The New Laborers" in *Europe and the People without History* (1982) for a discussion of how changes in the organization of capitalist production influenced the migration of labor on a worldwide scale in the nineteenth and twentieth centuries.

the size of the business they share are important factors in their decisions to emigrate. But in their cases, migration away from home is as likely to entail emigration overseas as to other cities in India. This choice of emigration abroad is partly a response to their inability to find new economic niches within urban India, where particular ethnic groups are likely to monopolize certain businesses, and partly a response to political pressures within the host society, as in the case of Mr. Kong's son Stephen.

Thus, in analyzing the trajectories of Calcutta Chinese families, I focus on both the internal dynamics of their developmental cycles and the external constraints on their ethnic role in their host society of India. These factors alone, however, do not account for the goals that motivate action. The Calcutta Chinese also attempt to manipulate the structures of family and host society to achieve certain ends. What are these ends?

The Ideology of Chinese Entrepreneurship

At the most general level, the Calcutta Chinese are motivated by goals of security and continual economic betterment; and they view business, as opposed to salaried employment, as the best means of achieving their objectives in the context of Calcutta. In later chapters of this book I examine the entrepreneurial ethic of the Calcutta Chinese in greater detail (including its ambiguities and contradictions); here I want to place this ethic in a larger context. The reader should be aware that entrepreneurial ideology does have deep roots within Chinese culture itself. In this case, values within the culture of origin work in conjunction with, and not against, the values held by the emigrants. That this is so is amply demonstrated by recent scholarship on the ideology of Chinese entrepreneurship, scholarship which draws on materials from Taiwan, the mainland, and overseas communities. This literature not only adds to our understanding of the goals that motivate Chinese entrepreneurs but also clarifies the relationship of these goals to the family.

Stevan Harrell, for instance, has identified what he calls a "Chinese entrepreneurial ethic, a cultural value that requires one to invest one's resources . . . in a long-term quest to improve the material well-being and security of some group to which one belongs and with which one identifies closely" (1987:94). He makes three important points about this entrepreneurial ethic: first, entrepreneurial efforts are dedicated to a group, and not just to individual enrichment; second, the group to which most individuals usually dedicate their entrepreneurial efforts is the family; third, the entrepreneurial ethic grew out of a culture in which "strategies of economic mobility (whether it be through labor, investment, study, diversification of holdings, or whatever) were what made the difference" (1987:219).

This third point refers to the fact that even in traditional China, an ideology of meritocracy prevailed. According to this ideology, one's station in life is determined not by birth or blood, but by achievement, whether it be as scholar-official or merchant. Of course, one can certainly argue about the degree to which this ideal was implemented in actual practice, but the important point is that it was one shared by many Chinese, especially those who migrated overseas for the express purpose of bettering themselves economically.[6]

Therefore, while the Calcutta Chinese are pariah entrepreneurs, one can use the word "entrepreneurial" to apply to the actions and aims of Chinese actors in indigenous Chinese settings as well. Richard Stites, for instance, points out that Taiwanese blue-collar workers often perceive their work as just a temporary way station between wage employment and self-employment in their own family business (1985: 237). The goal of self-employment makes sense in Taiwan, says Stites, because conditions of industrial work there are actually less secure than those of small business. Similarly, in Wong's study of Shanghai industrialists in Hong Kong, he notes that residents of this colony put a high value on business proprietorship as compared with salaried employment (1988:170). (Even the current conflicts over economic policy in the People's Republic of China indicate that entrepreneurial motivations still have a strong pull.)

At first glance, the observations of Stites, Harrell, Wong, and others

---

[6] One of the best studies of the value system of an overseas Chinese community is contained within an unpublished doctoral dissertation by Edward Ryan (1961) on the Chinese of Java. It is unfortunate that Ryan died before being able to turn this work into a book and to make it available to a wider community. But it is clear from his account that the community he studied, like the one I studied in Calcutta, was strongly motivated by an ideology of entrepreneurship. Says Ryan, in a quote which is one of my favorites, "It is highly unlikely that a Modjokuto Chinese would, in his fantasy life, see himself as a fearless fighter for an ideal, a great physician, or even a political leader. There is evidence, on the other hand, that identification would be expressed in the image of the business tycoon or a power figure dispensing summary justice and practical beneficences to his opponents and followers" (1961:14).

(see Niehoff 1987) do not seem to apply to Calcutta Chinese, like Stephen Kong, in their decisions to emigrate to Canada. The Calcutta Chinese in Toronto usually engage in wage labor, or earn salaries, working in assembly-line factory jobs or in modestly paid white-collar jobs such as secretarial work or computer programming (see Epilogue). On the face of it, these actions seem contradictory to the entrepreneurial ethic. But when one considers that workers in Canada generally receive good benefits compared with those in India, and that investing in business is extremely risky and takes much more capital in Canada than in India, then these actions make sense in terms of the values discussed by Harrell and Stites. For wage labor in Canada does fit into a scheme in which importance is placed on long-term security and continual improvement in a family's economic status, the very goals that Harrell identifies as being integral to the Chinese entrepreneurial ethic.

As Stephen Kong put it: "We are a business-oriented family at home in India, but coming over here you have to work for someone . . . they do their own business over there [that is, the rest of his family], and I do my own job here. I don't need help, they don't need my help . . . we're all doing very well."

Family Process

What is the actual decision-making process within specific Chinese families engaged in such entrepreneurial quests? And what is the relationship between this decision making and the structures of society and family which people must contend with in realizing their entrepreneurial goals? Unfortunately, few studies address such questions.

In the case of Calcutta Chinese tanners, both their status as a politically insecure minority group and the structure of their family developmental cycle are factors around which they model their entrepreneurial strategies. Just as their minority-group status is a given, so, too, they must mold their actions around the assumption that their family development will proceed along certain lines; that is, they assume that their families will grow and ultimately divide, that sons will inherit, that daughters will marry out. These aspects of family structure are givens of social life for most Calcutta Chinese.

But while actions must take account of these almost nonnegotiable

[25]

social facts, it is just as apparent that family members do manipulate the structures they live in very purposefully. I find it useful to think of both these elements, namely, the unfolding of family structure and the manipulation of its possibilities, as part of an ongoing family process— a process that involves the almost mechanical working out of the kinship system over time, but also the very conscious playing with its underlying potential.[7] The individuals in Mr. Kong's family in India, for instance, do accept and act upon certain basic premises in ordering their family life. I already mentioned that the principles of patrilocality and patrilineality (daughters marry out, and sons carry on the family line), equal inheritance for all sons, and the growth into and eventual fission of joint families structure the shape of family development among the Kongs and other Calcutta Chinese families. As Netting, Wilk, and Arnould state, "household rules are culturally defined and set limits on the possible structural solutions to instrumental problems" (1984:xxix). But as we will see in the case of Calcutta Chinese families, many different courses of action can be structured around the basic assumptions and principles that underlie their kinship system.

Furthermore, it is precisely because these basic principles are susceptible to such useful manipulation that they are reproduced at all in this particular setting. This last point is important. Stating that patrilineality or patrilocality are almost "nonnegotiable social facts" for Chinese in India does not mean that they are that way because they represent some sort of immutable essence. Certainly, from the standpoint of any particular individual born into the community, they may appear immutable and are taken for granted (part of what Bourdieu calls "the habitus" [1977]). But it is just as clear that these principles are continually reproduced by the actions of particular individuals, and one would have to assume that elements of family structure that proved totally unworkable in this setting would gradually change or be dispensed with altogether.

Likewise, as mentioned earlier, the entrepreneurial ethic of the Calcutta Chinese is not as simple or clear-cut as might appear at first sight. Not only are people torn between their belief in hard work as the engine of success and their acknowledgment that dumb luck may

---

[7] E. A. Hammel has utilized the notion of the household as process in his work on the Zadruga (1972). In this case, he is referring primarily to the structural changes that occur over time. When I refer to family process, however, I refer not only to structural elements of the domestic cycle but also to the manner in which family members manipulate such structures.

be the ultimate arbiter of financial success, but in addition, the goal of enhancing the material well-being of family members can itself engender familial conflict and competition, and even individual uncertainty. Do married sons work to enhance the well-being of their own conjugal families, and separate from the larger family of which they are a part? Or do they work for the benefit of the larger unit? We should never assume that family members have uniform interests. Discrepancies in power and location in the family structure among individuals differentiated by sex, generation, and age mean that the stakes of any particular course of action inevitably differ for each of them. To talk of the family as a nondifferentiated unit bound by a universally shared goal is rarely possible. As Netting, Wilk, and Arnould point out, "Decisions emerge from households through negotiation, disagreement, conflict and bargaining" (1984:xxii).

I take the position that the analysis of pariah entrepreneurs and middleman minorities can be particularly enriched by an emphasis on family process. Such an emphasis directs attention toward the way in which individuals and families within such groups utilize and act within their kinship systems to obtain their objectives and respond to both the existential and practical problems of living in their host societies. And, as pointed out earlier, such action has both temporal and spatial dimensions to it.

Of course, the fact that individuals *use* kinship structures to attain their goals does not preclude the fact that kinship relations themselves create powerful impulses for action.[8] We have seen that entrepreneurial efforts among the Chinese are usually conceived of in terms of family, rather than individual, benefit, and that such efforts among the Calcutta Chinese are bolstered by their position as a pariah ethnic

---

[8] In my view, an emphasis on strategy or process does not overlook the fact that kinship *does* provide a framework within which people can conceptualize and understand social relationships (see Schneider 1968; Yanagisako 1985). Indeed, the meaning attributed to particular kinship relationships in specific cultural settings can itself provide a powerful motive for action. If it is important to have many male descendants, for instance, one can expect an array of strategies through which people in a particular cultural context will attempt to achieve that goal, and to manipulate these conceptually valued relationships.

The role of "cultural schema" as motives has been discussed by Roy D'Andrade (1986), Claudia Strauss (1987), and Naomi Quinn (1986), among others. But the main point here is that by emphasizing the fact that people manipulate the kinship and other structures in which they live, one does not deny that kinship also creates meaning for people.

[27]

group. Finally, family structures themselves are not set in stone but are reproduced or even transformed in the process of being manipulated by family members. Family system, host society, and the values and ideology of the pariah community are therefore intricately interconnected. The relationships among them are the focus of this book.

Organization of the Book

I have begun by describing the Hakka Chinese of Calcutta as a group that monopolizes a particular economic niche while it remains politically powerless. In Chapter 2, I explain the role that the Hakka play within Calcutta's ethnic matrix. I examine how they fit into the larger scheme of Calcutta's ethnically organized economy, how they view others, how outsiders to the community view them, and how they responded to the initial attempts of a particular outsider, myself, to do research within the community. In short, I situate the Calcutta Hakka in terms of an ethnic geography of that city, hence emphasizing the spatial component of their role. In Chapter 3, I turn to the history of the community. I also explore the way in which the community's internal institutions have aided and abetted their entrepreneurial efforts and the reproduction of their ethnic identity. Thus, in the first three chapters of this book, I examine the Hakka community within the Indian context.

Next, I focus on the connections between family and enterprise. In Chapter 4, I take a closer look at the entrepreneurial ideology that fuels both familial and individual strategies. As I explain there, this ethic is not so simple as it might appear. The Dhapa Chinese acknowledge that entrepreneurial goals can engender seemingly contradictory attitudes and actions.

In Chapters 5 through 8 I explore the interconnections among family structures, entrepreneurial strategies, and the expansion and development of tanning firms in successive generations of Hakka families. In Chapter 5 I consider the relationship between business growth and the developmental course of families among first-generation tanners, and then in Chapter 6 I describe the internal organization of these family firms, paying particular attention to the critical role played by women, and to the sexual division of labor, property, and space. I continue the chronological narrative in Chapter 7, analyzing the processes of family division among second- and third-generation tanners and examining the manner in which these processes are used to disperse political risks and expand on and solidify economic gains. Throughout these chapters I pay close attention not only to the manipulation of patrilineal and patrilocal structures but also to the use of links to married daughters and affines for the purposes of business expansion and/or spatial dispersion through emigration.

In Chapter 8 I look more closely at the interaction of entrepreneurial goals and familial duties from the point of view of one Dhapa entrepreneur. As in Chapter 4, my emphasis is on contending imperatives. While entrepreneurial aspirations can be viewed as an aspect of familial obligations, they may also conflict with them, especially in relationships among brothers. The urge to profit may clash with as well as sustain familial obligations and feelings, as is revealed clearly in the recollections of Mr. Zhou, a moderately successful entrepreneur in Dhapa. His account of family relationships among his brothers, and between himself and his parents, evokes a complex picture of the interplay of entrepreneurial ideology and familial duties within the Chinese business family.

Finally, in the Epilogue I return to the subject of the "Calcutta" Hakka in Toronto. During my visits to Toronto, I was impressed with how family relationships had changed in order to meet the demands of life in this new setting. But I was also struck by the persistence of links with the "home" community in India and by the new dilemmas and decisions that immigration and changing economic circumstances had created for families spread across several continents. It is with an analysis of these temporal and spatial transformations in family and ethnic role, and of the relationship between them, that I conclude this study.

Chinese woman and Bengali vendor at early morning market in Dhapa.

[30]

[2]

Research in an Ethnic Matrix

The story about the Kong family, with which I began this book, may convey the impression that it was easy to establish rapport with members of the Calcutta Chinese tanning community. After all, on that day, my presence did little to dampen a heated family argument. But, in fact, as with most ethnographers who engage in field research, it took time for me to find a role and gain acceptance.

Anthropologists usually begin fieldwork as strangers with little knowledge of the culturally appropriate behavior for the contexts in which they do research. But this factor is not the only barrier to acceptance. Fieldworkers also come to a community with particular cultural, ethnic, and national identities. And the people they intend to study frequently have their own ideas and expectations about those identities. [1]

In my case, the process of gaining an entrée into the tanning community was somewhat more complex than that of the ordinary fieldworker; for I was associated not with one, but with two groups that were both clearly outsiders, but whose relationships to the Chinese community were quite different. As an American, I was identified by the Chinese as a foreigner and as a Westerner. But my husband was a

---

[1] One of the most infamous examples of this is the case of the British anthropologist E. E. Evans-Pritchard in his study of the Nuer people of the Sudan. The British government had engaged in an extensive military campaign against the Nuer prior to Evans-Pritchard's arrival, and as many later analysts have pointed out (e.g., Rosaldo 1986), this fact could hardly have been irrelevant to the Nuers' cold reception of Evans-Pritchard and certainly influenced the nature of the data he collected.

Bengali, and my use of his surname marked me as someone who was affiliated through marriage with the ethnic group that was numerically and culturally dominant in Calcutta. Both these identities influenced the manner in which I was viewed and created a number of apprehensions about my purposes.

In this chapter, I discuss and analyze this fieldwork experience. I do so not only to illuminate the conditions of my research but also to provide insight into the nature of relationships between the Chinese community and various categories of outsiders. This examination of my fieldwork is prefaced by a description of the setting of my research— the city of Calcutta. In particular, I introduce the reader to the diverse and important roles played by Calcutta's numerous ethnic groups and to the unique niche that the Chinese fill within this ethnic matrix.

The Setting: Ethnic Geography

Occupation and Ethnicity in Calcutta

Even before I came to Calcutta to do fieldwork, I was aware that it is a city in which ethnicity is a critical social, cultural, and economic force. Located in the Indian state of West Bengal, Calcutta has a great array and diversity of ethnic, religious, and caste groups—a population mix that results partly from its role as the preeminent city of northeast India. In addition to its teeming population, Calcutta has well-publicized urban problems—poor sewage, overcrowded and polluted slums, or bustees, multitudes of pavement dwellers, public transportation that is bursting at the seams—and has now been overtaken by Bombay as a center of industry. Yet despite all this, Calcutta continues to be a magnet that attracts migrants. They have come from the surrounding Bengali countryside, from the neighboring states of Bihar and Orissa, from the even more distant states within India (e.g., Gujarat, Punjab, Rajasthan, and Tamil Nadu) and from the neighboring countries of Bangladesh and Nepal (see Map 2). At one time, Calcutta hosted a sizable Jewish community and a smaller Armenian one.[2] This continuous migration to Calcutta has been augmented by

[2] Armenian merchants and their families arrived in Calcutta soon after it was founded at the end of the seventeenth century, and although there are only a few hundred remaining, they numbered in the thousands in the nineteenth century (Chaliha and Gupta 1990). Jews, most of them from Baghdad, migrated to Calcutta at the end of the nineteenth century and remained until the establishment of the state of Israel, when most of them emigrated there (Chowdhury and Chaliha 1990).

Map 2. The states of India. From Ashok K. Dutt and Margaret Geib, *Atlas of South Asia* (Boulder, Colo.: Westview Press, 1987), by permission of the publisher.

[33]

the great human waves associated with the partition of India in 1947 and by subsequent wars with Pakistan, culminating in the formation of Bangladesh in 1971, when millions of refugees poured into West Bengal and Calcutta. Indeed, throughout the period between 1881 and 1961, migrants from outside the state of West Bengal constituted over 50 percent of the city's population (Chakraborty 1990:11).

Founded at the close of the eighteenth century by traders belonging to the East India Company, Calcutta eventually served as the capital of British India, until political agitation and unrest forced the British to relocate the capital to Delhi in 1911. Calcutta's predominance as a major port and center of trade, finance, and industry has continued since the days of the East India Company (Lubell 1974:3), and indeed the Calcutta region preceded other parts of the country in the process of industrialization (Lubell 1974:14). Greater Calcutta is still the most populous city in India (Geib and Dutt 1987:32); in 1981 the population of the the Calcutta metropolitan district was 9.2 million, making it one of the ten largest metropolises in the world (Geib and Dutt 1987:132). Furthermore, unlike Bombay and Delhi, Calcutta is hundreds of miles away from any other major urban center (Lubell 1974:2, also see Map 3). Although the growth of the city is now said to be "merely" 25 percent per decade, or the same rate as India as a whole (Stevens 1983:3), the ethnic, caste, and religious diversity of the city continues to be a preeminent feature.

First, however, let me define what I mean by "ethnicity" within the context of Calcutta's social and cultural diversity. When I use the term, I refer to several types of groups: (1) immigrants from outside South Asia, like the Chinese and the Armenians; (2) people from South Asian countries other than India, such as migrants from Nepal and Bangladesh; and (3) people from Indian states outside West Bengal, who speak languages other than Bengali. In addition, many of these groups, all of whom can be referred to as "ethnic" groups within Calcutta, are subdivided along caste and religious lines. Hence, Hindu Bengalis, as well as Hindu immigrants from other states in India, have a multitude of different caste affiliations. And not only are most of these diverse caste groups endogamous with respect to marriage, but many are also associated with distinct occupational niches. Religion as well as caste divide the migrants. Thus, migrants to Calcutta from the state of Punjab include Hindus, Muslims, and Sikhs.

The differentiation of groups in Calcutta is therefore based on several cross-cutting categories, including language (see Table 1), reli-

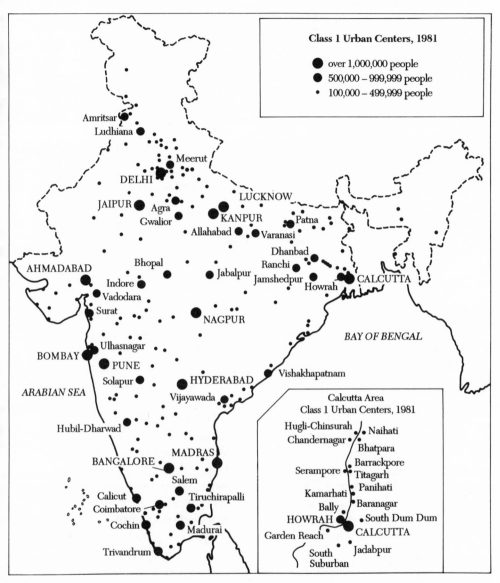

Map 3. Calcutta compared by population with other Indian urban centers. From Ashok K. Dutt and Margaret Geib, *Atlas of South Asia* (Boulder, Colo.: Westview Press, 1987), by permission of the publisher.

Table 1. Population of Calcutta, by language, 1971

Language	Number of speakers
Bengali	1,887,471
Hindi	731,853
Urdu	348,689
Oriya	42,252
Gujarati	26,939
Punjabi	20,237
English	15,784
Nepali	13,192
Chinese	7,606[a]
TOTAL	3,148,746

Note: Population does not include urban agglomeration, but only that within city limits.

[a]Of these Chinese speakers, 705 are listed not under the population of Calcutta but under that of the neighboring district, 24-Parganas. Almost all of these Chinese, however, are residents of the tanning district that straddles the border of Calcutta and 24-Parganas. Therefore, the larger number has been considered as part of the Chinese-speaking population of Calcutta.

Source: Census of India, 1971, Social and Cultural Tables for West Bengal, table C-V, parts A and B.

gion, caste, class, and regional origins. And each subdivision created by the combination of one or more of these categories tends to be associated with particular clusters of occupations. For instance, Hindi-speaking people include groups as varied as migrants from rural areas in the state of Bihar, which borders West Bengal, and Marwaris, a trading people with origins in central India. Whereas the Biharis are industrial laborers and operators of pushcarts and rickshaws, the Marwaris are industrialists and businessmen. South Indians, on the other hand, are commonly associated with clerical and administrative work (Bose 1968:39), and Sikhs are found in large numbers in the transport business (Bose 1968:38). Among Bengalis, who share language and ethnic affiliation, occupational differentiation is organized according to caste categories and/or regional origin.[3]

[3] For instance, Bengalis of the Subarnabanik caste, a traditional trading caste, were in the moneylending business from the early days of Calcutta's history. They have tended to gravitate toward insurance, banking, and landed proprietorship, and they also hold shares in such major industries as coal, jute, and textiles (Bose 1968:28). Upper-caste Bengalis are found in large numbers in professions like law, accounting, and engineering (Bose 1968:28). Finally, Bengalis who emigrated from Bangladesh,

Even the leather business is organized according to linguistic, caste, religious, and regional categories: the Hakka Chinese buy their rawhides from north Indian Muslims; they employ scheduled-caste[4] Bihari migrants as laborers and Nepalese as guards; and they sell their leather to Hindus, Muslims, and Sikhs from the state of Punjab.

Such ethnic variability might remind one of the ethnic diversity of American cities—New York, for example—but there is an important distinction here. Although ethnicity is certainly a major component of socioeconomic status in American cities, particularly among black and Hispanic populations, there is still a wide variation of income within each ethnic group. In Calcutta, however, as Brian Berry and Philip Rees point out in their study of its factoral ecology, the occupational differences between ethnic groups are greater than those that exist within them. The only exception is among Bengalis, where different castes are connected to different occupational roles (Berry and Rees 1969:490).

One reason for the continuing importance of ethnicity in the social structure of Calcutta is its economy of scarcity. According to Nirmal Kumar Bose, "because there are not enough jobs [in Calcutta] to go around everyone clings as closely as possible to the occupation with

formerly East Pakistan, are also internally subdivided on the basis of caste. Those who were agriculturalists have settled down on the outskirts of the city as gardeners and fishermen, whereas many of the middle-class refugees have found employment as skilled workers (Bose 1968:34).

Even within the major industries of West Bengal—jute and engineering, both of which are concentrated in the Calcutta metropolitan region—the labor forces are ethnically distinguished. The jute industry is dominated by a work force of Biharis, and a majority of laborers in the engineering industry are Bengalis (*Economic Review* 1979–1980: Table 4-10).

[4] The term *scheduled* caste is usually used to designate those groups known as "untouchables," in other words, those castes with whom contact is considered especially polluting within caste ideology. The sociologist R. J. Schermerhorn points out that the term originated during the 1930s when the British desired to categorize for census purposes those castes with whom contact "'entails purification on the part of high-caste Hindus,' a dejure definition. Lists or schedules of such castes were drawn up for the purpose of singling out those groups suffering civil and religious disabilities" (Schermerhorn 1978:29). There are problems with this definition, since all castes are hierarchically ranked and therefore contact between a relatively higher group and a relatively lower group, no matter what their particular identity, always entails the possibility of pollution for the higher group. Even among groups defined as untouchable, for instance, there is a hierarchy of relative purity. Nevertheless, the term is generally applied to those groups who are defined in a particular region as "the most defiled of all, the ones who can pollute all others" (Schermerhorn 1978:30).

which his ethnic group is identified and relies for economic support on those who speak his language, on his coreligionists, on members of his own caste and on fellow immigrants from the village or district from which he has come. By a backwash, reliance on earlier forms of group identification reinforces and perpetuates differences between ethnic groups" (1966:102).

To some extent, therefore, the Chinese are simply one among many different social groups in Calcutta that are affiliated with a particular economic niche. Like most ethnic, caste, and religious groups in this diverse city, the Chinese not only occupy particular economic roles but are endogamous with respect to marriage and social life. On the other hand, their status as foreigners associated with a country that has been engaged in hostilities against India, combined with their association with a particularly degraded occupation (leather making), lend a certain uniqueness to their role and give them even more of an outsider status than other migrants to Calcutta.

The Chinese Niche within India's Leather Industry

Just as Calcutta's economy is organized along ethnic, caste, and religious lines, so, too, the tanning industry itself is subdivided by social group. Before I continue this account of the Chinese role in Calcutta's ethnically variegated economy, it is important to place the Hakka tanners within the sociological and technical contours of India's leather industry.

Because India has an enormous stock of cattle, larger than that of any other country (UNCTAD 1971:26), it should not be surprising to find that the leather industry has long played an important role in India's economy. India is one of the largest producers of rawhides in the world, outproduced by only the United States and the former USSR. It is also a major exporter of finished leather, joined by the highly industrialized countries of Japan, West Germany, the United Kingdom, and Italy (*Encyclopaedia Britannica* 1982:764). During the 1970s, when many of the Calcutta Chinese were expanding their operations, only the jute, engineering goods, tea, and iron ore industries outranked leather and leather products in the export goods sector (*Economic Times* 1972:3).[5] By the late 1980s, the leather industry was one of the fastest-growing industries in India (Hazarika 1987).

---

[5] The tanning industry is one of three major subdivisions of this leather and leather products industry; the other two are the collecting, curing, and trading of rawhides,

Whereas leather tanning in Western countries is an activity totally integrated into the modern manufacturing sector, however, in India it is carried out at a variety of technological levels.[6] The tanning methods practiced within India are diverse, each corresponding to a different social, cultural, and economic context. Trade in leather and leather goods is centralized in the cities of Calcutta, Madras, and Kanpur, the three major centers of modern tanning in India; tanning also takes place in a multitude of villages spread throughout the subcontinent. To understand the role that the Chinese came to play within this industry, one must place them within a mosaic composed of different castes, religions, ethnic groups, technologies, and economies of scale.

The smallest and simplest tanning enterprises in India exist in villages where members of the Chamar caste, an untouchable caste traditionally associated with leather making, process leather from locally available vegetable matter such as bark and leaves. The leather they produce is used to fashion shoes and water buckets for use in agriculture. At the other end of the spectrum, there are large modern tanneries employing thousands. The most notable example of these in West Bengal is a tannery associated with the Bata Company, a Czech firm which is one of the largest footwear companies in India and in the world.

Between the tiny one-person operations of the villages and the large organized tanneries, there are two intermediate types of tanning organization in India. One of these, referred to as the East India Tanneries, can be found in the states of Maharashtra, Andhra Pradesh, Tamil Nadu, and Kerala. These tanneries originally specialized in producing semi-tanned leather which was then exported, but they ultimately shifted to production of finished leather. Small in size, employing from ten to twenty-five workers each, such tanneries use vegetable matter for tanning and do not require machinery (*AILD*, 1965–1966:24).

Unlike the East India tanneries, the fourth category of the Indian tanning industry consists of small and medium-scaled tanneries that are mechanized to varying degrees. Although most of these tanneries are modest in size, their total output was greater than that of the large

---

and the manufacture of leather goods like footwear, sporting goods, industrial goods, and army equipment (*All India Leather Directory* [*AILD*], 1965–1966:15).

[6] Leather making, after all, is one of the oldest of currently practiced manufacturing techniques—dating back to the ancient civilizations of the Chinese, Egyptians, and Indians, among others (*Encyclopaedia Britannica* 1982:760).

organized sector by the mid-1960s (*AILD*, 1965–1966:23, 25). Hence, they have played an important role in India's leather industry. The city of Madras, in the Indian state of Tamil Nadu, is the preeminent center for such tanneries. Recently the leather industry in Madras has been the recipient of government assistance, which has contributed both to the development of new tanneries and to the modernization of existing plants (*Calcutta Statesman* 19 July 1982). The Chinese tanneries in Dhapa also belong to this fourth category of tanning enterprise, but the Chinese have received no government assistance. Their primary sources of funding have been their families and community, as discussed in Chapter 5.

Of course, although the Chinese tanneries are classified in this fourth category of small and medium-sized mechanized enterprises, they range in size, technical sophistication, and productivity. Tanneries vary in the number and types of machinery they contain.[7] Even tanneries of equal size in terms of machinery inventory may vary in terms of productivity. In one tannery, the tanner may run a relatively small business and rent his excess capacity to tenants. In general, small businesses in Dhapa produce between 500 and 1,000 pieces of finished leather per month.[8] Larger businesses may produce up to 2,000 pieces per month, and the largest enterprises may produce 4,000 to 5,000 pieces of finished leather each month. Not only do larger and more profitable businesses produce more, but their margin of profit on each piece of leather is greater because they produce superior quality.

It should be emphasized that even small businesses now earn a good living by Indian standards. For instance, by 1982 a small tanning business that produced ordinary chrome leather might have earned a profit of ten rupees per piece of leather. If it produced 1,000 pieces of leather per month, which was not uncommon, it would still earn more than a highly placed white collar-professional at that time.

---

[7] Certain minimum requirements must be met if one hopes to produce leather in Dhapa. Every tanner must have at his disposal a few rudimentary machines: a rotating drum, to mix the hides in various chemical solutions; a shaving machine, to shave pieces of partly tanned leather to uniform thickness; a staking machine, to pound the leather to greater softness; and a grazing machine, to make the leather smoother and shinier. These machines plus a water pump are absolutely essential for even the smallest tanneries. In addition, larger and wealthier enterprises utilize a number of more sophisticated machines like the hydraulic press and the splitting machine, which produce higher-quality leather, and measuring machines, which mechanize a task that is performed by hand in most tanneries.

[8] On average, each piece of finished leather is between twenty-five and thirty square feet.

Most Chinese tanners, however, are reluctant to divulge detailed financial information. While doing my fieldwork, it was impossible for me to assess accurately a family's profits, not only because they certainly varied over time, but also because no family would ever make such information public, even to the most trusted of friends. It would be to no family's advantage to let tax collectors or even potential borrowers have a completely accurate reading of their affluence! One measure of firm size that was publicly observable, however, was the number of nonfamily workers employed in a business. This number was easily measured, and perhaps more important, most community residents themselves considered it a good indication of the relative prosperity of the owners.

In a sample of forty-six tanning businesses that I surveyed in the summer of 1985, I found a great variation in firm size as measured by the number of workers employed. The smallest business in this sample employed only four workers, and the largest, 150; but the median number of nonfamily workers was nine. Indeed, businesses in Dhapa that employed more than twenty workers were rare enough that most residents of the community could easily remember and identify them. Thus, while these businesses have certainly brought a good living to their owners, it is important to remember throughout this narrative that the overwhelming majority of them are still modest in size.

The Distinction between Center and Periphery

Ethnic, caste, and religious distinctions play an important role in both the Indian leather industry and Calcutta's economy. However, in addition to the strong association between occupation and ethnicity, Calcutta adds a geographical demarcation. Nirmal Kumar Bose examined this phenomenon extensively and charted the social, ethnic, and religious composition of Calcutta (1965, 1968). He demonstrated that there was a tendency for groups of higher caste and class to be associated with the center of the city, those of lower caste and class, with the periphery (see Map 4).[9]

[9] For instance, Bengalis of commercial and artisan castes (Subarnabanik, Gandhabanik, Kansaris, Tantubanik) are found in much greater numbers in the wards at the center of the city than in those at the periphery; on the other hand, scheduled-caste Bengali refugees are found in much greater concentrations in peripheral wards.

Likewise, among the non-Bengali population, a similar geographical arrangement is found. Bose indicated that the "commercial" and "bureaucratic" classes (e.g., the Marwaris and Gujaratis) are found in areas north, south, and directly east of the Maidan, a

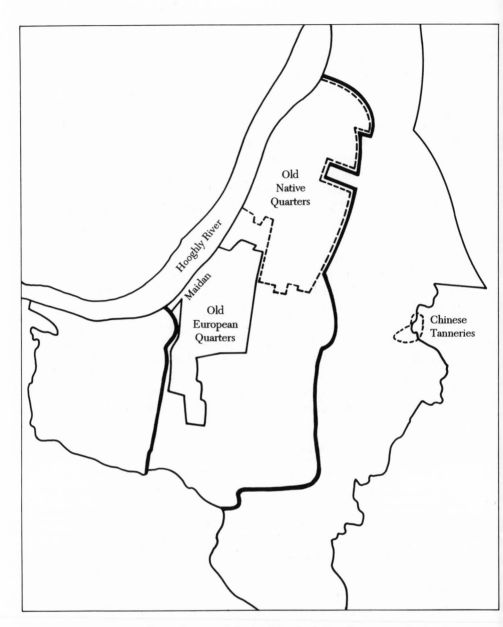

Map 4. Center and periphery in Calcutta. The thick line demarcates the border between the central area associated with higher castes and classes and the peripheral areas. Low castes and classes are concentrated in a greater number of wards outside this border than within it. Note the peripheral location of the Chinese tanning community. Based on information in Bose 1965 and 1968.

[42]

The primacy of the central area in Calcutta has continued since British times and results from the interaction of both political and economic forces. When the British founded Calcutta, they built an imperial stronghold, Fort William, near the river and surrounded it with a large open area called the Maidan. They did so as a defensive tactic. The fort was so strategically placed that although British troops could easily see attackers from inside (Lelyveld 1975:12), the fort itself could not be observed by outsiders attempting to close in. The British residential quarter adjoined this protected area. Presently, the Maidan functions as what the journalist Joseph Lelyveld calls "the city's lungs" (1975:12), the only open green space left. This area and bordering sections of the old native quarter continue to be prime real estate, partly because of their proximity to the open space of the Maidan and partly because the major shopping district is located in this central area. Therefore, the high value of the center in Calcutta is closely linked to its original importance in securing British military, political, and economic power and to its subsequent desirability for both residential and commercial use.

It is significant that both spatial and occupational demarcations distinguish ethnic, caste, language, and religious groups in Calcutta. And these distinctions are reflected in and help maintain social separation. Calcutta is not a melting pot. Instead, each of the many groups maintains its separation from the others, rarely intermarrying and conservatively guarding its own customs and ways of life. For instance, Calcutta's schools cater to groups according to language. There are Bengali, Hindi, English, Gujarati, and Chinese schools. Furthermore, many groups have their own associations, and few associations are based on a cross-ethnic membership (Tysen 1971). Indeed, in Calcutta questions of assimilation and acculturation are irrelevant. If the Chinese were to assimilate, for instance, with which group would they do so?

The existence of these relatively endogamous, occupationally demarcated, and geographically clustered subgroups, as well as the con-

---

large area of park which is usually taken as the center of the city and around which the Europeans used to live (1966:95). On the other hand, Bihari, Oriya, and Uttar Pradesh migrants, all of whom belong to laboring classes, are found in the northeastern, eastern, and southwestern peripheries of the city (Bose 1966:95). According to Bose, Muslims also divide themselves residentially on the basis of class: upper-class Muslims are found in more of the wards in the center of the city than at the periphery; lower-class Muslims are found in greater numbers in peripheral wards; and middle-class Muslims are found in equal numbers in central and peripheral areas (1968).

[43]

trast between center and periphery, bears some resemblance, on a larger scale, to the organization of Indian villages. But whereas in villages the division of labor is based primarily on caste, in Calcutta it is based on much more: caste, language, religion, and regional origin.

As in a village, however, the economic interactions of each group have not broken down the barriers between them, which are reproduced through social and domestic organization. Indeed, the multitude of groups in Calcutta resemble the collectivities alluded to by Fredrik Barth in his work on ethnic boundaries—"their agreement on codes and values need not extend beyond that which is relevant to the social situations in which they interact" (1969:16). While many of these groups interact in the economic sphere, their separate ethnic identities remain unscathed.

Most striking, both the ethnic organization of Calcutta and the caste differentiation of Indian villages are reflected in an opposition between center and periphery. Just as low castes and classes are associated with the peripheral areas of Calcutta, so, too, in many Indian villages the untouchable outcasts are frequently found in distinct quarters outside the village proper.[10]

Chinese Tanners—Peripherality and Impurity

One must be cautious not to stretch the analogy between village India and Calcutta too far, for the historical reasons behind the opposition of center and periphery differed in these two locations; the establishment of British military and commercial power was not a factor in the center/periphery distinctions in Indian villages, as it was in the colonially created city of Calcutta. In both cases, however, a knowledge of the values embedded in caste society is critical to an understanding of the contemporary social significance of these spatial oppositions, particularly the significance of the tanning community's location on the eastern periphery of the city.

The ideology that underlies the Hindu caste system is based on a distinction between purity and impurity. According to this ideology, organic waste products are impure, and so, by extension, are activities

---

[10] Of course, neither Indian cities nor Indian villages are unique in terms of the significant symbolic role played by space within them. As Walter Firey noted in a pathbreaking study, undertaken more than forty years ago, of the city of Boston, "space may be a symbol for social values" (1980:169).

such as eating, sex, defecation, and menstruation. Furthermore, all people, animals, and things may temporarily undergo states of pollution by engaging in such polluting activities or by contact and interchange with others who are in a more polluted state (see Kolenda 1985). But while all beings and things can be polluted, they may also be hierarchically ranked according to their relative degree of pollution. Occupation is an important component of such ranking, since certain occupations, by their very nature, expose their practitioners to greater contact with pollution.[11] For instance, those who deal with human waste (e.g., sweepers, barbers, and washermen) are always in a more impure state than those whose occupations involve less contact with pollution (e.g., priests).

Significantly, none of the occupations engaged in by Calcutta Chinese are associated with high-caste activities in traditional Hindu thought—whether it is the hairdressing, restaurant keeping, tanning, and shoemaking of the Hakkas, the carpentry of the Cantonese, or the dentistry of the Hubeinese. But of all these tasks, certainly tanning has the lowest status. In a system where status of groups is determined by the relative purity or impurity of their occupations, there is no doubt that tanning is viewed as one of the most supremely impure tasks, because of its association with dead cattle and the necessity of working with hides. Death pollutes by making the entire body a waste product, and the association with slaughtering of the sacred cow adds to the impurity of this connection.

As discussed in Chapter 1, it is not uncommon for immigrant minority groups throughout the world to engage in occupations that are denigrated by their host societies, or at least by the higher-status members of those societies. That the Chinese within India have taken

[11] Scholars are engaged in a broad and vigorous debate about the nature of the caste system in India, and the extent to which it is ideologically based. Some, like Louis Dumont (1970), assert that the ideology of purity and pollution underlies and orders the social relations that can be observed among castes. Others, such as Joan Mencher (1974), argue that this ideology is not shared by all castes. Still others, like McKim Marriott, maintain that the ranking of castes within villages cannot be explained solely in terms of relative purity and pollution (1968) but must be derived by an analysis of transactions of different categories of food between different castes. But although the degree to which the ideology of purity and pollution is universally shared and the degree to which all occupations can be ranked according to it have been disputed, no one would deny that work with rawhides and leather is considered an impure occupation within caste ideology, associated with castes traditionally placed in the category of untouchable.

[45]

up vocations associated with lower castes, or even with the work of untouchables, bears out this general pattern. Furthermore, their peripheral geographical position within Calcutta's urban space is in many ways analogous to that of an untouchable community within an Indian village. Given the traditional Hindu view of tanning as a polluting activity and the notion that those who engage in it should reside at the margins of their communities, the location of the Chinese tanning community in Calcutta should not come as a surprise.

The Chinese tanning community is in the eastern corner of Calcutta, adjacent to the city dump. The Indian residents of the areas that surround it (Tiljala, Tangra, and Tapsia) come primarily from the Chamar caste, a group traditionally considered untouchable, whose customary occupation was leather work (Bandyopadhyay 1990:79). The peripherality and isolation of the tanning district, as well as the association with an impure task, bring to mind the definition of *untouchability* used by Louis Dumont: "We shall define untouchability in the way that is most current by the segregation into distinct hamlets or quarters of the most impure categories. This feature is pan-Indian, as is the association with a religiously relevant function (quartering of dead cattle and consumption of meat, leather tanning, role in incineration or cleaning of rubbish and excrement, pig rearing and consumption of pork)" (1970:134). Charlotte and William Wiser, in their classic study of village India, *Behind Mud Walls*, also comment on the peripheral location of the leather workers in the village where they lived: "The *chamars* (leather workers) live a furlong from the rest of the village in a cluster of huts enclosed by mud walls. We have not made much progress in friendliness with them, chiefly because of the inconvenience in reaching them (1971:41). And Adrian Mayer notes in his study of a village in central India: "Everyone, including Harijans, can walk freely through all parts of the village. But people should go to the Tanner and Sweeper wards only on business, it is said; and some added that they should wash their feet afterwards . . . the Tanner ward is off the beaten track, and few people would go there for casual conversation in any case. It is also a naturally uncongenial place, for cow and buffalo hides hang drying between the houses, and there is a tanning pit in the middle of the houses which gives off an unpleasant smell" (1960:57). Likewise, few visitors go to Dhapa except those directly involved in the tanning business—workers, leather buyers, and the Chinese themselves.

Of course, considerations of purity and impurity are not the only factors that prevented the Chinese from setting up their tanning operations nearer to the center of the city. The Chinese themselves emphasize other considerations in the selection of Dhapa as their site for tanning. Dhapa, formerly a marshy and swampy area, had the requisite amount of available water, an essential for tanning. Furthermore, although close enough to the city to do business with buyers and suppliers, it was still relatively uninhabited and real estate was cheap. Conversely, Chinese shoe shops, whose original clientele was largely European and high-class Indian, had to be situated in the center of the city near the major shopping areas frequented by these groups.

While several explanations can be found for the tanning community's peripheral location, there is no doubt that this geographic marginality and their degraded occupation have served to isolate the Chinese tanners even more than other Chinese subgroups in Calcutta. These facts were driven home to me when I attempted to introduce myself to the tanning community.

Fieldwork in an Ethnic Enclave

Crossing Communal Boundaries

For most anthropologists, immersion in a new culture stimulates an ongoing conceptual comparison of the knowledge, habits, and ideas of that culture with those of their own culture and society. Yet in my case I frequently moved conceptually not between two cultures, but among at least three: that of the Chinese, my own cultural background as an American, and that of high-caste Hindu Bengali society.

Although I ultimately found a place to live near the Chinese community, and although my husband did not go with me into the field, I often moved between the Chinese and Bengali communities because of family obligations, social occasions, and festival days. Just as I would begin to immerse myself in the outlook, tempo, and style of life of one group, I found myself switching contexts.

Differences in life-style and outlook are far from subtle, and the most visible types of distinctions—those of dress and diet, for instance—reminded me daily of the differences between the two groups. Following the Hindu ideology of purity and pollution, most Bengali Hindus abstain from certain foods, such as pork, beef, and liquor, because they are considered defiling. Chinese, on the other hand, have few restrictions in their daily diet, and during such festivi-

[47]

ties as wedding banquets, they readily consume liquor and beer. Dress is also a significant mark of affiliation with one group or the other. Saris are the standard dress for adult Bengali women. Chinese women, however, never wear Indian dress. Married women wear Chinese pajamas in their tanneries, and even on visits to town; younger unmarried women wear Western dress, usually skirts and blouses. "Saris are pretty," a young Chinese woman remarked to me, "but no Chinese will wear one, or others [other Chinese] will pass remarks."

As I moved between one community and the other, not only did I find myself changing visible aspects of identity, such as dress and diet, in order to accord with each group's established practice, but I also found myself shifting the focus of my concerns. The segment of the Bengali community with which I was most frequently associated was upper-middle-class. Many were professionals or worked in white-collar jobs. Although a few were also in business, they did not usually discuss money and prices. Songs and music by such artistic luminaries as the great Bengali poet, Rabindranath Tagore, were focal points of cultural life. The Chinese of Dhapa, however, had few such "highbrow" tastes. Western pop music, or the pop music of Taiwan and Hong Kong, was standard musical fare. Money and prices were frequent topics of conversation. Mahjong and other forms of gambling were common forms of recreation.

While it was a bit disconcerting to switch contexts so frequently, this mobility did give me an opportunity to gain insight into two cultural milieus within one city. And I frequently had the unsettling experience of listening to the negative ethnic stereotypes with which individuals in each group characterized the other.

Visiting my Bengali relatives, for instance, I would often bring up my research among the Chinese. "Yes," said one of my husband's aunts, "Chinese are basically hardworking, but they can't be trusted, they're really *budmash* [a Bengali word that means "up to no good," "a scoundrel"]". These two themes, that Chinese work hard, but cannot really be trusted, were frequently sounded by Bengali acquaintances and relatives. One woman told me that she had a Chinese friend but ultimately, "I never know what she has up her sleeves."

Much of this attitude seemed to be related directly to the Sino-Indian conflict, and it was an attitude held not only by many Bengalis but also by numerous other groups in India. A common remark was that India had been "stabbed in the back" by China, a reference to the fact that before the outbreak of hostilities, relationships between the

[48]

two countries had appeared congenial. Whereas some individuals clearly differentiated between the Chinese who lived in India and those who lived in the People's Republic of China, others did not. One woman, for instance, told me that ever since 1962 she regarded all Chinese as her enemies. And even those who were not alive at that time, or not old enough to remember the events, still seemed to be affected by the conflict. Said one young man, "Everybody knows that China stole Indian territory, so Chinese can't be trusted." Furthermore, while most Chinese would bring up as one of the first topics of conversation the loss of rights many Chinese experienced, many Bengalis, as well as other Indians whom I met, would claim that they were not aware that the Chinese were deprived of their citizenship rights on account of the hostilities. When I raised the issue, some would insist that I had my facts wrong, or try to explain it by saying that those who had lost their citizenship must have done something wrong. There were "good" Chinese and "bad" Chinese, one acquaintance argued, and if you were a "good" Chinese you would definitely be allowed to be a citizen.

But political history was not the only factor that influenced the way Indians, particularly Bengalis, talked about the Chinese. The dissimilarities in diet were also frequently alluded to. As the anthropologist Fredrik Barth has pointed out, different ethnic groups often latch onto particular "diacritica," specific markers of difference, as a way of defining the boundaries between them (1969). In India, diet is an especially significant marker of caste, ethnic, and/or religious affiliation. Chinese are set apart from both Hindus, who generally abstain from beef, and Muslims, who abstain from pork. Where diet is such a critical concern and symbol, it is not surprising that it is one of the most frequently mentioned items when ethnic groups discuss and define one another. The apparent willingness of the Chinese to eat almost anything was often cited by Bengalis as proof of their peculiarity. As a cousin of my husband put it, "They do eat rice [a staple of the Bengali diet], but I also heard that they eat frogs and snakes!"

In addition to focusing on the impurity of food intake (a trait many Calcuttans believe is shared by all Chinese) many Calcuttans view the tanning area as particularly unclean. While I was doing my fieldwork, for instance, my sister came to visit me for two weeks; she fell ill for a few days, a rather common occurrence for travelers. But many of my Indian friends were sure that these health problems resulted from her being in the tanning district. Later, one of my friends wrote in a letter to my sister, "Next time you come . . . stay with us. It is difficult to stand Tangra [Dhapa] environment. Ellen has developed a bit of immunity."

In fact, for most Calcuttans, the tanning area is a place to be avoided. It is seen as a slightly mysterious, even dangerous location. One young college student, for instance, told of his reactions every time he passed the area on a bypass road. "Tangra [Dhapa] is considered a rather unsafe area for a variety of reasons . . . the moment somebody mentions Tangra the two things you think of are Chinese, and you don't want to be there . . . and people are rather intrigued by the Chinese because they have, you know, they have their 'walled city' [here he is alluding to the appearance of the tanneries from afar] . . . there are these huge walls, and you can't see inside . . . people think it's mysterious, you don't know what is going on, you kind of wonder what happens there." And, in a recent anthology of essays on Calcutta, Jawhar Sircar, a member of the Indian Administrative Service, writes of Dhapa: "The tanneries-cum-residences with high walls, fortress-like gates and huge padlocks" are "an exclusive domain where even the municipal authorities tread warily" (1990:64).

Although Calcuttans expressed a range of feelings about the Chinese, particularly about the Chinese tanning community, attitudes of hostility, avoidance, or, at the very least, puzzlement were not uncommon. The conflict between India and China, Hindu ideas about purity and pollution, and the structure of ethnic relations in Calcutta, a city in which economic role and ethnic identity are closely correlated for all groups, all contributed to the maintenance of these ideas.

Initial Contacts

Given the geographical peripherality of the Chinese tanning community, the impurity of tanning within caste ideology, and the mistrust and apprehension expressed about the Chinese in the political sphere, it is hardly surprising that no one had ever brought me to see the area during my first two visits to Calcutta, as a tourist in 1976, and as a graduate student in the summer of 1979. Indeed, even other Chinese whom I met, Chinese who lived in central Calcutta, spoke negatively about the place. Dhapa, they asserted, was nothing but a pile of mud and mosquitoes. A Hubeinese man added that everyone knew that the Dhapa tanners were a rather uncultured lot, prone to uncouth and extravagant displays of wealth.

Furthermore, the tanning process undeniably creates a terrible stench, and the tanning area is full of unpaved roads and paths. A bypass road connecting downtown Calcutta to the airport now skirts the community's borders, but there is really no reason for an outsider to pass through. In fact, convincing a Calcutta taxi driver to go there was usually a major undertaking. The typical exchange would go something like this: (To first driver) "I'd like to go to Dhapa." "Sorry." (To next driver) "I'm going to Dhapa." "Ten extra rupees please!"

I decided upon returning to Calcutta in 1980, therefore, that I should begin my inquiries with the president of the Overseas Chinese Association, a Hakka who lived in central Calcutta. For most non-Chinese, Mr. Zhang was the primary intermediary with the Chinese community. I, too, had learned of him by skimming through local newspaper and magazine articles about the Chinese community in which he was the primary source quoted. Later, I contacted him and arranged to meet him.

When I saw the staircase to his second-floor apartment, I was a bit shocked and almost disappointed. The stairs looked as though they were falling down, and the entryway was rather dilapidated. But when I entered, I observed that as with many Calcutta flats, this well-worn exterior concealed a fairly comfortable and plush interior. I saw a well-decorated apartment with fine wood furniture and many photographs adorning the walls. Some of these photos, pictures of Mr. Zhang with well-known Indian and Chinese leaders, such as Chiang Kai-shek, Jawaharlal Nehru, and Indira Gandhi, seemed to visually validate his claimed role of spokesperson for the Chinese community to the outside world.[12]

On that day, both Mr. Zhang and his wife were present. Mr. Zhang was a heavyset man who wore thick glasses. He had a tendency to quickly gloss over matters with a nervous laugh, and in my mind the

---

[12] Skinner (1968) has written a trenchant analysis of leadership in Southeast Asian Chinese communities that applies in parts to the situation in Calcutta. Leaders, he notes, were both agents of the state and representatives of Chinese interests, and were inevitably individuals of great wealth. But because such individuals had to be acceptable to the state as well as to the ethnic community, they were rarely militant articulators of ethnic group interests and thereby often "forfeited influence in their own communities" (1968:199). I was later to learn that Mr. Zhang fit this mold to some extent. He appeared to have more power and influence in the Calcutta Chinese community than he actually held, and while he was easily accessible to outsiders, he was not viewed by community members as an energetic spokesperson for community interests.

glasses exacerbated his indirectness, serving as another barrier between us. His wife, by contrast, was a petite woman with a direct manner of speaking. I introduced myself in Mandarin and was quickly ushered in and asked to sit down. I was offered the customary glass of cold soda and looked around the room as I searched for some polite small talk. I asked about the photographs, and Mrs. Zhang began to explain them to me. There were many pictures of her children, seven sons and two daughters, who were now dispersed throughout North America and India—one remained in Calcutta, several lived in Toronto and Vancouver, and still another lived in Washington, D.C. Indeed, the Zhangs had just returned from Canada where they had attended a son's wedding, and Mrs. Zhang showed me some recently developed photos of the wedding.

Slowly we got down to talking "business," and I explained to Mr. Zhang that I was interested in living with and writing my doctoral dissertation on the Chinese tanning community, and I asked him if he could help me find a place to live in Dhapa. Although I knew that Mr. Zhang was usually an intermediary between the Chinese community and the outside world, and that one role of such intermediaries was frequently to keep outsiders at bay (see Skinner 1968), I was hoping that Mr. Zhang would help me gain direct access to others in the Chinese community, particularly those in the tanning district.

"Where do you go to school?" he inquired. I replied that I was doing my graduate work at Harvard University. "Oh yes, that's a very famous university." Mr. Zhang seemed somewhat reassured as he responded. He then explained that he was also the principal of the Chinese school in the tanning area and that I should meet him there later in the week. This would give him time to think of a family that might be willing to take me in.

I visited the school a few days later. It was a large, imposing, though somewhat neglected-looking structure, with well-placed portraits of the Chinese nationalist leader, Sun Yat-sen, and the Indian independence leader, Mahatma Gandhi, overlooking the main assembly hall. The students, whose uniforms resembled those of the Boy Scouts of America, tumbled and ran about, their high-pitched voices joining to create a general air of commotion. But as the bell rang, they quickly ran to their classrooms. As each teacher entered the classroom, the students stood up in unison with the greeting, "Good morning, Teacher."

I was impressed with the discipline but soon learned that the students at Pei Mei School were as ingenious as children everywhere when it came to finding new and original ways to be naughty and have fun. Mr. Zhang had decided to ask me to teach English at the school. This arrangement would be good, he assured me, for it would enable me to meet families and to do my research.

After meeting with Mr. Zhang and some of the other teachers, I learned that the majority of the school's students were enrolled in first through sixth grades, and a smaller number continued through grade nine. Although instruction was in Mandarin, students also studied English and Hindi, and after graduation many continued their studies in "English medium" schools (those where English is the medium of instruction) so English was an important part of the curriculum.

I soon understood why Mr. Zhang had tried to enlist my services so eagerly. The school had once been the pride of the community. But, over time, English education had become more popular. Families reasoned that a background in English was useful if one emigrated and even within India itself. Attendance had slowly decreased from more than a thousand students in the 1950s and 1960s to only 250. And those children who attended for the purpose of gaining some familiarity with Chinese culture and language were usually enrolled for only the first few years of primary school. Teachers' salaries were extremely low, and because the tanning business was now prospering, few individuals chose to make teaching their career anymore; indeed, teachers were paid less than the average Indian employee in a tannery. Most of the teachers were young unmarried Hakka women who lived at home and who used their salaries as personal spending money. Since only a few teachers continued working in the school after marriage, the turnover rate was high, creating frequent problems of understaffing.

Because I had indicated that I was interested in living in the community for at least a year, and that I could communicate with the students in Mandarin, my services could be profitably utilized in the school. From my point of view, this was a good arrangement inasmuch as I thought that teaching in the school would provide an opportunity to meet people and to establish an identity and role in the community. Furthermore, since I was volunteering, I thought it might be an effective way of showing my goodwill toward the community.

Finding a place to stay, however, was more problematic. After agreeing to teach at the school, I asked Mr. Zhang about my living arrangement.

[53]

"It won't be easy to find a place to stay for six months," he began, "although some families wouldn't mind it if you stayed for two weeks or a month." Thinking that a short stay with a family would be better than none at all, and knowing that I could always move back with my in-laws, I indicated my willingness to try a short-term stay with a family, if one could be found. Mr. Zhang arranged for me to live with a Chinese widow who resided near the school and who was prepared to keep me for two months.

Mrs. Jia, my first landlady, lived in a small flat a short walk from the school. Her place had two bedrooms, one of which was used by her eighteen-year-old son, the other by herself and a fifteen-year-old daughter who was away at boarding school at the time. I would stay with Mrs. Jia in her bedroom, where we shared a bed and a dresser. But once her daughter returned from school for vacation, it would simply be too crowded. Although my stay was short, I learned a great deal from Mrs. Jia. She was a loquacious and friendly person, and she liked to share gossip about other community members. She also told me a good deal about her own history and that of her deceased husband—describing how and when he had immigrated to India, how he had become involved in the tanning business, and why, as a widow, she had found it too difficult to manage the business on her own and had finally sold it.

It was not long before I discovered that moving beyond Mrs. Jia's house and the schoolyard would require time and patience. Communication itself was not my chief obstacle. Most people whom I met were fluent in either Mandarin, which many had learned as students in the Chinese school, or English. Thus, although I did not know Hakka at the beginning of my stay, it was not impossible to speak with people. But it was difficult to go beyond formalities and courtesies.

People responded appreciatively to my knowledge of Mandarin and interest in Chinese culture, but there seemed no natural or defensible way I could ask them about their own families and experiences in India without being intrusive. When I tried, most of my queries were speedily brushed away. For instance, when I asked one woman, whom I had come to know casually, if I could speak with her about her family history, she responded, "We were not born in India, so we can't tell you much about Chinese life here." But in another case I was told, "We were born in India, so we don't know anything about China." When I objected that it was their own personal histories, and not the entire history of the community, in which I was interested, I was

[54]

usually referred to the former principal of the school, who was said to have investigated the community history in detail and to know everything I could possibly be interested in.

My Bengali surname often added to people's mistrust. On several occasions I introduced myself using my Chinese name, Ou Ailing. But early into the conversation someone would ask me if I was married or ask for my name in English. Inevitably a disappointed or mistrustful look would appear on people's faces as I replied that my surname was Basu, easily identifiable as Bengali. "They think you are with the CID [Criminal Investigation Department, the Indian equivalent of the FBI]," said Mrs. Jia. A teacher at the school advised me, "They think you are working for the tax department." My American identity did not help much either, since most community members believed that Americans had loose sexual morals and generally low standards of behavior.

Hakka Views of Outsiders

Indeed, there were few categories into which I could be placed that would not justify mistrust, or at least extreme caution on the part of community members. From their vantage point, Indians, Westerners, and, to a marked but somewhat lesser extent, non-Hakka Chinese, are outsiders; and these distinctions are clearly revealed through the terms by which they refer to these groups. In fact, these terms are used in situations that, for an outsider, sometimes create almost ludicrous juxtapositions.

Several years after my introduction to the community, when I was conducting research in Toronto, for instance, I met two sisters from the tanning community who had recently immigrated to Canada. We got together on a Sunday afternoon for a reunion and decided to visit the CN Tower, the tallest building in the city. I had my camera with me, and we all thought it would be nice to have a picture of the three of us in the vicinity of the famous structure. As a middle-aged, white man passed by, one of my friends shouted in Hakka to her sister, "Oh look, there goes a *fangui* [literally, "foreign ghost" or "devil"]. Let's ask him to take a picture for us!" The *fangui* in question took our picture, and my friends thanked him cheerfully, remarking afterward how nice he had been in helping us out.

Westerners are frequently called *fangui* in the colloquial speech of the Hakka of Calcutta. The word *gui* literally means "ghost," and

[55]

indeed, ghosts themselves have frequently been associated in popular Chinese religion with outsiders and undesirables, including bandits and beggars (see Wolf 1974). Yet despite the literal meaning of the word *fangui*, the term is used not only when consciously denigrating a foreigner but even in neutral or even positive situations such as the one I just described. Like the residents of the immigrant Chinese community in California described by Maxine Hong Kingston (1975), the Calcutta Chinese use the word *gui* frequently when referring to community outsiders. Indeed, the Calcutta Hakka use the word for "person" (*ren*) only in reference to Chinese people. Thus, Chinese are called *Tangren*, or literally "people of Tang."

Yet when specific subgroups of Chinese are referred to, as opposed to the Chinese people as a whole, the Hakka also make important distinctions. When talking about themselves, the Calcutta Hakka continue to use the appellation *ren*, or person. They usually refer to themselves as "people of Mei Xian," thereby distinguishing themselves not only from other Chinese, but even from Hakka who do not come from Mei Xian in Guangdong, the county in Guangdong from which all Calcutta Hakka originate. But the Calcutta Hakka use the word *lao*, a word which connotes a vulgar person, sort of a hillbilly or hick, when referring to the Cantonese or the Hubeinese. Thus, a Cantonese is referred to as a *Guangfulao*, rather than a *Guangfuren* (literally, a "Cantonese fellow" rather than a "Cantonese person").

In addition to differences in terms of reference, the Hakka distinguish between themselves and other Chinese groups in other ways. From the perspective of the Hakka, the Cantonese do not work as hard, are not as frugal, and depending on the speaker, are either more Indianized or more Westernized than the Hakka; in all cases, the Hakka are portrayed as more loyal carriers of Chinese tradition than other Chinese subgroups. "Those Cantonese," asserted one young Hakka man to me in denigrating tones, "they mix Hindi and English in with their Chinese." My first landlady in Dhapa, Mrs. Jia, liked to compare Cantonese and Hakka working habits, and would imply that Cantonese in Calcutta were less successful financially than the Hakka because they were overindulgent. "When Cantonese make money," she informed me, " they get lots of servants, eat with ivory chopsticks, and use tablecloths . . . but Hakka keep working hard."

The distinctions that Hakka make between themselves and other groups of Chinese in Calcutta are replicated in social organization. Lawrence Crissman has drawn attention to what he calls the "segmentary structure" of many overseas Chinese communities throughout the world. These societies are divided into progressively segmenting sub-divisions based on language, native place, and surname. It is only vis-à-vis non-Chinese that these overseas Chinese societies present a united front (1967). In Chapter 3 I examine the internal social struc-ture of the Calcutta Chinese community more deeply, but the impor-tant point to remember here is that the Calcutta Hakka definitely view even non-Hakka Chinese as a category of outsider.

In referring to all other categories of outsiders, however, the Hakka make a much sharper distinction, since in these cases the word *gui*, rather than the less negative appellation *lao*, is used. As indicated, Westerners are referred to as *fangui*, Indians, as *wugui* (literally, "black ghosts" or "black devils"). The word *gui* is also used when talking about an individual as well as an entire group. When referring to an individual Indian man, for instance, speakers will frequently append the word *gui* to his surname. Thus, "Mr. Sen" becomes "Sen *gui*."

In their speech, therefore, the Calcutta Hakka differentiate them-selves from two levels of outsiders: first, other speech groups among the Calcutta Chinese; second, Indians and Westerners.[13] Whereas Westerners are no longer numerous or highly visible as actors within Calcutta's ethnic landscape, and hence Hakka ideas about them are not constantly reinforced through interaction, this is not true of Hakka attitudes toward Indians.

Hakka interactions with Bengalis, for instance, often occur in set-tings that, for the Chinese, reinforce the negative stereotypes they hold. Chinese are most likely to encounter Bengalis when they have dealings with government bureaucrats. Because many Chinese are still classified as "foreigners," such contacts are not infrequent. Regis-tering yearly with the Foreigners Registration Office or making re-peated applications for citizenship requires numerous meetings with government officials, and such interactions are seldom pleasant expe-

---

[13] The definitions of *Westerner* and *Indian* are primarily cultural and contextual, rather than purely biological. This is illustrated by the fact that, although rare, Chinese families that have had no sons will sometimes adopt babies of non-Chinese descent when it is impossible to find a baby to adopt who is of Chinese descent. These children are raised as Chinese and considered Chinese. On the other hand, the children of mixed marriages between a Chinese and an Indian are not necessarily considered Chinese, even though they have some Chinese ancestry. They are usually classified, instead, according to the language they use at home.

riences. Indeed, one of the most frequent grievances I heard was that the only way to get anything done was to bribe an official. Less prosperous community members complained that because they did not have enough funds at their disposal to bribe effectively, they were at a perpetual disadvantage in securing citizenship papers or in getting business permits (e.g., export licenses).

Bengalis also meet with government bureaucrats, of course, and they are not strangers to unmotivated, inefficient, or even corrupt officials. But since the officials are usually from the same ethnic group to which they themselves belong, Bengalis do not conceptualize such interactions in ethnic terms. Rather, they tend to see this behavior as a sign of the times (*shemoi kharap*, meaning "times are bad") or as a symptom of bad government in general.

When Chinese encounter difficulties in their dealings with bureaucracy, however, they often blame the Bengali bureaucrats themselves, claiming that Bengalis are lazy and that the Bengali government workers will provide services only in return for a bribe. Furthermore, they assert that because they are Chinese, they can be taken advantage of more than other groups. After a disappointing inquiry about a delay in the processing of his papers for a passport application, one Hakka Chinese acquaintance complained that you could get it done very quickly if you gave extra money to the official in charge. "They all need money for their daughters' dowries . . . and they know we can't object because we are Chinese."

The feeling that Chinese will never be treated fairly only because they are Chinese is quite pervasive. One year before I arrived, a band of dacoits attacked a tannery.[14] Three people were killed before the dacoits fled across the marshy area bordering Dhapa. Most Dhapa residents felt that the police had done nothing about the incident and had not tried to apprehend the culprits because the victims were Chinese. Ultimately, the police did apprehend some people who they alleged were the perpetrators. But most Dhapa Chinese claimed that it took place only because they had complained to the Chinese Embassy in New Delhi and that the embassy had interceded with the police on their behalf.

Whereas Hakka interactions with Bengalis tend to occur in the bureaucratic sphere, their interactions with most other Indian groups

---

[14] *Dacoit* is a word commonly used in Indian English to refer to gangs of armed robbers.

are usually confined to the economic or commercial sphere. Hakka tanners sell their leather primarily to Hindu, Muslim, and/or Sikh Punjabis, and they buy their rawhides from Muslims who come from the Indian states of Uttar Pradesh and/or Punjab. Most of their employees are Biharis of the Chamar (leather-working) caste; others are Nepalese and north Indian Muslims. Bihari women are also employed as servants to wash clothes, do household work, or watch over small children (they do not cook since they are unfamiliar with Chinese cuisine). In short, Hakka interactions with Indians occur primarily in bureaucratic or economic contexts, where Indians are officials, workers, suppliers, servants, or customers.

These contacts require that the Hakka be conversant with a number of different languages. In their interactions with tanning workers, rawhide merchants, and leather buyers, their primary language is Hindi. Hakka who run shoe shops in the center of the city may also need to know some Bengali. And those who run restaurants or beauty parlors may use a combination of Hindi, English, and Bengali. Age also has a bearing on these language competencies. Younger community members, who have attended English medium schools, are more likely to be competent in English as well as Hindi. Older individuals, whose schooling was primarily in Chinese medium schools, are still likely to know Hindi, which they speak with their employees; but they are unlikely to be competent in English.

Of course, the fact that Chinese interact with Indians primarily in the economic sphere does not mean that such interactions are totally impersonal or cold. As I explain in Chapter 4, in order to secure credit on favorable terms, the tanners go to considerable lengths to demonstrate their trustworthiness to their suppliers, particularly the rawhide merchants. Occasionally, an extremely important supplier or buyer will be invited to a wedding feast. But attendance at a large life-cycle celebration, at which there are hundreds of guests, is the usual limit to the social intimacy that would occur between a Chinese and an Indian who had important business connections. Few outsiders ever have a chance to enter into close personal relations or interactions with the Chinese.

It is only in the English medium schools, to which more and more young Chinese are being sent, that their interactions with different Indian ethnic groups are not primarily economic or bureaucratic. But even in these settings, Chinese have a tendency to segregate themselves or to feel that they are excluded by others. One resident of

[59]

Dhapa reflected on his years in an English medium boarding school in this way: "There would be a lot of name calling . . . even in teamwork you are more or less left to the last . . . mind you there were some pretty good [Indian] friends that I still keep in touch with now . . . and it's interesting . . . I would get along better with another minority, such as Anglo-Indian, you know, or somebody they would consider different, such as an Armenian." While other young people from Dhapa talked of their experiences in English medium schools in a more positive way, many emphasized that even if they had Indian friends they would not bring them home. I observed that Indian school friends did visit, but only on rare occasions.

Establishing Ties

Naturally, I was not privy to all this information when I began my fieldwork. But I could detect that the community was tightly knit and that its members had a strong sense of outsiders and insiders. As time elapsed, I began to think that my chances of learning about and being accepted in the community were getting slimmer. Since Mrs. Jia was not prepared to keep me on a long-term basis, I would have to move to my sister-in-law's flat in north Calcutta after two months. But although I could continue teaching at the Chinese school, I now would have a long commute every day, and I would be removed from the casual and constant contact with the community that is so essential to research. After teaching my few classes in English, I would have no excuse to linger.

I feared that I would remain on the periphery of this tightly encapsulated community. There were other non-Chinese teachers at the school, a Burmese man who taught English and a Bihari who taught Hindi. Later in my stay, a young Bengali woman was hired to teach both English and Hindi. All these non-Chinese teachers always appeared to be rather forlorn and excluded, having little contact with the Chinese community beyond the school walls. Unable to speak Hakka or Mandarin, they could not take part in the animated banter of the other teachers. Indeed, on my first day at the school, the Burmese teacher, Mr. Than, had a loud argument with the principal over a cut in pay because of absence. He shouted that many Chinese teachers were often absent but had not had their pay cut. His exasperation and the isolation of the other non-Chinese teachers disturbed me, and I could also easily envision myself settling into a similar position.

Fortunately, my role at the school provided me with a view of some of the larger and more important ritual events in Dhapa. The school often sent delegations of teachers and students to attend the funerals of prominent men in the community, especially those who had given generously to the school. On such occasions, I frequently questioned people about the meaning of what I had seen. Although hesitant about giving the details of particular family histories, people were not reluctant to answer my questions about rituals, for the interest I displayed in learning about Chinese culture through these events was not threatening. The relationships established over such cultural matters thereby became an important bridge into the community and enabled me to meet more people and to communicate with them in a less intrusive way.

One day, when I was leaving the schoolyard, I crossed paths with Mrs. Qiao, whose family I had met through exactly this type of inquiry about ritual and religion. Her husband had once been a teacher in the Chinese school. Upon retirement he went into the business of making paper objects that are burned as offerings to deities; this business was quite lucrative in Dhapa because prosperity enabled people to enjoy a rather elaborate ritual life. After meeting Mr. Qiao, I frequently went to his house to question him about various rituals that I had observed.

On this particular day I was carrying several heavily loaded bags. I had been gradually moving my clothes and books from Mrs. Jia's house to my sister-in-law's flat and sensed a good opportunity to impress Mrs. Qiao with the difficulties I faced. I told her that I could no longer stay with Mrs. Jia. "It is really a lot of trouble, " I complained, "I have to travel an hour and a half to get to the school, and at this rate I'll never be able to get the information I need to write my thesis!" I do not know where I got the idea that Mrs. Qiao would think writing a thesis was important, but perhaps because I seemed so upset when I said this, I managed to convey a sense of urgency about the matter. Mrs. Qiao told me to come home with her for a few minutes while she explained the situation to her family. I understood little Hakka at this time. Nevertheless, from Mrs. Qiao's conversation with her family and with me, I gathered that she thought that I would have to take an important test when I returned home. She was apparently concerned that I would be questioned before a panel of imposing and stern professors and would be unable to answer them because I had spent all my time in India commuting.

After sitting and talking with the rest of her family for a few minutes,

[61]

Mrs. Qiao said, "Let me take you to my sister's house." I had known that she had a younger sister who had married a Bengali, and who lived very close to the tanning community. I also remembered Mrs. Qiao's sons telling me that the two sisters had very little contact now. Nevertheless, I was hoping at this point that something would turn up. "The only trouble with my sister is that her mother-in-law is really fierce [*hen lihai*]!" Mrs. Qiao remarked.

I wondered what Mrs. Qiao might be referring to, since she did not elaborate, but I assured her that in general I was accustomed to living in a Bengali household. I surmised that some of the problems Mrs. Qiao foresaw might reflect her view of Bengali life, particularly what she perceived as the restrictions of the Bengali diet. In fact, as it turned out, Mrs. Qiao was referring to the mother-in-law's excessive concern with matters of purity and pollution, including diet. Because widows who strictly follow Hindu dietary laws should not eat meat, onions, and garlic, they are often quite vigilant in guarding their own kitchens, lest one of these forbidden substances come in contact with, or pollute, the utensils they use in the preparation of their relatively purer food. Indeed, Bengalis even have a name for people whom they view as almost fanatically concerned with matters of purity and pollution (*chuchi bhai*), and it is commonly thought that such people are usually elderly widows.

Despite qualms about the mother-in-law, however, Mrs. Qiao decided it would be worth asking her sister if I could stay with the family. We hailed a rickshaw and proceeded to her sister's house, although Mrs. Qiao continued to mutter along the way about what a pain the old lady was. Later, I learned that the two sisters had a tense and troubled relationship. When we arrived at her sister's doorway, Mrs. Qiao called out her sister's name. It was the first time that she had visited her sister, Xiu Lilan, in a year. Afterward, Lilan complained to me frequently that she heard from her elder sister only when help was needed, or when a problem had to be solved. Sometimes this involved taking her sister and/or her family to a Bengali doctor and translating for them. At other times, it was to use Lilan's telephone, since Mrs. Qiao did not have one. This time I was the problem! And Mrs. Qiao was typically and deftly allowing her sister to handle it.

In any event, Xiu Lilan's household did become my permanent home in Dhapa, and moving into Lilan's house solved many of my difficulties. Lilan was an extremely interesting, complex, and formidable person who understood both Bengali and Chinese cultures thoroughly, while in her own behavior she unhesitatingly ignored many salient features of each. Having married into a Bengali family herself, she was less suspicious of my own ties to the Bengali community than were many other Chinese, and she helped me immensely in the task of understanding a society from which she herself had been marginalized since her marriage.

Lilan had fallen in love with a Bengali when she was sixteen. She married soon afterward and bore three sons whom she raised as Bengalis, speaking Bengali with them and sending them to Bengali schools. As with other ethnic groups in Calcutta, intermarriage between the Calcutta Chinese and outsiders is rare. During my stay, I learned of only one other case besides Lilan's in which a Chinese woman had married into a non-Chinese family. Indeed, most Chinese do not even marry outside their speech group. Lilan's husband died young, and she was a widow at thirty-three. Widowhood seemed only to exacerbate her problems—though, in truth, she did not go out of her way to avoid them. She did not dress as a proper Bengali widow would, in a white sari, wearing no ornaments. Nor did she abstain from eating meat. Thus she earned the disapprobation of many relatives on the Bengali side of the family. Even her youngest son, who was seventeen when I moved into the house, would voice his disapproval sometimes, although he would then be roundly scolded by his mother.

But if Lilan did not the fit the proper image of a Bengali widow, neither did she present herself as a typical middle-aged Chinese woman, wearing loose-fitting Chinese pajamas over a slightly extended midriff. Instead, she favored colorful saris as well as Western dress (e.g., skirts and pants) accompanied by a vivid combination of jewelry and makeup. Indeed, her attitude toward fashion was probably best summed up by a comment she made to me on the day I apprehensively decided to get my ears pierced. "If you want to look pretty," she unflinchingly asserted, "it has to hurt!"

All of this caused many in the Dhapa community to suspect Lilan of the usual ploy that Chinese have traditionally attributed to widows—trying to entice men.[15] And in this community it was usually implied

---

[15] The ideal of chaste widowhood has had a long history in China (see, e.g., Spence 1978:59–76, 99–132). But this very ideal has also meant that most widows become the objects of intense scrutiny and curiosity. As the novelist Lao Xiang states in a short story written in the 1930s, "'Gossip hangs around a widow's doorsteps.' The old saying still holds good today. Whenever people find a moment free, they like to watch what is

that the motives were economic. What better way to get access to and influence over a man's property and assets?

Lilan had no intention of altering her behavior to gain acceptance. But the facts of her life history, and her own presentation of self, meant that she was socially stigmatized and often excluded from the life of both the Chinese and the Bengali communities. I feared at first that Lilan's own marginal status would make it difficult for me to gain entrance into the community. But although Lilan often flouted many conventions, it was not because she did not know them. Indeed, she advised me on numerous matters. She understood that becoming accepted within the community was not simply a matter of avoiding cultural blunders, although that was important, but of interacting in a positive way with people through the establishment of flexibility and reciprocity in my relationships.

"People won't give away something so easily," she would say to me. "You have to have a good relationship with them first." Lilan emphasized that establishing such a relationship involved not only a reciprocation of friendship and time, but also an openness about myself and my intentions. Explaining who I was and why I was there was critical, and Lilan advised me to make use of an important community institution—the Chinese newspaper.

In this tightly knit society, no engagement, wedding, opening of a new business, settlement of a dispute, or funeral took place without a notice being given in one or both of the two Chinese newspapers. Announcements validated social activities. Even divorce, which was extremely rare, was always concluded with an announcement in the paper. To undertake an action without such an announcement, on the other hand, was to bypass others, something like a slap in the communal face. Only people who were quite arrogant (*jiao ao*) and had an

---

going on inside a widow's house, determined to find something there to keep idle tongues busy. When a woman becomes a widow, the best thing for her to do is to cover her face and weep all day" (Lin 1950:24–25). Interestingly, recent research suggests that in rural areas this ideal was not always followed for practical reasons. Margery Wolf found that in the Taiwanese village where she did research, filiality was more important than chastity. If a young widow gave birth to a son, and therefore carried on the line of her husband's family, many would turn a blind eye to her sex life (1972:201). Arthur Wolf, who analyzed population registers in Taiwan, found that in one sample of women born between 1856 and 1920 whose husbands died before 1940, 58.5 percent of those age twenty-four and under at the time of their husband's death had later remarried (Wolf and Huang 1980:226).

inflated sense of themselves, thinking they were "terrific" (*liao bu qi*), would ignore their fellow community members in this way.

Lilan advised me to print an essay in Chinese in which I introduced myself and explained my purpose. After following this advice, I found that many people who met me for the first time had already read the essay, and this made it easier to explain to them who I was. Little by little, people showed less wariness in their conversations with me. But more important, simply by using the paper as a forum, I had shown my respect for others and acknowledged their importance, rather than acting unilaterally.

The Chinese New Year celebrations presented further opportunities to establish and strengthen relationships. During this period, all the factories close for five days. Bearing small gifts, usually boxes of sweets or cookies, people pay brief social calls (*bainian*) to convey their good wishes for the new year. Lilan pointed out that these were perfect opportunities for me to solidify fledgling relationships with certain families, and this was indeed the case. It was a way of demonstrating that I appreciated their help and/or friendship. Many commented that through visiting I had displayed my good intentions (*hao xin*).

Over time, as I was able to build upon these beginnings, I made friends and was gradually included in more community and family social events. Slowly, the standards for interacting with me changed. Yan Baoxia, a close associate of Principal Zhang who was a pillar of the community, and whose family had been especially hospitable to me, liked to quote from a favorite Chinese aphorism: "You can rely on relatives when you're at home, but when you're away you have to rely on friends." He would add that this was a good system. I was away from home now and had to rely on friends, but it would all equal out in the end, since he would also need help, possibly even my help, when out of his element.

As a friend, rather than a complete stranger, I had involved myself in the reciprocities of multistranded social relationships—new relationships which also entailed new responsibilities. Indeed, these changes in my role were extended to my husband's family as well. Despite the initial mistrust of my Bengali connections, my in-laws ultimately found themselves playing host and being hosted by residents of Dhapa on a number of occasions.

In fact, the Calcutta Hakka liked to portray themselves as having greater degrees of friendliness and hospitality (greater *renqing wei*) than the Chinese of Taiwan and Hong Kong whom they regarded as hardened and more urbanized. At first, when I had been a mistrusted stranger and outsider, it was not necessary to demonstrate this hospitality to me, but as my connections deepened, this ethos of hospitality became a point of pride. It was not a one-way street, for I also began to internalize norms of social reciprocity and etiquette, feeling embarrassed (*bu hao yisa*) when I breached them. I began to learn on what sorts of happy occasions I should send a gift of cash in a red envelope (*hong bao*), and when it was appropriate to bring a small gift of cakes or fruit. And whereas attendance at weddings, funerals, house-moving ceremonies, and birthday celebrations was initially a simple strategy of participant observation, this changed when I knew the individuals involved. When a good friend's elderly grandfather died, for instance, I no longer showed up merely because I wanted to take pictures and observe, but also because I wanted to pay my respects. And I remembered to send shirting material, with a message of condolence pinned to it, in advance of my arrival at the funeral, for I knew that this cloth and other similar contributions would eventually be distributed to relatives of the deceased who had helped during the mourning period.

In my case, my job as a teacher alone would not have provided me with a legitimate social role in the community. For as I had discovered early in my stay, teaching at the school in and of itself did not necessarily mean that one interacted with individuals from the community in other settings. But teaching was a starting point. It gave me a reason for living in the community, and it gave me an identity and title beyond that of "the foreigner." When I first came to the community, small children would call out as I passed, "Look, here comes the foreign woman [*fanpo*]." But as I became known, they were more likely to shout that Teacher Ou (Ou Laoshih) was passing by.

My gradual assumption of a role and identity, and the establishment of good social relations with some of Dhapa's families, opened up the process of interviewing people about their own families and businesses. In addition to those with whom I had established particularly friendly relations, there were others who simply began to assume that since I already had heard something about them anyway, they might as well set the record straight. The statement "You have most likely heard that my brother and I divided our business," for example, would replace an attempt to portray a family as united and harmonious. In one case, the members of a family I met early in my fieldwork described their business as a united venture among five brothers. Several months later, when I interviewed the two younger brothers, I was surprised both at the vehemence they expressed toward their elder brothers, and at the details they provided me in their story of the division of family assets and their establishment of a new business together.

As time passed, a variety of people began to take an interest in my project for diverse reasons. Some would state that no one had ever before written a book about their community, and therefore it was important that I include a particular detail that they thought was especially significant. They would excitedly tell me of some item I simply must not forget, such as the Qingming Festival, when people visit their ancestors' graves, or a reception given to the soccer team from the People's Republic of China, the first such open exchange with a group from the PRC in twenty-five years.

Some took a more parental stance toward me, seeing me as a young woman who had taken on too much, and who would reap no return on her efforts but for their role in getting me on the right track. For them, it was important to advise me on all aspects of life, not just on my research. For instance, one man who had been a very important source of information persistently advised me about my future career plans. Why go into academics, he asked, when I displayed a natural entrepreneurial spirit? Instead, he insisted, I should go into business and be my own boss.

But although some of Dhapa's residents took an interest in me and my research, I did not lose sight of the larger picture. Clearly, for most individuals from the Chinese tanning community, interactions with other ethnic groups were channeled within economic and bureaucratic contexts in which they did not feel that notions of social reciprocity (e.g., face, human feeling, friendliness, and hospitality) were relevant.

The observations of Fredrik Barth in his important work on ethnic boundaries seem most relevant here. As he states, in most societies characterized by multiple ethnicities, "the ethnic boundary canalizes social life—it entails a frequently quite complex organization of behaviour and social relations. The identification of another person as a fellow member of an ethnic group implies a sharing of criteria for evaluation and judgement. It thus entails the assumption that the two are fundamentally 'playing the same game'" (1969:15).

As I was discovering, the notion that ethnic boundaries contain and structure social life was powerfully relevant in assessing social relations in Calcutta. While expressions of hostility and antagonism between Chinese and Indians continued to be personally unsettling throughout my fieldwork, I realized that they were caused by historical, cultural, and sociological factors. As I have indicated in this chapter, the structure of ethnic relations in Calcutta, in which economic role and ethnic identity overlap strongly, was one reason for the maintenance of strong dividing lines between the Chinese and other groups; ethnic relations were indeed channeled and limited to a narrow range of interaction. In this respect, the Chinese community was not unique but simply operated according to the established pattern of ethnic relations in Calcutta. The association of the Hakka with the denigrated occupation of leather work compounded their isolation, as did their unique historical experience in Calcutta, particularly in connection with the Sino-Indian Conflict of 1962. In the next chapter, I examine this historical experience in greater detail and assess its impact on the structure of the contemporary community.

[3]

The Emergence of an Entrepreneurial Community: History and Social Organization

Graceful and quietly tasteful Chinese artifacts adorn the interior of Thomas Liang's living room. Thomas is a ten-year resident of Canada and the younger of two sons from a Calcutta Chinese family that owns a substantial tanning business. It is the summer of 1986, and I am interviewing Thomas at his home in suburban Toronto. I am curious whether Thomas thinks he has experienced any hostility or even subtle discrimination as a Chinese in Canada. But for Thomas, what is most important is not his status as a minority group member in Canada but the switch from being a member of a small minority community in India to a numerically larger one in Toronto. "There are more Chinese around [in Toronto]," Thomas asserts, ". . . you're not singled out." And then, comparing this situation with that in India, he continues, "I guess that the war [the Sino-Indian conflict of 1962] had something to do with it . . . [the] hostility. They feel that just because you're Chinese, you are the enemy of the country."

Thomas's response, his reference to the impact of the Sino-Indian conflict on the Indian Chinese, and his feeling that it caused ordinary Indians to view all Chinese as enemies, are typical of the feelings expressed by almost all Indian Chinese whom I have met, both those who remain in India and those who have emigrated. Certainly, as I have already indicated, the impact of the conflict has been enormous, playing a large role in the subsequent strategies of both individual Indian Chinese and their families. Nevertheless, the Chinese in India, in particular the Chinese of Calcutta, had a long history in India prior to this pivotal period, and it is important to view the impact of the

[69]

Portraits of the Indian nationalist leader Mahatma Gandhi and the Chinese nationalist leader Sun Yatsen hang behind the principal of the Chinese school in Dhapa as he addresses the audience during its graduation ceremony.

Sino-Indian conflict on the Calcutta Chinese within a larger historical and social context.

In this chapter I focus on the historical background of the Chinese community in Calcutta, paying particular attention to the emergence of distinct economic roles for each of the three Chinese groups: Hakka, Hubeinese, and Cantonese. I conclude the chapter with a consideration of the internal organization of the Calcutta Chinese community. Not only is this organization instrumental in maintaining and reproducing boundaries between Chinese and other ethnic groups, and between Hakka and other Chinese, but it also establishes the local institutional context within which individual Chinese families and individuals work out their particular economic strategies.

History

Early Settlement

Although the majority of adult residents in Dhapa, the Chinese tanning district, are only second- or at most third-generation residents of India, Chinese settlement in India dates back to the eighteenth century. In fact, Indian Chinese trace their historical origins, as opposed to their personal ones, to the arrival of a Chinese sailor in Calcutta in the 1770s.

This sailor, referred to as Atchew or Acchi in English, and as Yang Da Zhao in Chinese, is said to have arrived on a ship from Guangdong to Calcutta under the command of a British captain. Various myths have been told about this sailor. According to some stories told to me by Calcutta Chinese, two stowaways were seen by the captain, who then accused Acchi of smuggling them onto the ship. But the stowaways magically transformed themselves into pieces of wood, and Acchi then knew they were deities. He took them ashore and placed them on land around which a Chinese temple was eventually built.

When Acchi's name is mentioned, most residents of the Chinese tanning community also relate an anecdote about how Acchi outwitted Warren Hastings, the British governor-general of Bengal. According to this story, Hastings agreed to grant Acchi as much land as could be covered on horseback in a day, and Hastings, it seemed, severely underestimated Acchi's riding abilities. Acchi succeeded in covering so much territory that he secured for himself a large tract of land on

[71]

the banks of the Hooghly River, downstream from Calcutta. It is said that he then recruited workers from China to grow sugarcane.

Factually, there is a historical record of Acchi and his settlement. From this record it does appear that the Chinese whom he brought to India came to work for him as indentured laborers, for in a 1781 letter addressed to Warren Hastings, Acchi begs for assistance after some of these laborers have apparently escaped upstream to Calcutta:

HON'BLE SIR AND SIRS,—The kind protection which I have hitherto experienced, and the encouragement, afforded my small colony by the grant of lands, which I have cultivated with some success, induces me to trouble you with this address, and to request your assistance, without which I am afraid it will be impossible for me to retain my people in my service to keep them to their duty. It is unnecessary to enlarge upon the ruinous consequence of suffering these people, whom, at great expense, have brought to so great a distance under indentures to serve me for the space of —— years to be spirited and enticed away. The persons who have thus want only endeavour'd to injure me are Chinese who have deserted from Macao ships and remain in Calcutta without any apparent means of subsistence, therefore, beg that these vagrants may be severely punished, if detected in such practices, for the future, and that orders may be given to assist me in recovering any person deserting from my service, and that no one may be allowed to protect or employ any of my indented servants.

I have, etc.,
(Signature in Chinese) Atchew
Witness Chas. Rothman
Calcutta, 29th October 1781
(*Bengal Past and Present* 1909:138)

That Acchi enjoyed the support of the government is also evidenced by the following government advertisement, published just a few days after his request regarding the indentured laborers:

Fort William, 5th November 1781
Whereas it has been represented to the Hon'ble the Governor-General and Council by Atchew, a native of China now under the protection of this Government, that several ill-disposed persons have endeavoured to entice away the Chinese labourers in his employ who are under indentures to him for a term of years. Notice is hereby given that the Board wishing to grant every encouragement to the Colony of Chinese under the direction of Atchew, are determined to afford him every support and

assistance in detecting such persons and bringing them to condign punishment for inveigling away his people or affording them shelter from him.

> By order of the Hon'ble Governor-General and Council
> (Sd.) J.P. Auriol, Secretary
> (*Bengal Past and Present* 1909:138–139)

We can also surmise that Acchi died within two years of his problems with his laborers, for in a 1783 letter, an attorney for the East India Company attempts to extract payment from the executor of Acchi's estate (*Bengal Past and Present* 1909:139).

Apparently, the Chinese residents of Acchi's colony not only grew sugarcane but also manufactured sugar and liquor. In an 1804 advertisement the estate is offered for sale. Not only land, but also buildings, sugar mills, and stills are mentioned in the advertisement (*Bengal Past and Present* 1907:204). This advertisement, through its announcement of the sale of all productive assets in the area, indicates that the Chinese community in this area was short-lived. Further development of the community proceeded in Calcutta.

The original settlement area, however, still retains reminders of its existence. The town is named Achipur, after the name of its Chinese founder. A tomb, said to be Acchi's tomb, and a Chinese temple stand there. Every year during the first few weeks after the Chinese New Year, hundreds of Chinese from Calcutta visit this site and make offerings at the temple. It is believed that Tudigong, the spirit of the land to whom the temple is dedicated, is particularly efficacious.

Origins of Chinese Residence in Calcutta

The first Chinese who actually took residence in Calcutta may have been the runaway sailors and indentured servants referred to in Acchi's letter. Whatever their origins, the first references to Chinese living within Calcutta proper date from that period. In a 1784 advertisement in *The Calcutta Gazette*, for instance, a Chinese man, referred to as Tom Fatt, offers his services as a cleaner of water tanks. The same man is said to own a rum works and a cabinet works, and to make sugar and sugar candy (Seton-Karr 1864:34).

Relationships between Chinese and the government in this early period seem to have been somewhat similar to those that existed between diaspora Chinese and colonial governments throughout much of Southeast Asia, where the "kapitan system" provided the structure by which Chinese and the government related to each other. In this arrangement, an intermediary from the Chinese community, one who was agreeable both to the community and to the colonial administration, handled all communications between the authorities and the Chinese. He frequently was responsible for administrative tasks, like the extraction of revenues from the community, as well as the registration of marriages, births, and deaths. Therefore, the representative chosen would be one who not only was capable of representing Chinese interests to outsiders but also was familiar with the language and culture of the authorities—and so could interpret their wishes to the Chinese (Skinner 1968).

Similarly, in Calcutta an attempt was made to find a figure who would function in a fashion analogous to the kapitans of Southeast Asia. A 1788 memo from the police office states: "A number of Chinese have settled in Calcutta, who, tho' in general sober and industrious, yet when intoxicated commit violent outrages, particularly against each other and as thro' the difficulty of procuring an interpreter it is almost impossible to ascertain who are the delinquents . . . we humbly propose that one of the most respectable among them be appointed chief captain, who shall have certain authority over the rest. . . . A man named Amu who superintends the rum works of Mr. Somber . . . and who speaks English appears to be the most proper person" (Sinha 1978:52).

Although this reference and others are evidence that a Chinese community did exist in Calcutta as early as the 1780s, the numbers remained low throughout the nineteenth century. And like many overseas Chinese communities in the first stages of development, this one was composed primarily of males who married or cohabited with local women.

In the Calcutta police census of 1837 the Chinese population is listed as 362 (Sinha 1978:43), and in an 1858 article in the *Calcutta Review* the population of Chinese is estimated to be about five hundred (Alabaster 1975:136). In the same article the author alludes to the lack of Chinese women and the fact that Chinese men therefore cohabited with Indian or Anglo-Indian women (Alabaster 1975:143–144). One may infer that these women were Anglo-Indians or perhaps Indian women who had converted to Christianity, based on the author's remark that the sons of such unions were "sent to Roman Catholic schools, their mothers generally belonging to their religion" (Alabaster 1975:144).

[74]

However, the author also makes clear that the offspring of such marriages retained their Chinese identity: in spite of their attendance at Catholic schools, "so soon as they have mastered a little writing and arithmetic, their fathers withdraw them, and if unable to send them to China, make them study Confucius at home." The author continues in characteristically Orientalist fashion, "Thus even if, as the good fathers say, they do become indifferent Christians while at School, they soon lapse back into Paganism when their great Master's works are set before them" (Alabaster 1975:149).

These mixed unions, therefore, did not produce a class of people who were clearly identifiable as half-Chinese. In those days, a mixed union always involved a Chinese man and a non-Chinese woman, and the children were brought up as Chinese. Since marriage in Chinese society is customarily patrilocal, women marrying into their husband's families, it is more likely that the children of such marriages will be brought up with their father's cultural identity, since they will be surrounded by their Chinese relatives. Such patterns have also been noted in the early years of settlement of other overseas Chinese communities, also in cases where the overwhelming majority of migrants were male (see Patterson 1975 and Loewen 1971). At present, marriages between Chinese and non-Chinese are extremely rare in Calcutta. When they do occur, the ethnic identity of the children is still determined by that of the father (since most of the local Indian kinship systems are also patrilocal, it is likely that the children of a Chinese woman and an Indian man would take on the cultural identity of their father as well, since they would be raised in an Indian environment). Among the Calcutta Chinese, there is no group of people similar to the mestizos, the offspring of mixed marriages between Chinese and Filipinos in the Philippines (Omohundro 1981).

Growth of the Community and Increase in the Female Population

By 1876, the Chinese population of Calcutta had grown to 805 (*Report on the Census of the Town of Calcutta* 1876:22).[1] But according

---

[1] Also in this census report is the statement that the majority of Chinese live in three areas of the city—Burrabazar, Colootola, and Bowbazar (Bowbazar is now known as the old Chinatown of Calcutta). Few Chinese reside in this area today. Nevertheless, there remain reminders of the community's presence, including several Chinese temples, district association headquarters, and Chinese schools. Colootola is now a Muslim area and contains one of the two rawhide markets in Calcutta where Chinese tanners purchase their hides.

to the 1876 census report, few Chinese females lived in the community, only sixty-four, and, because of this small proportion of Chinese women, most Chinese men continued to wed Eurasian women.

Not until the first few decades of the twentieth century did the sex ratio in the Chinese population change. While the total Chinese population in Calcutta grew modestly from 1,640 in 1901 to 3,542 in 1931 (*Census of India, 1931*, 1933, vol.6:112), a significant change occurred in the proportion of men to women in the Chinese population. Indeed, between 1911 and 1931 the ratio of men to women in the Calcutta Chinese population changed from eight to one to four to one. And in succeeding decades these proportions were reduced considerably.[2]

This increase in the population of Chinese women was due partly to births within the community, but it is also explained by the fact that as male Chinese immigrants began to succeed economically, they would go back to China for an arranged marriage and return to India with their brides. Indeed, by the 1930s, the practice of marrying and cohabiting with native women was rare.

Tidings of economic success in India, coupled with increasingly difficult circumstances in China, contributed to a steady stream of Chinese immigrants to India during the 1930s and 1940s. By the 1951 census, the number of Indian Chinese had increased to 9,214 (*Census of India, 1951*, 1953, vol.1:18). And prior to the outbreak of the Sino-Indian conflict, the population of Indian Chinese had climbed to 14,607, of which almost six thousand were females (*Census of India, 1961*, 1964, vol.1, part 2c[ii]:149). The majority of these Chinese still lived in Calcutta. However, about two thousand of them had moved their residence to Bombay, where they became involved in the restaurant, shoemaking, and dry cleaning businesses.

The Sino-Indian conflict of 1962 reversed the trend of continuing increases in the population of Indian Chinese. Several thousand Chinese either were deported or returned voluntarily to China. By the late 1960s, emigration to Europe, Australia, and North America had begun, a trend which continues today. The Chinese population de-

---

[2] According to the 1911 census of Bihar, Bengal, Orissa, and Sikkim, Chinese men in these areas (most concentrated in Calcutta) outnumber Chinese women by eight to one (*Census of India, 1911*, 1913, vol.5, part 1:174). Ten years later, in the 1921 Census of Calcutta, the proportions have altered, and men outnumber women by only five to one (*Census of India, 1921*, 1923, vol.6:21). By the time of the 1931 census, the proportion of men to women has declined further, to four to one (*Census of India, 1931*, vol.6:94).

clined from more than fourteen thousand in 1961 to under eleven thousand by 1971.[3]

Chinese in Calcutta are currently subdivided into three subethnic groups: Hakka, Cantonese, and Hubeinese. Although the census has never differentiated among these subgroups, the numerical dominance of the Hakka is clear both to knowledgeable outside observers as well as to the Chinese themselves. Because the Hakka are preponderant, many Cantonese and Hubeinese learn to speak Hakka so that they may communicate effectively with this group. Calcutta Chinese claim that the Cantonese community was also quite large in the past, but they say that in the aftermath of the 1962 conflict, Cantonese have emigrated from India at a faster rate than Hakka.

The Emergence of Occupational Specialties

The three Chinese subethnic groups have long been associated with particular occupational specialties. The Hakka are concentrated in shoemaking and tanning, the Cantonese in carpentry, and the Hubeinese, the smallest community, are dentists. In addition, both Cantonese and Hakka run restaurants, the Hakka own and operate beauty parlors, and until the early 1950s, Chinese women in the tanning district were in the illicit liquor business. Finally, Cantonese were renowned as fine shipfitters until the conflict of 1962. (Since they were considered a security risk in the strategic river port area, they were barred from working there.)

These occupational niches emerged very early. As noted earlier, Tom Fatt, the Chinese individual referred to in the 1784 advertisement of *The Calcutta Gazette*, was said to have a cabinet works and a rum works, among other assets. In a *Calcutta Review* article of 1857, the author refers to carpentry and shoemaking as the major vocations of Calcutta's Chinese residents: "Silently advancing they have driven all competitors out of the field; and now as shoemakers, ship-carpenters and hogslard manufacturers they reign unrivaled" (Alabaster 1975:136). The author also indicates that it was the Hakka who were associated with shoemaking (Alabaster 1975:139) and the Cantonese with carpentry (Alabaster 1975:150). Thus, the main outlines of the present-day occupational divisions within the Chinese community had

---

[3] Of these, 7,873 (of whom 3,504 were female) were living in the state of West Bengal, the majority in Calcutta (*Census of India, 1971*, 1975, series 1, part 2C [ii]:70).

already been forged by the midnineteenth century: Cantonese were associated with woodworking and Hakka with leather work.

Origins of the Tanning Community

Although this Hakka association with leather work dates back almost 150 years, the tanning community of Dhapa is more recent in its origins. The first Chinese tanners came to Dhapa, a swampy area at the eastern periphery of the city, around the year 1910. These tanners were shoemakers, and they probably thought they would produce leather for use in shoemaking. The process of tanning soon took precedence, however, owing to its profitability.

During these early years, the Chinese produced leather through the vegetable tanning method—a process which utilizes the "tannin" found in various types of vegetable matter, such as plants and tree bark, as the active ingredient in leather making. In the beginning, they worked without machinery, much as village tanners of the Chamar caste do throughout India.

World War I provided the Chinese tanners, still not exceeding ten in number (De 1972:237), an opportunity to buy machinery. Several European concerns had liquidated and retransferred their capital to England at the end of the war, enabling the Chinese to purchase their machinery cheaply (*All India Leather Directory* [*AILD*], *1965– 1966*:7). Further opportunities were provided for the Chinese during the European exchange fluctuations of 1920–21 when many European tanneries shut down, and between 1922 and 1926 when several Indian tanning companies failed (De 1972:237). Thus, ownership of tanneries "changed from the hands of Europeans and Indians to the Chinese, from large scale units to smaller ones" (De 1972:237). During this period the number of Chinese tanneries increased to thirty. Undoubtedly, the Chinese practices of living in their factories, utilizing family labor, and running the machinery nonstop helped them economize and may have given them the edge over both Indian and European tanners. Chinese tanners also switched to chrome tanning, a process that is faster and technologically more advanced than vegetable tanning. The majority of the Dhapa Chinese continue to use this method today.

During World War II, most of the large organized tanneries in India were placed under the control of the government according to the Defence of India rules. These tanneries were allowed to sell only to the government, and the leather produced provided for almost all the needs of the army under the Eastern Command. The obligation of the large tanneries to supply leather for military use made it possible for the small-scale and cottage tanneries, including those of the Chinese, to capture the home market (De 1972:239). These small tanneries received numerous orders from the United Kingdom for upper shoe leather, which the large tanneries were unable to supply.

The tremendous demand for leather created by the war led to a rapid expansion in the number of Chinese tanneries, which increased to seventy during the war years (De 1972:240). Chinese who had lived in Calcutta and engaged in other trades, as well as new immigrants from China, joined the growing ranks of tanners. By the mid-1960s, there were more than eighty-two tanneries housing almost three hundred businesses; many establishments were shared by a number of tanners, some of whom rented the use of machinery from the tannery owner (*AILD, 1965–1966*:26).

During 1980–82, the period when I lived in Dhapa and conducted my initial fieldwork, there were approximately the same number of businesses as in the mid-1960s—297 to be exact. But whereas the number of businesses did not continue to grow after the 1960s, there were more than 176 separate factory buildings as compared with the eighty-two that stood in the mid-1960s. During that intervening period, many tanners constructed factories of their own, and the proportion of those who conducted business as tenants diminished. Furthermore, many businesses had expanded and increased their productivity.

The community, therefore, experienced three types of business growth. The first occurred through migration. From its origins prior to World War I through the mid-1960s, migrants from other parts of Calcutta as well as those born in China moved to Dhapa to try tanning. Subsequently, this migration diminished considerably, and some community members even began to leave Dhapa by emigrating abroad. The community experienced the second type of growth through expansion in the scale and productivity of businesses, as tanners succeeded and then moved from tenant to owner status. Finally (as I describe later), the number of businesses in the community increased as single businesses were divided among descendants.

I discuss all these processes in detail in Chapters 5 and 7. It is important to emphasize here that the tanning community, which began as a small settlement of Chinese manufacturing leather by hand, had grown substantially by World War II and was by then well established.

The Impact of the Sino-Indian Conflict

No study of the Chinese tanners would be complete without examining the profound effect of the 1962 conflict. Not only did it influence family and business strategies, but it also had an impact on community life and on the relations between Chinese and their host society.

Unlike the Chinese of Southeast Asian countries, where ethnic Chinese form a substantial minority within the populations, the Chinese community in India was left to itself and encountered few political problems with their hosts prior to the 1962 conflict. As with overseas Chinese communities in other areas of the world, the revolution in China generated repercussions within the community. Both the Guomindang (the Nationalists) and the Communists had their partisans, and each faction ran its own Chinese language schools and newspapers. The conflict between them was public, and few felt any fear about voicing vocal support of one group or the other.

In fact, before 1959, when Sino-Indian relationships were good, identification with the Communists was more acceptable than with the Guomindang. Many of the teachers in the pro-Communist school had come from China, and some Chinese businesses within India received loans from the Bank of China. Both Indians and Chinese often quoted Nehru's famous comment, "Hindi Chini Bhai Bhai [Indians and Chinese are brothers]," to give me an idea of the nature of the relations that existed then.

Many Indian Chinese became citizens of the People's Republic of China. This was achieved easily by visiting the Chinese consulate and declaring Chinese citizenship. Indeed, the Indian government looked favorably on those who took out PRC passports (Ganguli 1973). According to Shao-chuan Leng and Jerome Cohen, those who did not become citizens of the PRC were usually regarded as "stateless" (1972:270).

While some Chinese were regarded as stateless and others had PRC citizenship, there were another nine hundred or so who either had applied for and been granted Indian citizenship or were simply considered citizens because they were born on Indian territory after the constitution went into effect in 1950.

The border dispute of 1959 marked the beginning of a change in the official Indian attitude toward its residents of Chinese descent. The central government ordered the registration of all Chinese living in India. And between 1959 and 1962 many Chinese (about two hundred, according to mainland sources) were deported to China; the deportees included teachers in the pro-Communist Chinese schools, staff members of the pro-Communist Chinese newspaper, and merchants and shopkeepers thought to be sympathetic to the Chinese government (Leng and Cohen 1972:272).

Many Chinese are bitter about the fact that conduct previously considered commendable, in the light of amicable relations between China and India, was now viewed as grounds for expulsion from India. During the days of Hindi Chini Bhai Bhai, such acts as welcoming Chinese delegations at airports were considered not only pro-Chinese but pro-Indian as well. Suddenly, Chinese who had participated in these activities might be viewed as security risks—much to their surprise.

The outbreak of armed conflict on a larger scale in 1962 exacerbated the situation for the Chinese in India. Although the Chinese say that they experienced few personal expressions of hostility from ordinary Indian citizens, they all emphasize that this period was very difficult for them. Chinese nationals were not allowed to leave their city, village, or registered address for more than twenty-four hours unless granted permission in writing from their registration officer. In addition, they were not permitted to live in certain restricted areas, like Assam, without a permit, even if they were Indian citizens (Leng and Cohen 1972:274).

Since the leather-producing area of Dhapa borders Calcutta district, these restrictions on movement meant that when Chinese men left the area each day to go to the rawhide markets in Calcutta, they would be circumventing the law if they did not apply for a permit, since technically many of the tanneries were in 24-Parganas District and not within Calcutta's official city limits. Chinese stated that during and after the conflict, individuals were checked as they passed through a gate on the road to the tanning area.

Of course, some Chinese were Indian citizens at the time of the conflict. In order to include them within the purview of the aforementioned restrictions, the administration found it necessary to extend the definition of *foreigner* to include "any person who, or either of whose parents, or any of whose grandparents was at any time a citizen or subject of any country at war with, or committing external aggression

[81]

against India" (*Acts of Parliament, 1962*, 1963:231–232). Since few Chinese could be found who at the very least did not have grand-parents who had been citizens of China, and since China was now a country at war with India, the effect of this provision was to deny citizenship to almost all Indian Chinese.

The provision was also used as a basis for the Foreigners (Intern-ment) Order of 3 November 1962. It resulted in the internment of more than two thousand Indian Chinese in a camp in the Indian state of Rajasthan, where many remained for several years.[4] This order "authorized the arrest without warrant and the detention of any for-eigner who is reasonably suspected of 'having acted, of acting, of being about to act, with intent to assist a country at war with or committing external aggression against India, or in a manner prejudicial to the public safety or to the safety of any building or machinery'" (Leng and Cohen 1972:275).

Thus, many Chinese who had expressed a friendly attitude toward mainland China or who held PRC passports were either sent to the internment camp in Rajasthan, or jailed, or served with a notice to "quit India." Additionally, some Chinese who were employed in facto-ries lost their jobs. Cantonese Chinese, many of whom were shipfit-ters, were particularly hard hit since, as noted earlier, they were considered a security risk in the strategic river port area.

Finally, after protests by China and negotiations between the two countries, it was agreed that those Chinese who wished to return to China could be repatriated and thereby leave the internment camp. In the spring of 1963, China sent ships to Madras, and almost twenty-five hundred Indian Chinese were repatriated (*The Times of India* 1963a, 1963b, 1963c).

Arrest, deportation, and internment powerfully disrupted the lives of many Calcutta Chinese families. For instance, Xiu Lilan, my land-lady in Calcutta, saw her father arrested and deported to China, while her mother and her siblings, except for her eldest sister, were served with "Quit India" notices. The story of her family's relationship to both China and India is filled with tragic irony and is emblematic of the

---

[4] Americans will readily recognize the parallels between the attitudes of the Indian government, and the actions taken by their own government during World War II, when Japanese-Americans were interned in camps. Not until 1990 did the American government officially apologize for this breach of its own citizens' rights. Many works exist on this historic episode, among them Peter Irons's *Justice at War* (1983).

problems faced by many Calcutta Chinese who became victims of events beyond their control in both countries.

When Lilan's father first emigrated to India, he continued to send money back to China, thinking that he would eventually retire in China. These funds were confiscated during the 1949 revolution. Despite this, her father later became known as a prominent supporter of the People's Republic of China, and he sent all his children to the school run by the mainland Chinese. One of Lilan's brothers voluntarily moved back to China in the 1950s, rising quickly in the bureaucratic echelons there. Indeed, just before the outbreak of hostilities between China and India, he was about to be appointed China's consul-general in Calcutta, an achievement which many Calcutta Chinese considered a great honor.

It was precisely these close connections with China, once viewed as a source of pride, that marked her family as a collaborator with an enemy country when hostilities broke out in 1962. Only Lilan and her eldest sister, who were both already married, were not forced to leave India. The family's luckless timing continued in China, where the Cultural Revolution began to unfold in the late 1960s, only a few years after they arrived. Unwelcome in India, her father soon became equally stigmatized in China, where, as a returning overseas Chinese businessman, he fell into the despised social category of former capitalist.

Most of Lilan's siblings, as well as her parents, ultimately succeeded in emigrating from China to Hong Kong in the late 1970s. But they had experienced nearly two decades of harassment in two different countries, each of which was supposed to be their "home."

Pressures from the Indian government also had an impact on the factional competitions within the Calcutta Chinese community: some individuals went to the authorities and denounced their opponents. Many Chinese today think that some members of the Nationalist faction identified prominent pro-Communists in the community, thus leading to their arrests and/or deportations. In one case, they say, competition between business rivals led one to identify the other as a Communist sympathizer and thus to his internment.

The effect of the conflict was to turn the tables on the internal divisions and struggles within the Chinese community. For many years thereafter, public identification with Communist China, either by individuals or by organizations, completely disappeared. The recent thaw in relations between India and China has somewhat relaxed the atmosphere within the community. While I was in Dhapa, the

Chinese soccer team was invited for a banquet, the first time a visiting Chinese delegation of any kind was entertained there in more than twenty-five years. However, despite the fact that India has no formal diplomatic relations with Taiwan, the Guomindang faction continues to control all the prominent organizations within the Chinese community—including the major newspaper, the Welfare Association, the Overseas Chinese Association, and the Chinese language schools.

Although Sino-Indian relations have improved, the Chinese of India still have an unresolved political status. As it currently stands, those Indian Chinese who were born in India after January 1950, when the constitution went into effect, are automatically considered Indian citizens. But those born before 1950 have to apply for citizenship, even if they were born on Indian soil. Indian Chinese who do not succeed in acquiring Indian citizenship are issued a Certificate of Identity and are virtually stateless persons. Although these stateless persons no longer need to register with the police every time they leave their town of residence, they are still required to register annually with the Foreigners Registration Office, where they are granted permission to remain in India for twelve more months.

Most Chinese in India think that acquiring Indian citizenship can greatly diminish trouble and harassment. Once citizenship is acquired, annual registration is no longer a necessity. Furthermore, Indian Chinese who have only a Certificate of Identity have difficulty traveling to other countries, since this certificate does not have universal recognition.

While the Indian Chinese recognize the usefulness of Indian citizenship, they complain that it is difficult to acquire. As noted earlier, they assert that wealthy Chinese are more likely than those of lesser means to be granted citizenship because they can bribe officials. Furthermore, they say that even the most trivial reasons are cited as a rationale for not granting citizenship to an applicant. For instance, they claim that attendance at an athletic meet in which Chinese teams participate may be noticed and later used against an applicant. Or they claim that they may be told that citizenship is being denied because they are unable to write in an Indian language, even though many Indians are not literate in their own languages.

If one considers the provisions of the Indian constitution, the present-day treatment of the Chinese is certainly an anomaly. According to the provisions of Article 5 of the constitution, the vast majority of Chinese who resided in India before 1950 should also be citizens, since this article states that anyone living in India at the time of the commencement of the constitution and who had been born in India, or had at least one parent born in India, or had been a resident of India for at least five years was to be considered an Indian citizen.[5] Yet these individuals must apply for citizenship, which is not always granted.

The experiences of the 1962 conflict—the internments, arrests, deportations, and denials of citizenship—as well as its aftereffects, have contributed to a sense of alienation from the host society, but these are certainly not the sole causes. As I indicated earlier, the boundaries between Chinese and other groups in Calcutta are also maintained by that city's ethnic and economic organization. And the marginality of the Dhapa Chinese is further compounded by their role in a polluting occupation.

Furthermore, the internal institutions of Chinese society in India reinforce the divisions between Chinese and other ethnic groups, as well as among the three Chinese subgroups. These institutions play a critical role in regulating and supporting economic behavior and in defining and enforcing moral and social norms. In keeping questions about social conduct strictly within the purview of Chinese community members, they play a crucial role in defining and maintaining ethnic and subethnic group boundaries. It is to an analysis of these institutions that I now turn.

Organization of the Chinese Community

Among the Calcutta Chinese, language group, native place, and surname serve as the most critical internal divisions within the community. Indeed, these categories provide the framework for Chinese social organization.

Distinctions based on language are critical. Since the Hakka clearly differentiate themselves from Cantonese and other Chinese subgroups in their terms of reference, it is not surprising to find that the three subgroups of Chinese in Calcutta—the Hakka, the Cantonese, and the Hubeinese—share only a few institutions. One such institu-

---

[5] The Citizenship Act of 1955 was meant to cover those born after the constitution went into effect. It "provides for citizenship by birth (born in India on or after January 26, 1950), by descent, by registration, by naturalization, and by incorporation of territory" (Leng and Cohen 1972:270).

tion was the school that had been affiliated with mainland China and which was closed after the 1962 conflict. The school's faculty had come from China, classes were conducted in Mandarin, and students came from all three speech groups.

At present, only the Overseas Chinese Association and one of the two Chinese newspapers have clientele or members who cross speech-group lines. The Overseas Chinese Association has both Cantonese and Hakka officers, and the larger of the two newspapers is read by Chinese from all three speech groups. (The smaller paper is read only by Hakka because it was founded as a result of a split between two factions of a Hakka tanners association.)

Institutions serving the needs of different language groups cooperate with one another occasionally. There are now three Chinese schools in Calcutta in which classes are conducted in Mandarin, and which are affiliated with a pro-Nationalist faction of the community which also controls the Overseas Chinese Association. Although the students at two of these schools are Hakka, and the students at the third school are Cantonese, these schools occasionally come together for celebrations such as Double Ten Day, the day which commemorates the birth of republican China. There is also a fourth Chinese school, run by the Catholic church. Classes at this school are also taught in Mandarin, and students are drawn from both Hakka and Cantonese communities, although the Hakka predominate. I pointed out in the preceding chapter, however, that the importance of these Chinese schools is diminishing; student enrollment has decreased because of the growing popularity of English medium education among the Chinese.

Therefore, primary social interaction takes place within language-group boundaries for most individuals in the Hakka community. Intermarriage between people of different language groups is rare; it is so rare that the cases of intermarriage between Cantonese and Hakka can be individually named. Similarly, intermarriage between Hakka Chinese and Indians hardly ever occurs. And at major social functions of the Hakka, like weddings, only a few non-Hakka guests are in attendance. Undoubtedly, the occupational divisions among the three groups have helped maintain the social divisions. Only one tanning business in Dhapa is run by a Cantonese family, and interestingly, their son has married a Hakka woman who speaks Hakka with their children.

As discussed in Chapter 2, several theorists, most notably Lawrence

Crissman (1967), have drawn attention to the segmentary structure of overseas Chinese communities, pointing out that although united in dealings with the outside world, they are divided according to progressively segmenting subdivisions based on language, native place, and surname. In the case of the Calcutta Chinese, their organization varies slightly from this segmentary structure. Rather than progressively segmenting on the basis of language, native place, and then surname, each language group has divided itself internally along one of these bases only.

For the Cantonese community, native-place associations form the primary subdivisions, and they have no organizations corresponding to surname group membership. Their native-place associations correspond to the different areas of Guangdong Province from which Cantonese immigrants came.

The Hubeinese, on the other hand, have only one association, the Hubeinese Association. The fact that their numbers are relatively few may be one reason for their lack of internal subdivisions. Furthermore, many Hubeinese work as dentists, and their residential arrangement is the least centralized of all the Chinese subgroups. Not only do they live in many areas of Calcutta, but they are dispersed throughout numerous other Indian cities. Therefore, their association serves as a focal point for a community that is otherwise quite scattered.

Organization of the Hakka

Because the Hakka of Calcutta all emigrated from Mei Xian in Guangdong, native place cannot constitute an important principle of division among them. In addition, they are quite numerous, and although many Hakka have migrated to other areas of India, the tanning district and the shoe shop area are still concentrated communities of Hakka Chinese residence. Thus, the most important subdivisions within the Hakka community are based on surname group.

The Calcutta Hakka commonly use more than fifteen surnames. Each of these surnames, except for the uncommon ones, is associated with a group that elects officers, raises funds, mediates disputes of its members, exercises social control through elected officers (who almost always belong to the most senior generation), and assumes certain responsibilities during major life-cycle events, as well as for festivals in the annual ritual cycle. For instance, if someone in my surname group

[87]

is to be married, at least one person in my immediate family will attend the wedding. The same applies to funerals, birthdays, and house-moving celebrations. Furthermore, at least a few members of a surname group will volunteer on such occasions to help out with the various tasks that need to be done.

Each surname group has its own surname association with a budget. Money is collected through contributions, by lending money at interest, by selling tanning chemicals, and through the operation of rotating credit associations (discussed in Chapter 5). These surname associations are pan-Indian. That is, their members include all Hakka belonging to that surname group regardless of whether they live in the tanning community, in other areas of Calcutta, or even in other Indian cities. Even individuals who have emigrated abroad, but who return to India for a visit, will often make a contribution to their surname association.

Some of the money thus collected is used for religious activities. For instance, during the spring and autumn ancestral rites, not only do individuals visit the graves of their ancestors, but in addition, surname groups gather to worship collectively at the graves of surname group members. The larger and richer surname associations may give a banquet for their members in conjunction with these ceremonies. Surname associations also give loans; for example, they lend small amounts of money to help a member start a business or pay for air passage when emigrating abroad.

Surname groups also exercise social control functions, many of which impinge on economic activities. The mediation of family disputes is one such area where the intervention of surname group elders is often critical. When brothers divide their property, for instance, the agreement is usually finalized in the presence of surname association representatives. Their intervention becomes especially significant when the brothers are unable to reach an amicable agreement (see the discussion in Chapter 7).

Marital problems are another arena in which surname group representatives may intervene. In the Dhapa community, if a man abuses his wife, she may take the matter to his surname association. The members, in turn, can pressure him by threatening to isolate him— barring him from important surname group functions, for example, or refusing to attend his functions. Since social isolation is extremely difficult to endure, even the threat of such tactics is usually sufficient to bring the offender into line. A refusal to attend an important social affair—a wedding, for instance—would be an insult to the entire family. In a community where the number of guests at a social function is important grist for the gossip mill, a small turnout can cause one to lose face and respect in the public eye. Indeed, one of the problems faced by Mr. Kong's daughter in Toronto was that when she began to have marital troubles, there was no authority to whom she could turn, as she would have expected in Calcutta.

Surname group elders may attempt to go beyond settling disputes. They may also try to exert social control in a more active way by preventing individuals from violating what they perceive to be the established norms of the community. For example, they may pressure or discourage widows who are thinking of remarriage, an act which is still uncommon. They may remind a widow that by remarrying she will forsake her claim to her son and to his support. In at least one case of which I am aware, elders of a surname group made it clear to a widow, who was carrying on a discrete relationship with another man, that her present course of action was preferable to marrying him. Marriage would mean publicly dissolving her social and economic ties to her husband's surname group, which would exclude her from their social celebrations and from possible financial help. Upon reflection, this woman decided that the elders' assessment of her situation was accurate. She decided against remarriage, despite the fact that this was a conservative community that basically frowned upon extramarital relationships. She often stated that she enjoyed inclusion in her husband's family activities, and while she realized that she was presently an item of gossip, this was preferable to severing ties with her husband's surname group, an action which would involve a much more public loss of face.

Surname group leaders take an interest in the activities of surname group members not only because they may reflect badly on the doers but also because they reflect back on the leaders themselves. If an individual acts in a way disapproved by the elders, people will comment that the offender "shaved off their beards," or, in other words, that the group leaders lost their dignity through their inability to exert their influence on the deviant.

Of course, what usually happens is that surname group leaders simply do not take up lost causes and thereby avoid the subsequent loss of face. A particularly notorious example concerned a woman who successfully persuaded her husband to send his elderly mother back to China, where the old woman's youngest son still lived. The daughter-in-law in this case reasoned that by ridding herself of her husband's mother, she could more easily emigrate with her husband and children to the United States. In effect, she had kicked her mother-in-law out of the house and also made a fool of her husband. Community members considered her actions outrageous. The daughter-in-law's image was reduced still further because it was assumed that her mother-in-law's diet and standard of living would decline in China, a change which would be hard for anyone, but which would be a particularly difficult adjustment for an eighty-two-year-old woman. Although the elders of the husband's surname association discussed the case, they ultimately did nothing during the years in which the family remained in India. (Even after qualifying for immigration to the United States, most families must wait for several years before their number comes up.) Knowing the woman's personality and her family situation—the knowledge that she would ultimately be leaving the community certainly had a bearing on her ability to ignore moral norms—the surname elders in this case concluded that no amount of pressure would dissuade her. Thus, why risk the inevitable loss of face when their efforts would fail?

In some cases, where the limits of surname group power have been reached, individuals in the tanning community have another option; they may turn to one of two tanning associations for help. Although personal matters, like disputes between mothers-in-law and daughters-in-law, are usually not within their purview, they do intervene in property disputes between brothers when the surname associations have failed to bring about a settlement. Negotiations between tannery owners and their Indian workers are also handled by the two tannery owners associations.

But even here, the influence of the surname associations is felt. Since the head of the more recently formed tanning association belongs to one particularly powerful and numerous surname group, his association includes almost all individuals from that group. He also publishes a Chinese newspaper, to which only members of his association subscribe. Likewise, all members of an equally numerous rival surname group belong to the other tanning association (and read the other newspaper).

In the past, the rivalry between these two tanning associations, and the two large surname groups associated with each of them, was quite intense. During the 1960s, the groups argued over control of the Chinese school in Dhapa. These arguments were exacerbated by political divisions. The group that ultimately took control of the school was adamantly pro-Guomindang and pro-Taiwan.[6] The rival group, the one that had broken away to form a new tanning association and newspaper, was somewhat more neutral, although it, too, was hardly sympathetic to political trends on the mainland. For a long time, members of the two large surname groups connected to these tanning associations would rarely intermarry, and they would not publish announcements of family events in the newspaper associated with the other group.

Over time, however, as the generation of community leaders that came to power in the 1960s has aged, and as the political tensions of the period have waned, these divisions have become less and less important. Certain formalities, such as publishing wedding announcements in the paper associated with one's surname group, are still followed, but marriage, friendship, and economic cooperation now span the boundaries of these two formerly opposing factions.

Not only do surname and tanning associations provide an organizational rubric within which individual Hakka families live out their social and economic lives. They also play a critical role in reducing the intervention of non-Chinese in their lives. The Cantonese and Hubeinese associations serve the same function, as do the few organizations that all three subgroups share. During my stay in Calcutta, for instance, a set of brothers who ran a Cantonese carpentry firm became involved in long and expensive litigation against each other. Most Hakka with whom I spoke regarded their actions as the utmost in folly. All brothers will eventually quarrel, people told me, but why allow outsiders (in this case, the Indian legal system) to become involved?

There is no doubt that the organizations discussed in this chapter play an important role in regulating and influencing the economic lives of most Hakka tanners, but it is from within the family itself that we can best understand the development of Hakka businesses, and it is family members—past, present, and future—who are the intended beneficiaries of this entrepreneurial drama. In the next chapters, I take a closer look at the histories and geographic dispersion of particular Hakka families. First, however, I must examine the ideology that underpins their entrepreneurial efforts. For it is more complex and internally contentious than it appears at first glance.

---

[6] Political polarization based on attitudes toward the People's Republic of China and Taiwan is common among overseas Chinese communities throughout the world. For a description of this polarization in an American Chinatown, see Bernard Wong (1982). At the same time, reforms of the past decade in China, and the coming to power of a new generation in Taiwan, have helped to lower the intensity of their ideological battle and to lessen the fervor of those who are strong partisans of either side.

Friends and relatives play mahjong at the groom's house on the night before the wedding.

[4]

Profit, Loss, and Fate:
Gambling and the Entrepreneurial Ethic

A story was told to me by a Chinese resident of Calcutta: "Qiao Tanming's mother and Chen Guozhang's mother were two sisters in China. They went to a fair where children were sold. One man had a bamboo pole over his shoulders with a basket hanging down from each side. Inside of each basket was a small baby. Chen's mother immediately grabbed the good-looking baby, so the other woman had no choice. But later on when both children were grown men, they immigrated to India. And, the man who had been the homely sickly looking baby was the one who ultimately prospered." Qiao Tanming, the homely but ultimately prosperous individual in this story, was the epitome of success, status, and moral virtue in Dhapa. He grew to be very wealthy, and even after his death, his business, under the management of two of his sons, was one of the largest in the tanning community.

Even now, when people talk about how Tanming gained his wealth, they always mention the qualities they value most. It is said that he worked extremely hard—in the words of an oft-quoted saying in Dhapa, he "gave his heart, sweat, and blood [*chu le xin, han xue*]." Furthermore, Dhapa residents praise Tanming's extreme trustworthiness and reliability, most frequently referring to the day he traveled through torrential monsoon rains to pay a rawhide merchant on time. This effort so impressed the merchant that he always gave Tanming excellent hides on favorable credit. Tanming is considered to have been canny and farsighted too; he was the first tanner to recognize the value of certain types of machines that are now used almost universally in Dhapa.

That Tanming should be admired for achieving great wealth is in keeping with the values most prevalent among the Hakka Chinese tanners. For there is no doubt that in their community, status is primarily determined by wealth. Other personal qualities, for example, the tenacity, perseverance, and intelligence of Qiao Tanming, are valued precisely because they are useful in entrepreneurial pursuits. At the same time, it would be wrong to interpret Tanming's efforts as only an attempt to gain individual status, for as I make clear in this chapter, entrepreneurial goals and aims among Hakka tanners also fit into a larger familial strategy that extends even to the afterlife.

In this chapter, I analyze the values of the tanning community, and I contrast these values with those of other non-Hindu groups within India. Although I focus on the strong entrepreneurial ethos of the Hakka tanners, I also examine its limits. As with all groups of people, the values and behavior of the Dhapa Hakka do not fall into neat and consistent categories. Furthermore, the entrepreneurial ethos itself contains contradictory imperatives. In the final section I look at this problem in terms of the popular activity of gambling and attempt to explain the complex ways in which gambling articulates and reinforces the contradictions within the community's dominant entrepreneurial ethos.

Status, Wealth, and Business

What is perhaps most striking about all the Indian Chinese, as compared with other non-Hindu minority groups, is that the caste system has exerted so little influence on either their ideas or their organization. In India, most non-Hindu minorities have been powerfully affected by the caste system. For instance, many tribal groups from the Indian subcontinent have been incorporated into the surrounding society as castes. They have attempted to raise their status, not by rejecting Hindu practices, but by imitating higher-caste customs, such as abstaining from eating beef. In so doing, they have indicated their acceptance of the basic premises of the caste system (Srinivas 1966:6). Furthermore, Indian Christians and Muslims, whom one might expect to have renounced caste as a result of their ideological traditions, have castelike divisions within their populations (Dumont 1970:206–207, 211). Even groups that immigrated to India from other countries (e.g., Parsis and Jews) have come to replicate some elements of caste within their own group structures.[1]

Despite the all-encompassing nature of the caste system, none of the Chinese subgroups in Calcutta has fallen into the patterns described here. They explicitly reject caste ideology in favor of a status system based almost exclusively on wealth. This fact was clearly illuminated for me one day, shortly after I had settled into Lilan's house, when her nephew took me to visit and to introduce myself to some families in Dhapa. On the way home, he told me that under normal circumstances he would not even speak with the families we had just met. "They might know me as my father's son," he remarked, "because my father taught at the Chinese school for so many years. But they're rich people, and they only talked with me today because I brought you along."

Although the Hakka tanners are united in the face of outsiders and almost all of them are prosperous compared with middle-class Indians, there are still sharp differences in wealth among them. These distinctions are socially significant. One community member explained this to me in starkly sociological terms: "We don't have castes. Your blood doesn't matter. We have classes. What matters is how much money you make." This high priority accorded to the achievement of wealth as a measure of status is not atypical of overseas Chinese societies in other parts of the world.

G. William Skinner has discussed the importance of wealth in Southeast Asian overseas Chinese communities, both as a criterion for leadership as well as a measure of status (1968). As he points out, one reason that wealth is the primary component of status in these com-

[1] Parsis not only adopted caste notions about commensality but also assimilated Hindu notions of purity and pollution. In 1903, for instance, a Parsi judge expressed his opposition to the idea that Parsi priests could admit lower-caste Hindus into the Parsi community without first "'making them give up their unclean professions'" (Fischer 1973:94).

Among some groups of Indian Jews, castelike patterns were also present (I use the past tense here, because most Indian Jews have now emigrated to Israel and other countries). The Cochin Jews of the south Indian state of Kerala, for instance, were internally divided into castelike divisions with prohibitions on intermarriage (Mandelbaum 1939:424) and on entering each other's temples (Strizower 1962:112–113). And the Bene Israel, a Jewish community centered in Bombay, had endogamous subdivisions, with one subdivision considered particularly polluted in the sense that both commensality and intermarriage with them was forbidden (Strizower 1962:30).

munities is because most Chinese emigrated in order to better their economic positions. "Unlike the Jews," says Skinner, "the Chinese went abroad in the first place specifically to make money, and unlike the Jewish *diaspora*, that of the Chinese excluded the traditional elite of their homeland. In consequence status for overseas Chinese was almost a direct function of wealth" (1968:195).

Since status within the Calcutta Chinese community is based almost exclusively on wealth, there is no concept, as in caste ideology, that certain occupations or social groups can be compared in terms of relative purity and impurity. Nor is there any sense that social status can be inherited and is not dependent on one's present social situation. (Caste ideology ranks a multitude of endogamous groups in terms of their relative purity and pollution. Furthermore, one inherits one's caste: no matter how one may change one's life situation, one cannot change caste.) Indeed, from the point of view of the Calcutta Chinese, any job is worthwhile if it is a profitable source of income. Whereas caste ideology ranks tanning as a polluting occupation, one performed only by a particular untouchable caste, Dhapa Chinese consider it a good business, because it is so lucrative.[2] The Chinese also believe that tanning is far superior to white-collar desk jobs, where salaries rarely amount to more than a fraction of the earnings possible in even modestly successful tanning businesses.

In fact, according to the Calcutta Hakka, running one's own business, in whatever line presents the most possibilities, is the ideal economic activity and, unless circumstances make it absolutely impossible, is far superior to salaried employment. Not only do they see business as providing a greater income than salaried employment, but

[2] The differences between the Calcutta Chinese view and the stance held by one who accepts the premises of the caste system were made clear to me in an interview I conducted at the Leather Research Institute in Calcutta. One of the officers of the organization pointed out that although a certain percentage of seats at a leather technology institute are reserved for Chamars, the untouchable caste traditionally associated with leather work, and although completion of coursework at such an institute would mean a good-paying job with a large leather manufacturer, few members of this caste apply for admission.

Since the basis for the stigma that Chamars suffer is the polluting occupation they traditionally followed, those who are in a position to apply to an institute of higher education are unlikely to apply in a field that had served as the basis for this stigma. Chinese have not become involved in tanning as the result of training in institutes. But what these practices make evident is the difference between evaluating tanning from within the caste system, as a polluting and stigmatizing occupation, and from without, as a potentially lucrative profession.

in addition, they feel that by going into one's own business one has more control over one's own life. That business means family business is an assumption so deep that it is rarely discussed. And in fact, of the 297 tanning businesses that existed in Dhapa in 1982, only two were partnerships involving nonrelated individuals.

The high value placed on entrepreneurship as a way of life was one of the themes that was most frequently and explicitly articulated to me. For instance, one of my good friends and best informants, Mr. Zhou, was always perplexed about why I would want to return to the United States to teach. One day, while discussing the advantages of business as opposed to salaried employment, he asked me, "If you wanted to start a business, what would you do?"

"Well, I would borrow money and invest it," I replied.

"There you go, it's taking you so long to do your research, but you would know exactly what to do to go into business." As he shrugged his head, Mr. Zhou added, "You'll never do well when you work for others!"

Indeed, for Mr. Zhou, it was difficult to understand why one would choose work other than business if given the option. In his view, salaries were fixed and limiting, whereas business opened up the possibility of multiplying one's resources exponentially through the application of one's own efforts. One of his favorite sayings, composed of four four-character phrases, was that there are four types of people: first, those who harm themselves and others (*hai ren hai ji*); second, those who help themselves but harm others (*hai ren li ji*); third, those who harm themselves to help others (*li ren hai ji*); and fourth, those who help themselves while helping others (*li ren li ji*).[3] And, as if he were quoting straight from Adam Smith and Jeremy Bentham, Mr. Zhou would then proceed to expound on the evident superiority of the fourth type—those who help themselves and thereby benefit others. This happy outcome, he would add, can most easily be achieved by engaging in one's own business.

A corollary of this preference for business was the assumption that no one with intelligence wallows for long in the shadows of an employer. "You can never keep a good foreman," one factory owner told me, "because if he is any good, he'll start a business of his own."

---

[3] The use of such four-character phrases is pervasive in everyday Chinese speech as well as in written texts. They are used for many different purposes, including greeting, congratulating, enjoining, or describing recognizable traits or situations. Their compactness and economy of expression are usually lost in translation.

Clearly, for both Mr. Zhou and other members of the Dhapa community, one goal of such business activities is to increase the material well-being of oneself and one's family. But not only is it the pursuit of a more comfortable life that makes wealth desirable in Dhapa, it is also the status that accompanies it, and the ability to influence and to be respected by others.

The importance of wealth can be felt in many ways in the Hakka community. Whether an individual or family is *hen you qian* (very wealthy) or *mei you qian* (poor) is usually the first item mentioned in any discussion about them. The in-betweens excite very little comment. It is wealthy men who serve as community leaders; for example, they are the ones who head business associations. Furthermore, community social life is focused on the ceremonies and celebrations that surround major life-cycle rituals, providing numerous opportunities for wealthy individuals to validate publicly their financial success. The wealthiest families stage more lavish and larger weddings and birthday celebrations than other families, and the number of tables at a reception (ten people to a table) may be the talk of the town for several days before and after it is held (more than fifty tables is usually cause for extended comment). Likewise, more people attend the funerals of wealthy individuals than those of less prosperous individuals, even though the criteria that supposedly determine who should attend such functions are constant.

Indeed, because wealth is so critical to status, I had to quickly change my graduate student ways of relatively frugal and simple living. When I first moved to Xiu Lilan's house, for instance, I used to walk to the school every morning. It was not far, not even a twenty-minute walk. Lilan and some other acquaintances kept urging me to take a rickshaw or to buy a bicycle or motor scooter. Much to their relief, I finally did buy a bicycle. They had worried that because I walked, people would think I was poor and would look down upon me. Later, when my parents came to visit me in Calcutta, Lilan constantly reminded me to let people know that they were staying in the best hotel in Calcutta.

This emphasis on wealth does not exclude other characteristics from garnering status for a family or individual within the community (see the discussion in the following section). Nor does it mean that a wealthy individual will truly be respected in all cases. For instance, if community members believe someone gained wealth through cheating, or some other unfair means, they will certainly call him a "scoundrel" (*jian zei*) behind his back; yet a person who is not rich but who works loyally for his or her family will be granted a certain degree of respect. But no one denies the importance of achieving wealth as an ultimate goal. And many other qualities are valued precisely for the part they play in enabling a family to achieve prosperity.

The Ideal Qualities of an Entrepreneur

Among the qualities most highly esteemed in this drive toward prosperity are diligence, tenacity, and hard work. Stories abound within the community about individuals who prospered because of their unstinting labors. Many people, when asked about their past, like to quote the aphorism "toil and endure hardship" (*ke ku nai lao*).[4] Dhapa tanners pride themselves not only on the amount of time they spend in their work but also on the fact that they are willing and able to perform tasks that many would consider unpleasant. They explain that although they employ Indian workers, they themselves have no hesitation in performing many laborious chores within their factories. The architecture of the tanneries abets this process of participation in hard factory labor. Few tanneries have formal offices. Instead of wearing office clothes and supervising from a distance, most Chinese tanners usually plunge into the work themselves, working in baggy pajamas and torn T-shirts at the side of their Indian employees. Indeed, the Dhapa Hakka enjoy telling stories about the amazed reaction of buyers from abroad, who constantly confuse the tannery owners with the tannery workers.

In addition to hard work, frugality is much admired. Saving one's resources is often touted as a reason for an individual's business success, and families that have lost wealth over the years are often said to have done so because of the wasteful practices of succeeding generations. Closely tied to this stress on frugality is an emphasis on being able to plan well, making intelligent use of one's resources. In fact, on New Year's Eve people like to hang three vegetables over their stoves, the names of which are homonyms for intelligence, diligence, and the ability to make good plans (*cong cai*, *quan cai*, and *suan cai*).

Nevertheless, the same emphasis on intelligence also means that

---

[4] A more literal, but less elegant, translation of this phrase would be "work hard and put up with hard work." *Ke ku* is also translated frequently as "endure hardship." But the English word *endure* is somewhat passive, and the Chinese words *ke ku* imply not the mere endurance of something but the fact of actually working very hard. Likewise, *nai* often suggests patience. Thus, one not only works hard but puts up with the condition of working hard without complaint.

[99]

there are limits to the importance placed on frugality and hard physical labor. As many explained to me, the ultimate aim is to have enough money to be able to spend without worry. Commenting on my habit of taking the crowded buses instead of taxis, one friend pointed out that although my frugality was admirable, I would be better off if I simply figured out a way to earn more money!

Factory owners also tend to retreat from hard physical labor as they become wealthier and are able to employ more outside laborers. In this way, the Dhapa tanners are similar to the peasants and small-scale entrepreneurs in Taiwan. When Stevan Harrell asked the residents of Ploughshare village in Taiwan what a "good fate" was, for instance, they almost all replied, "lots of money and freedom from physical labor" (1985:209). And, as Justin Niehoff found, the goal of household manufacturing enterprises in Taiwan is to grow "to the point where hired labor can supplement, and eventually replace, the labor of family members" (1987:279).

Two final qualities, those of trustworthiness (*laoshi*) and reliability (*kekao*), are also seen as integral to business success, and unlike frugality and an emphasis on hard physical labor, these qualities are not considered dispensable once prosperity has been achieved. If you cannot demonstrate your trustworthiness to community members, you will probably never get loans and financial help from them. And if the same qualities are not revealed to your suppliers and buyers, they will stop doing business with you. The story about Qiao Tanming struggling through the drenching monsoon rain, in order to pay his supplier, was often recounted in discussions about important qualities for business success.

Therefore, many of those who eventually started their own tanning businesses, and even built tanneries of their own, stress the importance of having good personal relationships and a trustworthy reputation in order to achieve business success. This emphasis is not peculiar to the Chinese of Calcutta. Indeed, it is discussed in much of the literature on overseas Chinese business. Donald DeGlopper, for instance, discusses the importance of trust in its many aspects in his examination of business practices in a Taiwanese town (1972:315).

Like the Chinese of Java, whom Edward Ryan studied in the early 1960s, therefore, "a particularly valued type of personality is one which combines integrity, with cleverness, nerve and skill" (Olsen 1972:262). Nevertheless, the possession of all the most valued entrepreneurial attributes—diligence, intelligence, reliability, and frugality—is much less likely to receive acclaim in Dhapa if despite all one's efforts, the ultimate result is business failure. In the worst-case scenario, people will hint that some misdeed in the past was the cause of the present bad fortune. They will point to the mistreatment of a child, sibling, or spouse in earlier years, for instance, and explain that an individual's current hardships are retribution for such thoughtless behavior. This is illustrated by the manner in which people spoke about one man of relatively modest means. Years earlier he had broken off his engagement after his fiancée was crippled in an accident, and he subsequently married another woman. His failure to prosper was usually referred to in a rather unsympathetic manner. Hadn't he been completely unjust in abandoning his fiancée? And weren't his adverse circumstances exactly the fate one should expect for such bad behavior?

Religion and Entrepreneurial Values

The notion that good behavior and wise investment can have considerable influence on one's future even extends into ritual practice and conceptions of the afterlife.

Ritual life among the Hakka Chinese of Calcutta restates the importance of economic success and prosperity in a twofold manner. First, the symbolism of money and material goods is critical to expressions of the relationship between gods, departed spirits, and humans. Second, the rituals, by their very extravagance, are an index of the prosperity that the participants have achieved in their present lives. Like the Chinese businessmen in the Malaysian town studied by Donald Nonini (1979), therefore, Calcutta Chinese both invest in their future prosperity and display their present success through their religious practice.

The use of monetary symbolism is not unique to the Dhapa Chinese, for the metaphor of money and monetary relations is a pervasive concept in Chinese popular religion, especially in expressions of the soul's relationship to its incarnations. After the introduction of Buddhism into China, the belief that a person's soul is reincarnated in another being after death became infused in popular religious thought. But in its Chinese variant, this belief in reincarnation took on a curiously monetary expression—souls do not just get reincarnated, they need funds to do so.

[101]

Hill Gates examined this infusion of monetary metaphors in Chinese popular religion. In the Taibei neighborhood where she did fieldwork, her informants explained that souls en route to reincarnation borrow large sums of money from celestial treasuries. These sums are "used to purchase a body for reincarnation, the rest defrays the cost of the individual's particular lot in life, a matter determined prior to birth. Some, indebted for large sums, will receive wealth, high rank, and other blessings in life while those who give less must live with correspondingly straitened means" (1987:268).

As a result, individuals are constantly attempting to pay off these debts throughout their lives. Burning paper money to the gods is one way of paying off this debt, and even after one dies, one's relatives burn large amounts of spirit money, for as Gates explains, one needs to "pay off the account . . . if the spirit is to enter unencumbered into a new and presumably more fortunate incarnation" (1987:268).

In Dhapa, such monetary symbolism is a pervasive part of ritual life. The entire process of reincarnation is conceptualized in rather concrete terms in which large amounts of money and material goods are necessary for a fortuitous celestial journey. In fact, the accoutrements of modern living often appear prominently, both as paper replicas which are burned as offerings to the departed souls, and in accounts of the spirit world.

"Suppose you live in India now, but after you die you come back as an African," my first landlady explained to me one day. "How will you get to Africa? By boat? By car? The best way is by airplane, but for that you'll need money, because the ticket is so expensive."

The entrepreneurial values of wise decision making and careful planning are also embedded in tales of celestial life. For instance, many individuals emphasized that it was not enough to pay off old debts; it was better, through wise investment and intelligent foresight, to build up credit. As several people told me, if one presents offerings of enough spirit money during one's lifetime, one can pay off one's debts from one's present incarnation and start to build up equity for the next round.

I should point out here that in Dhapa, and indeed among all the Chinese of Calcutta, what we would call popular Chinese religion, a set of practices influenced by Buddhist, Taoist, and Confucian values and symbols, is the overwhelmingly dominant form of spiritual orientation. But Chinese in Dhapa do not conceive of religious orientation or identification as a matter of exclusivity. Many young people, for

This paper money vault was burned as an offering to the gods by a family whose tannery had been robbed. It is believed that such an offering will build up heavenly credit for those who provide it, and may even help forestall further financial disasters in one's present life.

instance, will identify themselves as Christian to gain admission into a mission-run English medium school, since these schools are considered high quality and since Chinese believe that it is easier to get in if you are Christian. In fact, community members sometimes make disparaging remarks about the importance of religious orientation in the social identity of Indians, stating that they cannot understand why differences in religious identity should provoke enmity and even riots. It is not uncommon in Dhapa for each member of a given family to describe his or her religious identity differently—some identifying their religion as Protestant, others as Catholic, and still others as Buddhist.

Nevertheless, despite the fact that Chinese will convert to Christianity as a practical move, primarily to gain admission to certain schools, only a few individuals in Dhapa have been married in a Christian church, and funerals are never conducted in a Christian manner.

Indeed, religious images not commonly found in Chinese popular religion usually get incorporated into the same cycle of monetary and material offerings that I have described. For instance, during the Bengali holiday dedicated to the worship (*puja*) of the Hindu goddess Kali, who is the patron deity of Calcutta, an older Chinese woman whom I knew tacked up a picture of Kali at an altar with Chinese gods. She then proceeded to propitiate Kali by burning paper money and setting off firecrackers, an act that set off her younger family members into wild paroxysms of laughter, since Hindus traditionally propitiate their deities with fruits and flowers.

Certainly, Dhapa residents find it hard to imagine spiritual life without a comfortable collection of modern consumer goods and status symbols. One of the most unforgettable offerings I ever saw go up in smoke was a life-size three-dimensional paper replica of a Fiat car, complete with clear cellophane windows and a paper chauffeur, also life-size and three-dimensional, at the steering wheel. Neatly stacked inside the car were wads of paper money—this to pay for the chauffeur's salary and for gas.

This elaborate construction had been occasioned by the death of an elderly gentleman with a moderately successful tanning business. His two sons, who inherited the business, and his five daughters, who had all married into wealthier families, held a ceremony every week for the first seven weeks after their father died. This period (*zhongyou*) is believed to encompass the time between an individual's death and his or her soul's reincarnation in another being. It is the time during

[104]

A life-size paper image of a Fiat car, replete with chauffeur and paper money to
pay him, was burned as an offering to a recently deceased relative several weeks
after his funeral.

which the soul wanders, and since one wants the soul to be reincarnated in the highest form of being possible, one makes extensive
offerings during this period. The family in question staged a particularly elaborate ceremony on the fourth week of this process. It was on
that occasion that they invited Buddhist priests to their tannery to
conduct services, at the end of which the Fiat and all its accessories
were burned as offerings to their father.

The display did not go unnoticed by the family's neighbors. For days
afterward people talked about the car, the ceremonies, and most significantly, the cost of the entire production. Indeed, this episode illustrates the second manner in which the ritual life of the community
both underscores and supports a status system based on wealth. Ritual
life in Dhapa is an important arena for broadcasting credentials as a
financially successful family. Commissioning a craftsman to construct
elaborate paper offerings, such as the Fiat car, cost no small fee, but as

[105]

Dhapa residents would openly state, usually with a resigned chuckle, this was all part of the "competition."

To a cynical Western outsider, such open admissions appear to negate the sincerity of the actors or even cheapen the meaning of the ceremony. But for residents of Dhapa, such elaborate displays are not only unobjectionable but absolutely necessary. In the case of a funeral, what is important is that the ceremony does honor to an elder who has died. A small and inexpensive ceremony would be judged unfilial and disrespectful. Since the ceremony I described was in honor of a recently deceased father, its extravagance was in perfect accord with the cultural requirements of filiality. It created a "win-win" situation in which the display of one's wealth, with subsequent validation of one's status as a well-to-do family, was also appropriate social behavior, required by the criteria of filiality and respect for one's elders.

The accumulation of wealth is itself seen as filial behavior, since it enables one not only to look after one's parents in the present life but also to guarantee that their afterlife will be adequately provided for. The intent of the actors is not important in such cases, as long as the behavior is appropriate to their social role—in this case, behaving in a filial manner toward parents. As Sulamith Heins Potter indicates in a recent examination of emotion in a Chinese cultural setting, the actual content of one's feelings, though personally important, is not socially significant, as long as one behaves in a manner appropriate to the relationship; and such behavior is a matter of doing rather than simply expressing one's feelings. A Chinese villager told her, "We Chinese show our feelings for one another in our work, not with words" (Potter 1988:205). And Potter goes on to conclude, "The Chinese devote endless attention to work and the rewards for work. But in speaking of work, they are also speaking of social connection and the affirmation of relationship in the most fundamental terms they know" (1988:206).

Seen in this light, entrepreneurial, familial, and religious values are all mutually reinforcing in Dhapa. The hard work, frugality, and careful planning entailed in the entrepreneurial ethic are also the means by which responsibilities toward family members are fulfilled in this life and the next. And not only is the afterlife understood in monetary metaphors, but its very essence necessitates the pursuit of prosperity in one's current life, so as to better provide oneself and one's immediate ancestors with a fortuitous afterlife and reincarnation. Finally, what matters in all of this is what one does, rather than what one may merely feel. Indeed, it was in talk of labor and sacrifice, or the lack of these qualities, that family member's connections with one another were most emotionally articulated.

It was not uncommon during my interviews, for instance, for middle-aged men who were wealthy tannery owners to describe tearfully their mothers' sacrifices on their behalves. A mother's selling of her wedding jewelry, or making and selling of prepared foods or liquor, so that her son could go to school, or start a business, was a frequent theme in such stories. Likewise, one of the most bitter descriptions of a sibling that I ever heard was directed at a brother who had not provided his share of his mother's funeral expenses, thus endangering the ability of his other brothers to display appropriately their filiality at her funeral.

Potter contrasts the Chinese attitude with the American by an allusion to the American bumper sticker "Have you hugged your kid today?" (1988:182). Certainly, from the point of view of the Dhapa Chinese, it would be much more appropriate to ask, "What have you done for your family members to ensure their well-being in this life and the next?"

Gambling and the Entrepreneurial Ethic

Despite the emphasis on hard work and wise investment, many forms of gambling, the most popular of which is the game of mahjong, are abundant in Dhapa. At weddings, birthdays, and gatherings of friends and family, during Hindu holidays when the workers take off, and even during strikes, the gamblers come out. How common it is at these events to hear the crisp sounds of mahjong tiles clicking against one another, as they are mixed by intense players, who execute their moves without pause, and who sit for hours as the stakes rise. But it is not just mahjong. Card games, lotteries, trips to the Calcutta racetrack, and betting on the outcome of almost any sports event round out the options for the would-be gambler.

Nor are the stakes a matter of petty cash. In an afternoon of particularly keen play, thousands of rupees may crisscross the tables. How can the widespread practice and acceptance of many forms of gambling fit into a community that so thoroughly adheres to the practices and attitudes described in this chapter? To answer this question, I must first delineate the social contexts in which gambling occurs.

First and foremost, gambling is a mainstay of large celebrations that mark individual and familial changes in status and role. Weddings, for instance, are usually preceded by a full night of mahjong playing, and the gambling continues the next day both before and after the wedding feast. In this context, gambling is primarily an activity of men, and it should also be noted that when men gamble together they do so with their generational equals. Male friends and family of the groom will gather at his house, gambling away large sums of money which at other times would be invested wisely and husbanded carefully. Similar situations occur during house-moving ceremonies and birthday celebrations for elders—these are all large displays of hospitality to which several hundred guests may be invited. Indeed, the gambling that goes on during these occasions is part and parcel of the general atmosphere, in which display rather than conservation of wealth is temporarily the order of the day. All these events are preceded and followed by a night and day of gambling, primarily mahjong playing.

But one need not wait for important celebrations to gamble. Gambling within the home, including both mahjong and card playing, is a popular activity, and in this context women may be as active as men. Like men, women gamble with their peers. "Sisterhoods," which are groups of five to ten women who are of approximately the same age and who have formalized their relationship before a deity, frequently gamble with one another. A lunch gathering by a group of women who call themselves the "ten sisters," for instance, may be preceded by a few hours of mahjong and card playing. Of course, men also gamble at home, but they do so less frequently than women. There are two exceptions: one, when tannery workers go on strike, in which case everybody seems to pass the time with mahjong, and two, during the week of New Year festivities.

The week of the New Year celebrations is one context in which men and women gamble within a circle of family rather than with those of the same generation and sex. But here, the week is structured around a juxtaposition of control and abandon so far as monetary resources are concerned. On New Year's Day, gambling is forbidden and diets are vegetarian (the vegetarian diet is also viewed as purifying, and many individuals use this day to visit a local Buddhist temple built by the Hakka community). On New Year's Eve, on the other hand, and on days two, four, and six after the New Year, gambling is allowed, and meat is not forbidden.

The fact that gambling is enjoyed during the New Year, but confined within certain days, helps to explain how it can coexist within a community that normally stresses more reproductive attitudes toward money. As with the New Year celebrations, gambling usually occurs in contexts that are ordered and bounded—not only in terms of time and place, but even in terms of one's partners.

The distinction between gambling that is bounded by and confined to social occasions, and what we might term compulsive or uncontrolled gambling, parallels the distinctions made by Chinese in other contexts regarding the consumption of alcohol. As Stevan Harrell points out in an article on drinking in rural Taiwan, alcohol may be consumed in vast quantities but is not considered a problem if its consumption is confined to certain specified social occasions. As he states, "Drinking is not itself a problem, but wrong drinking is" (1981:50).

There is no doubt that the Calcutta Hakka condemn gambling when done to excess, when it spills out from these specified social contexts into other areas of life. Heavy gamblers, for instance, are seen as exceedingly undesirable marriage partners, and a common way of alluding to a person's laziness is to say that he or she wiles away time playing mahjong. And whereas a successful entrepreneur will rarely be taken to task for his gambling, an unsuccessful one may find his bad luck blamed on a gambling habit.

Although those who gamble may never realize a net profit, those who control gambling certainly do. The control of gambling is itself a form of entrepreneurship, and among the Calcutta Chinese such opportunities are not ignored. Profits from running lotteries (many of which are small-scale operations, with several family members as shareholders) can provide a sizeable addition to a family's income.[5]

But there is more significance to gambling than the fact that games like mahjong provide a venue for socializing, or that lotteries are profitable for those who run them. Gambling can also be understood as a part of life linked more with notions of fate than with individual control and power.

Although the Dhapa Chinese clearly subscribe to the notion that through good behavior and wise investments one can exert considerable influence over one's future and even one's afterlife, they also leave

---

[5] That gambling is itself a business is relevant not just in the case of the Calcutta Chinese. In a study of numbers gambling in African-American neighborhoods, for instance, Ivan Light (1977) found that numbers gambling banks became both a source of revenue and a vehicle for savings.

[109]

room in their worldview for the acknowledgment that sometimes even the best of efforts may result in failure. Thus, an individual who has done all the right things—worked hard, invested wisely, saved money, and behaved properly—may still fail to prosper. In such a case, that individual's circumstance may be explained as the simple result of a bad "fate" (*mingyun*).

This use of the concept of *fate* to explain business failure has been analyzed by Stevan Harrell, who notes that it is often employed in Chinese folk ideology as a "post-hoc rationalization, a catchall explanation when others fail, a way of acknowledging that even the most moral and diligent human beings cannot necessarily guarantee their own success in life" (1987:101).

Clearly, therefore, the Dhapa Hakka leave space in their entrepreneurial values to acknowledge that even the best of efforts may fail, and that complete control of the outcome is impossible, and gambling is one area of life where one's skill and hard work are even less deterministic than in business. If fate may undo one's best entrepreneurial efforts, it is even more likely that a highly skilled mahjong player can be wiped out at the end of an afternoon of high-stakes play.

Indeed, the Dhapa Chinese often use the image of gambling to demonstrate the connections between fate and business success. One of the wealthiest men in the community, Xi Taiguo, once related a part of his life story to me in this way. Taiguo ultimately built one of the largest enterprises in Dhapa, a large export business with more than 150 employees. But he had suffered through a prolonged period of failure before achieving his current success, despite his inheritance of a tannery and tanning business from his father. Unable to sustain that business, he had to lease out the tannery. He then lived on the income while spending his days at the racetrack and playing mahjong—hardly a story of enduring bitter labors and overcoming adversity!

Nevertheless, Taiguo told me, something must have been going right, because his luck at mahjong that year was phenomenal; he won nearly every time he played. And even his sojourns at the racetrack resulted in a business coup, for there he befriended a Punjabi man who worked for the State Trading Corporation and who told him that gloving leather was a hot item for exporters. On the basis of this tip, Taiguo was able to borrow money and start his own business again, a business that ultimately prospered beyond any success he could have imagined at the time.

While Taiguo's story also included spates of hard work and study, there is no doubt that he believed luck was a significant factor in his success, and he described his gambling luck as a foreshadowing of his luck in business. One's fate in business, therefore, like one's fate in gambling, is viewed as beyond one's ultimate control. Business success is explained as a combination of hard work and good behavior, with a little bit of luck; and as with gambling, it is understood that the factor of risk cannot be eliminated.

This necessity of taking risks in order to make any gains, and the manner in which gambling reenacts this tense relation between danger and profit, came out clearly in a discussion I had about gambling with my friend Mr. Zhou. "Why do people gamble?" I queried. Mr. Zhou, shrugging his shoulders, responded, "They just gamble; there is no reason." But then he added a significant evaluation about the character of gamblers. "Do you think they are not clever?" he asked rhetorically. "No! It is the *clever* one who gambles. Can the stupid person take any action? No, they can't!"

"But isn't it dangerous to gamble?" I insisted.

"It's luck." Mr. Zhou continued. "What is luck? You only get luck if you do something first. You won't know if you have luck until you do something. It's just like business."

"But in business you need skill too," I pressed.

"It's the same in gambling," Mr. Zhou insisted. "It's a question of skill and luck; they're both the same."

Of course, even though gambling is a part of life that allows for abandon and acknowledges fate for its outcome, one is normally advised not to participate to the point where one's financial resources will actually be threatened. Most people are expected to confine—and succeed in confining—their gambling to particular times and places. Furthermore, the compulsive gambler, the person who is unable to quit after great losses, will be roundly criticized. The very fact that gambling *is* "play" distinguishes it from business activity.

As Mr. Zhou stated in our conversation about gambling, both business and gambling involve luck and skill. But, he was quick to add that "you *must* do business to live. Business is very critical. You don't *depend* on gambling, but you depend on business."

Indeed, when Calcutta Chinese immigrate to North American cities like Toronto, they quickly revise their gambling habits to fit their new financial situations. In Toronto, most Calcutta Chinese take jobs as assembly-line workers. They may still gamble at important celebrations, but the stakes are drastically reduced. In India, the lowest

[111]

denomination passed around the mahjong tables was 100-rupee notes (the equivalent of $10, but with a value in India more comparable to $100). In their straitened circumstances in Toronto, Calcutta Chinese gamble with one-dollar bills and even small change.

Finally, it is important to remember that although frugality and wise planning are highly regarded, they are not values in themselves but tools to be used for the betterment of one's family, including one's ascendants and one's descendants. That is why people consider it much less desirable to hoard meager savings than to have ample money to spend, including money that can be sacrificed at the gambling table.

From the point of view of Calcutta's Chinese tanners, gambling and entrepreneurship are both activities where one plays with fate. Successful players in both areas are those who know how to minimize losses and maximize gains. But, as I explain in the next section, gains cannot be defined in identical ways in these two areas.

Calcutta Chinese Gambling in Broader Perspective

As the preceding discussion has made clear, the Calcutta Chinese belief in economic rationality is far from total, and they view gambling as reproducing the complex interplay of purposiveness and fate that characterizes their ability to effect economic outcomes. Gambling, I have suggested, is chiefly differentiated from entrepreneurship in the community by its degree of containment. When gambling breaks through the boundaries in which it is usually confined and becomes unrestrained, it becomes a symbol not of the interplay of fate and control but of total failure and lack of discipline. Hence, economically unproductive individuals, or individuals who whittle away fortunes, are usually described as compulsive gamblers.

The work of Edward Devereux, who in the late 1940s wrote an unpublished doctoral dissertation on gambling in the United States, is relevant here. Devereux indicated that capitalism was laden with contradictory values, for example, "thrift versus consumption" and "prudence versus risk-taking" (Downes et al. 1976:23). Since gambling is both socially and spatially segregated, Devereux claimed, both wastefulness and risk taking can be condemned without the critique explicitly implicating the overall economic system (Downes et al. 1976:24). Devereux's work, however, does not explain why gambling would appeal to entrepreneurs themselves. Indeed, it would lead one to conclude that gambling, as both a censured and a spatially separate activity, would not be engaged in by those whose activities are central to the functioning of capitalism. And, in fact, Devereux felt that gambling was more common among those who were not tied to the "constraints of middle-class life" (Downes et al. 1976:27).

Such a conclusion fits well with the data of Donald Nonini, who studied gambling among Chinese in the Malaysian town of Pekan Tebu. Nonini found that the working-class Chinese in this town preferred a more anonymous style of gambling. Lotteries were popular among this group, asserts Nonini, because "other forms of gambling in a community of poor neighbors and acquaintances pose a threat to ongoing social relations: for one's winning implies another's loss, diminishing a scarce base of resources and endangering reciprocity between people," but the lottery "operates beyond this community and thus does not threaten its social and moral basis" (1979:705).

Curiously, unlike Calcutta Chinese businessmen, the Chinese business class in the Malaysian town studied by Nonini rarely played mahjong and only occasionally bought lottery tickets. Nonini explains the difference between these working-class lottery players and the nongambling business class of this Malaysian town through an examination of entrepreneurial ideologies. The Malay Chinese businessman, Nonini explains, fears gambling because he believes his capital must circulate and he worries that through gambling he will lose both his capital and therefore his credit worthiness (1979:706). The working-class Chinese residents of the same town, however, see lotteries as the only possibility they have of earning extra money.

Nonini then points out that this difference between working-class and business-class Chinese attitudes toward gambling is reflected in religious practices. The working-class Chinese ask gods through spirit mediums for winning lottery numbers. But these are mere requests. No offerings are made, which would oblige the gods to reply. Businessmen, on the other hand, participate in ceremonies that "ostentatiously and publicly" honor the gods; "by their material offerings and service, these men, all or mostly merchants, place the god in a position of obligation to them" (1979:708). Chinese businessmen maintain that unlike money lost at mahjong tables or lotteries, funds spent in such public rituals will generate a greater return and are therefore not wasted. Indeed, one of Nonini's working-class informants remarked that "'Chinese businessmen believe they can bribe even the gods themselves'" (1979:708).

Nonini's work is particularly relevant to my own, because he connects gambling, religious belief, and entrepreneurial values. But unlike the gambling-averse businessmen of Nonini's town, the Calcutta
Chinese entrepreneurs are inveterate gamblers. What explains this
difference?

One answer lies in the type of gambling preferred in these two
divergent instances. Nonini's working-class Chinese gamblers preferred the lottery *precisely* because of its anonymity, because winning
did not directly entail a fellow community member's loss, thereby
endangering reciprocal social ties.

On the other hand, although lotteries do exist within the Calcutta
Chinese community, the game of mahjong is by far the most dominant
form of gambling. Here, the observations of Francis Hsu are relevant.
In his comparison of American and Chinese cultures, Hsu asks whether there is a relationship between gambling and entrepreneurship in
the Chinese context. But interestingly, Hsu rejects the notion that
there is any connection. Says Hsu, whereas the Americans will "bet on
practically anything from sports to presidential elections, the Chinese
prefer games with familiar and well-defined situations such as mahjong. . . . American gambling usually is individually conceived and
individually engaged in. . . . Further, organized gambling in America
is a highly impersonal affair, carried on without equipment and between strangers" (1981:317). Hsu goes on to contrast Chinese and
American gambling by stating, "Chinese gambling games are invari-
ably played with certain tools; the participants sit in definite positions,
know each other, and meet together regularly" (1981:317).

Hsu concludes that not only is Chinese gambling more "competitive" than American gambling, since Chinese wager on games of skill
whereas Americans bet on sporting events and other happenings over
which they have no control, but in addition, since Chinese usually
gamble with those they know, Chinese gambling is more social than
American gambling and therefore related to concerns about face.

Unfortunately, Hsu's distinctions cannot be applied in all Chinese
contexts. They simply are not relevant to many of the forms of gambling popular in Chinese societies.[6] For instance, racetrack betting,
dice, and lotteries all have great popularity in contemporary Chinese
settings and are examples of more anonymous, less "competitive"

---

[6] For further details, see my discussion of the varieties of gambling in Chinese
societies throughout history and in different overseas communities (Basu 1991a).

gambling than games played around a table, like mahjong. On the other hand, Hsu's observations can be usefully employed in the analysis of gambling among the Calcutta Chinese since the most prevalent form of gambling among the Calcutta Chinese occurs among acquaintances, friends, and relatives. Therefore, like the gambling that Hsu characterizes as most characteristically Chinese, it does have ramifications in terms of one's social relations, prestige, and face.

But a further question remains. Why are these entrepreneurs drawn into this more competitive, less anonymous form of gambling? Remember that social status in this community is almost directly determined by wealth. Gambling for high stakes in this setting, as long as it remains contained and does not threaten one's ability to earn, can be an indication of success, a demonstration that one has enough money to gamble large amounts away without apparent consequences. For instance, Mr. Zhou often claimed that gambling with wealthy men increased one's chances of winning, since they were not very careful with their money.

Certainly, when community members describe occasions of mahjong playing, it is not the humdrum exchange of small change, but the large wins and losses that are recounted again and again. When I questioned Mr. Zhou about gambling, for instance, he immediately began to recount a New Year's session of gambling with three of the wealthiest entrepreneurs in the community. "We all started out with 20,000 rupees [about $1000] on the table, and another 20,000 rupees promised," he said. When I reacted in disbelief, he indicated that in terms of community practice during New Year celebrations, these amounts were not extreme, and he asserted that many people could lose or win "one lakh" (100,000) of rupees over the course of one New Year's holiday.[7]

The public display of one's wealth, through indifference to its loss, is therefore one of the attractions of mahjong for Calcutta's Chinese entrepreneurs. This contrasts starkly with the motives of Nonini's working-class Chinese gamblers who actually play for a small profit. Nonini states, "Pekan Tebu working-class people gamble . . . so frequently and with so much fervor, because it is only through the magic of winning a lottery that they can accumulate capital at all" (1979:705). Calcutta's Chinese entrepreneurs, like many other overseas Chinese

---

[7] As a unit of measurement, one lakh is equal to the number 100,000. It is a measure commonly used in India.

entrepreneurial communities, utilize a large array of strategies to accumulate financial capital—including rotating credit associations and borrowing from other community members. Thus, if gambling presents any true possibility of amassing "capital" for them, such gains must be considered in the realm of "symbolic capital" (see Bourdieu 1977) rather than material assets.[8]

But we must also remember that such symbolic gains are intrinsically and fundamentally connected to real economic power. As Bourdieu reminds us in *Distinction*, "Economic power is first and foremost a power to keep economic necessity at arm's length. This is why it universally asserts itself by the destruction of riches, conspicuous consumption, squandering, and every form of gratuitous luxury" (1984:55).

However, the description of gambling as a sort of inverted form of conspicuous consumption cannot fully explain its appeal to the Calcutta Chinese. Why this particular form of consumption rather than others? Why the appeal of gambling in particular? We must remember that the wealth of the Calcutta Chinese, unlike that of many segments of the French bourgeoisie whom Bourdieu describes, is not based on the acquisition of skills in educational institutions, nor is there enough wealth to pass it down through the generations. As a pariah entrepreneurial community, the Calcutta Chinese can make a living only through entrepreneurship in a few restricted areas. Their good fortunes are also dependent on continued work in their family firms, and therefore, as noted earlier in the chapter, their central ethos emphasizes the attitudes needed to succeed in business and make a profit. Hence, gambling is much more than a form of conspicuous consumption for them. It reenacts the central pitfalls and risks of real-life entrepreneurship. To understand exactly how this occurs, we need to turn to Erving Goffman's ideas about what he calls *fateful action*.

Although Goffman's analyses of social interaction are directed at Western industrial societies and so would not ordinarily be expected to be of much use to the sinologist, they are surprisingly pertinent in this case. Fateful action, for Goffman, has three characteristics. First, it is "problematic" (1967:164), that is, it refers to activities that are "not

---

[8] As Bourdieu states, we must in our analyses "extend economic calculation to *all* the goods, material and symbolic, without distinction, that present themselves as *rare* and worthy of being sought after in a particular social formation—which may be 'fair words' or smiles, handshakes or shrugs, compliments or attention, challenges or insults, honour or honours, powers or pleasures, . . . etc." (1977:178).

yet determined but about to be" (1967:152). By this, Goffman means that action is problematic if the outcome is determined within the period of action. Many problematic actions, of course, may also have long-term consequences which may be realized years later. But actions that only have long-term consequences are not problematic within this definition. In addition to being problematic, fateful action must be "consequential." For Goffman, this means that such action must "spill over into the rest of life and have an effect there" (1967:162). Finally, actions must be, in Goffman's words, "undertaken for what is felt to be their own sake" (1967:185). Says Goffman, "fateful activities . . . *are* socially defined as ones an individual is under no obligation to continue to pursue. . . . No extraneous factors compel him to face fate in the first place; no extraneous ends provide expediential reasons for his continued participation" (1967:185).

Gambling easily falls under Goffman's schema of fateful action. Indeed, according to Goffman, "gambling is the prototype of action" (1967:186), since it is "a species of activity in which self-determination is celebrated" (1967:214). Earning a living, on the other hand, does not qualify as action in this schema. For while it is surely consequential, it is not "problematic." The outcome of one's activity may not be clear for years or even decades. In action, on the other hand, especially in games and contests, the "outcome is determined and payoff rewarded all in the same breadth of experience" (1967:156).

Such contests, says Goffman, are also great opportunities for displays of character, for one has ample chances to demonstrate how one acts "in the face of sudden pressures" (1967:217). Indeed, Goffman uses the term *character contest* (1967:246) to describe such fateful action, and he asserts that "each individual is engaged in providing evidence to establish a definition of himself at the expense of what can remain for the other" (1967:241).

Returning for a moment to Mr. Zhou's comments about gambling, we find that Goffman's observations are strikingly pertinent. Mr. Zhou's contention that "there is no reason" that people gamble, for instance, accords well with Goffman's definition of action as activity undertaken for its own sake. And when Mr. Zhou asserts that it is only "clever" people who engage in gambling, because it is only the clever who can take *action*, he defines gambling not as an addictive vice, but as an action freely chosen and as a showcase for the actor's capabilities and willingness to take the risks that might bring rewards.

Interestingly, Goffman's notion of character contests is remarkably

[117]

similar to, and may indeed have influenced, Clifford Geertz's use of the term *deep play* to describe games in which "much more is at stake than material gain: namely, esteem, honor, dignity, respect—in a word—status" (1973:435).[9] But it should also be pointed out here that the aspects of Calcutta Chinese gambling that so strikingly resemble Goffman's character contests and Geertz's deep play are most prominent in the gambling that occurs among adult men, as opposed to gambling that occurs among family members of both sexes, or among women.[10] This is because it is among adult men that the stakes are likely to be highest and the risks greatest. It is in these games that the potential rewards and dangers of risk taking are most resonant.

Indeed, the organization of gambling in the community—with adult male peers engaging in the highest stakes and the riskiest games— parallels the sexual division of labor in day-to-day entrepreneurial activities. I discuss this sexual division of labor more fully in Chapter 6, but for now, I need only mention that while both male and female family members in the community participate actively in the running of their businesses, it is male family heads who engage in what community members say is the riskiest business activity—buying the rawhides from which leather is processed. This decision is held to be the most critical and dangerous because if the hide is bad, no amount of processing can create a good piece of leather from it. And if the hide merchant overcharges the tanner, no amount of skimping on the manufacturing process can result in a profit.

But whether we choose to view high-stakes gambling among the Calcutta Chinese as deep play or as character contests, the aforementioned observations still leave us with a difficult paradox. Earlier in this chapter, I indicated that gambling was nonproblematic only when it was controlled, confined within certain special times and places. Yet

[9] Geertz had obviously read Goffman before writing his essay on the Balinese cockfights, and he cites and then utilizes Goffman's term *focused gathering* to describe the cockfights. (For a definition of this term, see note 11, below.) He does not, however, cite Goffman's later book *Interaction Ritual*, which is where Goffman develops the notion of *character contests*. My supposition that Goffman influenced Geertz's development of the concept *deep play* is based on its similarity with *character contests*, and on the fact that Goffman had written such an extensive analysis of gambling and other games, matters absolutely essential to Balinese cockfights, which contain both a gambling element and a competitive one.

[10] Here again there is a marked parallel to Geertz's description of the Balinese cockfights in which the "deepest" matches occur among socially prominent men rather than among women, children, or men who are not socially prominent (1973:435).

it is the wealth of the players and the chance to risk large sums of money—characteristics that reflect or have an impact on actual social life—that make certain gambling matches so attractive.

How can gambling exist in a realm that is apart from everyday life and still be intrinsically connected to it? How does the conspicuously social creep back into the game? And if gambling is set apart, why does it so meaningfully portray the central contradictions of the community's ethos? Why, for that matter, should the social identity of the gamblers make a difference in the degree to which the match proves exciting? Goffman would answer that although games may "disguise . . . the flow of socially significant matters into the encounter" (1961:73), they can never completely stop that flow. Inevitably, "the wider world must be introduced, but in a controlled and disguised manner." And, adds Goffman, "individuals can deal with one another face to face because they are ready to abide by rules of irrelevance, but the rules seem to exist to let something difficult be quietly expressed as much as to exclude it entirely from the scene" (1961:77).[11]

Gambling among the Calcutta Chinese, therefore, does not really exist apart from social life. But it may exclude or invert social realities as well as merely reflect them. It is therefore multifaceted. It mimics and reenacts both the risks and possible gains of entrepreneurship, but it does so within an arena contained by both temporal and spatial restrictions. It brings individuals face-to-face who are well aware of their relative place on a ladder of social status as determined by wealth. Yet winning or losing a particular gambling game is not determined by one's place in this social hierarchy.

Furthermore, unlike an actual decision to invest in a particular enterprise, gambling—like the fateful action discussed by Goffman—collapses the moments of decision and consequence. One does not have to wait years to learn the ultimate outcome. And unlike the desired results of real investment, which can only be financial gain, gambling allows the player to benefit in more varied ways. One can win money, it is true, but one can also gain prestige by displaying one's

---

[11] Goffman characterizes games, including gambling games, as *focused gatherings*. By this term he means events in which the participants have "a single visual and cognitive focus of attention" (1961:18). During such games, Goffman contends, participants abide by "rules of irrelevance" (1961:19) in which certain "properties of the situation . . . [are] . . . considered irrelevant, out of frame, or not happening. To adhere to these rules is to play fair. Irrelevant visible events will be disattended; irrelevant private concerns will be kept out of mind" (1961:25).

wealth and/or character—in part by exhibiting indifference to the loss of large sums.

It would be easy to view gambling among the Calcutta Chinese as merely an illicit and adventuresome diversion from the daily demands of business. Certainly, the fact that it occurs at important rites of passage—weddings, funerals, birthday celebrations for elders, and the like—serves to underscore its role as a diversion, placed back-to-back in these cases with rites that mark serious and necessary turning points in life.

But gambling does more than simply provide a venue for thrill seeking, although no one would deny that this is part of its appeal. For gambling in the Calcutta Chinese community simultaneously mimics and revolts against, reinforces and undermines the compulsions of the market with which they must necessarily deal in their daily lives. Perhaps it is best to see gambling as an expression of the contradictions inherent in their entrepreneurial ethos, an orientation which acknowledges both fate and skill as elements in business success, and which understands the roles of both prudence and risk taking. It is an outlook that gives status to those with the most wealth, but which thereby acknowledges the possibility of shake-ups in the status system when family fortunes change. Finally, while the community's ethos places emphasis on prudence, saving, and wise investment, it also admits that the ultimate aim is to be beyond want, to earn enough money to enjoy the luxuries of life, and to not worry about economizing. Gambling reflects this aspect of the ethos by dispensing with frugality, at least within the temporal boundaries within which it is expected to be confined.

But we must keep in mind that the rigors of daily enterprise around which the Calcutta Chinese organize their lives subsume such expressions of contradiction within one overarching goal—to earn a profit, to create ever more successful and expanding businesses. (As I explain in Chapter 8, this goal is usually a means of fulfilling family obligations, but it may sometimes conflict with them.) In the next chapter I examine the family histories within which individuals struggle to meet, and sometimes realize, their entrepreneurial objectives.

[5]

No Instant Success:
The First Generation

"It took me twenty years, twenty years to build this tannery. I didn't do it overnight." Ma Hongzhang, a successful tannery owner in his mid-fifties, is relating his life story to me. He speaks these words slowly and with emphasis, to make sure that I do not miss them. Visiting many of the now substantial tanneries with their plush living quarters, one can easily forget the simple truth revealed by Mr. Ma's statement—most Calcutta Chinese went through years or even decades of hard work before they achieved their present levels of economic success. Others did not succeed at all and left the tanning area for other parts of India or for different countries.

In this chapter, I concentrate on the experiences of men who founded the first generation of tanning businesses in Dhapa. Some were also first-generation residents in India; that is, they immigrated from China. Others were born in India but had no predecessor in the tanning business. My account draws heavily on the experiences of eighteen men who successfully started tanning businesses and ultimately built or bought factories of their own. I interviewed eleven of these men, the other seven were already deceased when I did my fieldwork, but I gathered information on them in the course of compiling family genealogies. The business histories of these first-generation tanners are summarized in Table 2. In addition to utilizing information about these eighteen individuals, I also draw on material from thirty-three genealogies that I collected during my fieldwork. These genealogies encompass the histories of eighty-eight existing businesses in Dhapa, almost one-third of the total.

Father (center), daughter, son-in-law, grandchildren, and other relatives enjoy a New Year's feast together in their tannery.

Because my focus here is on the experiences of male entrepreneurs, when I refer to *first-generation tanners* I mean men. But the reader must keep in mind that this term is merely a convenient shorthand for "men who founded the first generation of tanning businesses." When it comes to analyzing the actual work involved in making these businesses a success, we must take into account women's very substantial contributions of labor and even income. Women's critical roles in Dhapa's tanning businesses is the subject of the next chapter.

Arrival

Mrs. Jia, my first landlady in Dhapa, sat me down one day after I returned home from a frustrating attempt at fieldwork. I had tried to

Table 2. Life history and business development of first-generation tanners who became owners

Name	Birthplace	Age/year of arrival in India	Years spent as tannery worker	Years spent in nontanning work	Years spent as tenant	Tannery bought or built, year	Tannery bought or built with partner or by self	No. of offspring businesses
Yuan Qide (d. 1975)	China	14/1897	0	16	0	Built, 1913	Self	5
Wei Guangrong (d. '62)	China	16/1906	0	35	0	Built, 1941	Self	4
Kong Tienhua	China	19/1922	0	8	0	Built, 1930	Partner (brother)	8
Zhou Xianfeng (d. '54)	China	25/1925	0	25	4	Bought, 1948	Self	2
Xi Feiyuan (d. 1966)	China	16/1928	0	2	8	Built, 1938	Self	1
Pang Zhijian	China	18/1930	6	0	4	Built, 1940	Self	3
Qian Weigang (d. '81)	China	15/1932	0	16	32	Built, 1980	Partner (son)[a]	2
Mao Yisheng (d. 1989)	China	22/1936	0	3	10	Bought, 1949	Partner (unrelated)[a]	1
Yan Baoxia	China	19/1937	0	5	31	Built, 1973	Self	2
Fei Shengchan	China	17/1938	10	0	19	Built, 1967	Self	1
Qiao Tanming (d. '67)	China	18/1939	9	0	2	Built, 1951	Self	1
Tan Qiyun	China	17/1937	3	20	11	Bought 1971/built 1974	Self	1
Yuan Dongtai	China	23/1947	0	0	20	Built, 1967	Self	1
Song Yifu	China	20/1949	2	20	0	Built, 1971	Self	1
Ma Hongzhang	India	—	0	0	15	Built, 1970	Partners (wife's brothers)[a]	1
Gan Qianjin	India	—	7	0	28	Bought, 1970	Partner (unrelated)	1
Jiang Yongzhi	India	—	3	1	20	Bought, 1966	Partners (brother) (unrelated)[a]	2
Xue Youcai	India	—	0	10	10	Bought 1968/built 1971	Bought w/partner (unrelated)[a] Built w/brother	1

[a]Collaborator had separate business.

interview the members of a family about the history of their business in Dhapa. But, in fact, I did not yet know them well enough to discover anything but the most superficial details.

"You want to know about how people came to Dhapa?" she asked. "Okay, I'll tell you about my husband." She proceeded to describe his difficult childhood. Born in Mei Xian, Jia Wenzhi was orphaned when he was eight years old, at which time he was sent to live with a paternal uncle's family. This uncle, and his wife, apparently mistreated the young boy, which created a powerful desire in him to seize any opportunity that offered a way out. Then, as Mrs. Jia told me, "one day a Chinese man came back to the village from India—he had three things which nobody in the village had: leather shoes, a Western jacket and tie, and a gas lantern. Everybody was very impressed."

This exposure to a returned overseas Chinese from India evidently had a marked impact on Wenzhi. When he was sixteen, he negotiated with a merchant who went back and forth between Hong Kong, India, and China. For 3,000 rupees, the merchant agreed to escort him to India. Of course, 3,000 rupees was, in Mrs. Jia's words, "a great amount in those days." Wenzhi managed to borrow this money, however, and was soon on his way to Calcutta.

Upon his arrival, the young migrant stayed at the headquarters of his surname association, and surname group elders found a temporary job for him at a shoe shop. But he was not happy with this job. As Mrs. Jia informed me, "He was very depressed and said he did not want to do this kind of work, but that he wanted to work in leather making instead. So he came out to Dhapa. The year was 1935. For three years he really sweated it out! He was given no pay at all, just food and lodging. He awoke at 4:00 A.M. and worked until noon. At that time, the Indian workers left, but after lunch he continued working until 8 P.M.!"

A few years later, according to Mrs. Jia, her husband did succeed in receiving wages for his work, and after several more years of "bitter labor" and careful saving he succeeded in setting up a small tanning business as a tenant in another tanner's factory. These early years of hard work took their toll. Mrs. Jia's husband died of stomach disease in the 1970s, the result, said Mrs. Jia, of a work schedule so intense that he never took the time to eat and digest his food properly.

Even if we make allowance for literary license, Mrs. Jia's story about her husband contains many themes that were echoed in the stories I collected of other men who founded tanning businesses. Although they arrived during different periods, the men who founded the first generation of tanning businesses had much in common. The great majority of them had been born in China. Like Mrs. Jia's husband, many had been orphaned or had lost one parent at an early age, and the economic distress inflicted by such events was undoubtedly one reason for their decision to emigrate.

Even when the migrants had not suffered such personal losses, it was still family economic circumstances within China that compelled them to find new ways of making a living. Kong Tienhua, the father of loquacious Mr. Kong, came from a teacher's family that had encountered hard times. Forced to engage in exacting physical labor, dragging boats attached to ropes through inland rivers, Tienhua was eager to escape when in 1918, at the age of fifteen, he learned about India from an opium trader. But an older brother emigrated first, traveling with the opium trader and engaging in smuggling for a few years before he settled down to a job making wooden shoe forms (lasts) in Calcutta. Tienhua did join his older brother a few years later, and after working in a shoe shop for several years, both brothers started tanning together in Dhapa. Kong Tienhua told me one day in 1982 when I interviewed him, "There were hardly any tanners then [in 1928], and there was no electricity. We built huts and used a forty-horsepower steam engine. Electricity only came during World War II."

Like Mrs. Jia's husband and the Kong brothers, almost all the male migrants were young and single, in their late teens or twenties, and many of them came to India with itinerant merchants who traveled between these countries and traded in either legal or illegal goods. Often, as in the case of Mrs. Jia's husband, the young immigrants would have to pay fees to these merchants in return for being escorted to India. (All the early immigrants stressed the ease of crossing borders in those days. None applied for visas or permits to come and go from either country.) Only after successfully starting a tanning business, or attaining other gainful employment, would marriage be considered. At that time, a man might return to China to marry. Hence, it is important to keep in mind that unlike male migrants, Chinese women who emigrated to India usually did so as brides.

Similar family processes were frequently at work in a young man's decision to come to Dhapa, regardless of whether he arrived in the tanning district as an emigrant from China or was born and raised in India. In both instances, these actions can be viewed as part of a process of dispersion of individuals and diversification of a family's

[125]

economy. These processes, as Myron Cohen has noted, were a "grim necessity" (1970:32) when forced upon poor families, and a shrewd method of expanding the scope of economic activities when undertaken by wealthy families.

For most new arrivals in Dhapa, it was the aforementioned "grim necessity" that was usually closest to the truth. As I stated in Chapter 1, all those who emigrated from China came from Mei Xian in Guangdong Province, many from rural areas. This district had one of the worst man-to-land ratios of all the districts in Guangdong during the 1930s and 1940s (Cohen 1968:25), a period during which many of the migrants arrived in India. Even those who were born in India, however, such as Ju Suanjing, usually moved to the tanning district because of their family's poor economic circumstances.

Occasionally, young men who came to Dhapa were diversifying a prosperous family economy. Xue Youcai's father operated two successful shoe shops with his brothers in the most fashionable shopping district of Calcutta. Sensing that tanning was an emergent industry and would be even more lucrative, Youcai proceeded to Dhapa, where he started a small tanning business as a tenant with funds provided by his family.

Many first-generation Hakka male immigrants to Calcutta used personal connections to gain entry into both the host country, India, and the tanning community in particular. A great number of these immigrants had links with either a relative or village mate already residing in India. At the very least, as in the case of Jia Wenzhi, they made use of the help provided by their surname associations. In some cases, their acquaintances employed them as tannery workers, an experience which gave them valuable technical and business knowledge.

In other cases, male immigrants followed or preceded family members whose marriage to a Chinese in India had already been arranged. Fei Shengchan, for instance, came to India to work for his sister's future father-in-law. His sister's marriage to this man's son had been agreed to years before, when both families were still in China and their children were young. Subsequently, her fiancé's family migrated to India and started tanning. Shengchan followed them to India several years later, and they hired him as a worker. He worked for eight years and then married the owner's daughter (that is, his sister's sister-in-law). Two years later he set up his own business as a tenant in the same tannery. It would be another nineteen years, however, before he would build a tannery of his own.

Sometimes the migrants joined brothers who sent for them after gaining a foothold in tanning, as was the case for Kong Tienhua. Indeed, this process continues today. While I was in Dhapa, this occurred in two different families who were associated with flourishing tanning businesses. In one instance, an emigrant came from China with his wife and children to join two brothers who were already operating a joint business. In the other case, the new arrival was also married and had two teen-age sons. But his four brothers in Dhapa each ran a separate business, even though three of them shared the same factory building. His brothers insisted that once the newly arrived brother had learned the trade, he would have to begin a business of his own as a tenant.

Not all of the first-generation male migrants came to the tanning district immediately upon arrival in Calcutta. Some worked in other occupations in the center of the city. Mao Yisheng, for instance, worked as a tailor after his arrival in Calcutta. Three years later he moved to the tanning district. Some individuals worked for many years in other occupations before switching to tanning. Wei Guangrong worked for thirty-five years as a shoemaker, before selling his shoe shop and coming to Dhapa to start a tanning business.

Even after arriving in the tanning district, not everyone became involved in tanning from the outset. Tan Qiyun was a tannery worker for three years after his arrival in India, but he then spent twenty years selling tanning chemicals to other tanners before becoming involved in tanning again as a tenant. Another migrant, Qian Weigang, spent six years in the liquor business in Dhapa, after ten years of work in a Calcutta shoe shop, prior to becoming involved in tanning.

It is important to note that in these early days, male migrants traveled back and forth between India and China—working for a few years in India, for instance, then going to China for marriage, and then returning to India again with their brides. Indeed, Kong Tienhua returned to China in the late 1940s, when he had already been married for many years and had lived in India for more than two decades. When he came back to India, in 1953, his adult sons and wife were startled to learn that he had married a second wife, a turn of events which, as I explain in the next chapter, had important consequences when family assets were divided.

Later on, however, historical exigencies interfered with the ability of Dhapa Chinese to maintain connections, financial and otherwise, with relatives in Mei Xian. The souring of relations between China and India in the post-1962 atmosphere made it difficult to openly pursue ties with mainland Chinese kin. But recently, with the relaxing of relations between China and India, coupled with the liberalization of Chinese economic policy, a number of Dhapa Chinese have begun to rekindle their connections with their relatives in Mei Xian. And their growing prosperity has enabled them to provide financial aid to family members. Wealthy Dhapa Chinese have also begun to contribute funds to their ancestral villages for public purposes such as bridges and schools.

Founding a Tanning Business

Before building a tanning business of one's own, most Dhapa Chinese began businesses as tenants in others' factories. (*Tenants* is their word; outsiders might use the term *contract operator* to describe this relationship.) This system of tenancy, as well as a less commonly utilized system of leasing, continues today, and I need to briefly summarize the details of both these arrangements in order to explain how these systems have enabled individuals to start new businesses.

Tenants pay a fee to the tannery owner for each piece of leather they produce. In return, they are allowed to use the tannery owner's machines, although they hire their own employees. If a tenant is renting in a large tannery, he may have at his sole disposal one machine of each type necessary for leather production. But in tanneries where there are several tenants, they will have to share machines, taking turns in using them. While there are fewer tenants than owners in Dhapa—sixty-eight of the 297 businesses were run by tenants in 1982—it is important to keep in mind that most first-generation tanners, who eventually succeeded in building tanneries of their own, began their tanning businesses as tenants. Indeed, as I mentioned in Chapter 3, the number of factory buildings in Dhapa increased enormously between the 1960s and the 1980s, in part because many tenant tanners built factories of their own.

Unlike tenants, whose rent is set in accordance with their productivity, those who lease tanneries pay a set monthly fee regardless of their output. In return, however, leasers are given unlimited access to the owner's machines and factory space. Such monthly fees tend to be relatively expensive. But if a tanner's output is high, leasing a tannery may actually save him more money than working as a tenant, since higher productivity does not mean that he pays more rent. Leasing a tannery is therefore a sound investment for a tanner whose business is very productive, but who is not yet ready to build a tannery of his own, an undertaking which would require the raising of enormous capital.

These systems of tenancy and leasing provide some benefits to individuals on both sides of the arrangement. From the point of view of tenants, tenancy provides an avenue to start a business without the expense of building or buying a factory. Tenancy also helps the owner. It not only supplements his income but is an efficient means of absorbing excess capacity. Leasing, on the other hand, is a good arrangement for tannery owners who need an income, but who are unable to run a business themselves. For instance, one man in Dhapa is currently leasing his tannery to his nephew, since he is too ill to run his own business and all his sons have emigrated to Canada. Leasing his tannery guarantees him a monthly income. Furthermore, since leasers pay a fee by the month rather than per piece of leather produced, the owner's monthly income is not contingent on the amount of leather the leaser manufactures. Even if this nephew were to produce nothing in a given month, his uncle is assured of an income. Finally, leasing makes sense for those who own tanneries but do not have a lucrative business. In such instances, they may partition their tanneries and lease half to another tanner.

What sort of funds are needed to start out as a tenant? Although the actual amount has varied greatly over the years because of the changing value of the rupee, the obligations toward which these funds need to be applied have remained fairly constant.[1] Basically, to commence tanning as a tenant one needs enough money to purchase chemicals, to buy several batches of rawhides, and to pay workers for a number of months. After this, if one succeeds, one can carry on the business through continuous reinvestment of one's profits. A good relationship with some of the rawhide merchants is also invaluable, since they will then extend favorable credit terms, insisting on payment for a batch of rawhides only after the sale of finished leather.

As mentioned earlier, starting out as a worker helped to acquaint many first-generation tanners with the technical aspects of the tanning process. But it was also a useful way to build the reputation of trust-

---

[1] In the 1930s, one could become a tenant with an investment of 700 rupees, but during the early 1980s one would need at least 20,000 rupees (about $1,700 at the time).

worthiness and competence that was necessary to secure loans. For instance, Ju Suanjing, who had come to Dhapa when his family's shoe business failed and who had no relatives in the tanning business, asked his employer for assistance when he began thinking of embarking in business for himself. Because Suanjing had already shown himself to be knowledgeable and efficient, the employer was willing to advance to him a batch of rawhides on credit. Suanjing used these rawhides to make leather for himself during times when the employer's tanning work was already completed.

But even if an individual has an employer who is willing to back him up, or a relative who is willing to lend him money, this is usually not sufficient in itself to start a tanning business. Other means of raising funds are also necessary. The most common resource is the rotating credit association, used by Chinese on the mainland as well as overseas. To make use of a rotating credit association, an individual has to find a group of people who are willing to deposit money into a fund on a monthly basis. Each month all the money in the fund is lent to a different participant. Whereas those who have not yet borrowed deduct a certain percentage from their monthly payments, those who already have borrowed pay the full amount. In this way, those who wait to collect their money until the end of the cycle receive more than they put in. Those who need the money immediately receive a smaller total amount than they ultimately pay into the fund, but they are able to quickly gain access to a substantial sum.

In Chinese, this process of organizing a credit association is referred to as *qi hui*, which literally means "to start up an association." As discussed in Chapter 4, reliability (*kekao*) and trustworthiness (*laoshi*) are important attributes for all entrepreneurs. And without a reputation for these qualities, a would-be entrepreneur will probably be unable to gather enough participants to make a rotating credit association feasible.

Partnership is another arrangement by which aspiring tanners can put together the funds necessary to go into business. In some cases, young Chinese men who have been workers for a few years will pool their funds and start in business together as partners. Take the example of Mao Yisheng. After working in Calcutta as a tailor for three years, he pooled his savings with two other recent migrants. However, partnerships are rarely long-lasting; once the partners have established themselves, they usually split and form their own businesses. In Dhapa today, there is only one business—that of Gan Qianjin—in which two unrelated partners work together and share profits, and they have been doing so for more than twenty-six years.

Brothers may also set up partnerships for the purposes of starting a business. Among the family histories I collected, I found two instances where two or more brothers who had been working separately pooled their savings and started a business together. Yet even partnerships between brothers eventually break up, although they tend to last longer than those between nonrelatives.

Kong Tienhua's case offers a good example of such a partnership between brothers. They pooled their savings in order to start their tanning venture. Their partnership lasted for eight years, after which each continued tanning on his own. The case of Jiang Yongzhi and his brothers offers another example of such a temporary partnership. Their father, who had been a merchant, died in 1939 when they were all young. For several years Jiang and his brothers were compelled to earn their living by performing odd jobs. But in 1946, Jiang and one of his brothers combined their savings and began business as tenants. In 1966, in conjunction with a friend who ran a separate business, the two Jiang brothers finally succeeded in purchasing a tannery. But shortly thereafter, in 1969, they began to conduct separate businesses. By contrast, a third Jiang brother did not join his brothers in business but formed a partnership with a nonrelative.

Another means of raising funds is a variation of the partnership model. In this arrangement a worker who has knowledge of tanning processes but few financial resources teams up with an individual who has funds but little technical knowledge. I already mentioned Xue Youcai, who grew up in a prosperous shoemaking family in Calcutta, but who decided to go into tanning. Although his family financed his venture, he lacked technical knowledge. The problem was solved by forming a partnership with a man who lacked funds but who taught him the technical aspects of leather making.

Before the Sino-Indian conflict of 1962, a few individuals took advantage of yet another financial option: they received loans from the Bank of China, which until then had a branch in Calcutta. Both Ma Hongzhang and Qiao Tanming took out loans when they decided to start tenant tanning businesses.

Finally, women have also contributed to the fund-raising process. In earlier days, some of the women of Dhapa made their living in the illicit liquor business. People asserted that this was usually a female rather than a male line of work, for they believed the police would go easier on women in the trade than on men. Moreover, liquor making was often the sole means by which a widow could support herself and her children. In ten cases among the family histories I compiled, women's liquor businesses were so profitable that the owners could eventually underwrite their sons' tanning businesses. However, despite the belief that women would be treated less harshly by the law, there were instances in which they received severe penalties. In the 1940s, one woman in the community was killed by an excise officer, as he shot his way through the door of her family's residence in a raid on her liquor-making operations. (See chapter 6 for a detailed discussion of women's role in Dhapa's tanning businesses.)

Success and Failure

It is critical to remember that, even though many individuals were successful in starting tanning businesses, many of those who attempted to start their own business as tenants did not succeed at all. Many of the Dhapa Chinese who were unsuccessful left the tanning district. Some opened restaurants in other parts of India, and others emigrated to foreign countries. A few of them did remain in Dhapa but changed their occupations. One man, for instance, became a restaurateur and caterer whose business is extremely popular with the Chinese. He caters weddings and other large occasions, often preparing food for as many as five hundred people. In another case, a failed tanner utilized his artistic talents by constructing ritual artware— paper representations of real-life objects which the Chinese burn as offerings to the gods. This thriving business is continued by his son; it is now so lucrative that Dhapa residents complain, "If you want to buy a real umbrella, it will cost you twenty rupees. But a paper umbrella costs fifty rupees."

Sometimes people failed in their first attempts to establish a tanning business but went on to succeed on the next try. Ju Suanjing, for instance, spent eight years as a tannery worker before attempting to establish his own enterprise. He failed in this initial venture, spent another twelve years as an ordinary tannery worker, and succeeded in his second attempt. And Qian Weigang spent six years in the liquor business after his fledgling tanning enterprise collapsed. He then returned to tanning and succeeded in establishing a business as a tenant. After many years as a tenant, he collaborated with his eldest son, who already ran a separate business, in building a tannery. Qian Weigang died shortly thereafter, and his tannery is now shared by his two sons, each of whom runs a separate business.

Finally, the fortuitous nature of historical circumstances, particularly the impact of wars, played a role in the success of a number of first-generation tanners. As I mentioned in Chapter 3, World War II led to an increase in the demand for leather and an explosion in the number of tanneries. Indeed, several tanners mentioned this themselves, stating that World War II provided a terrific boost, since leather was in great demand for use in army boots and other war materials. "We used to work until 10:00 P.M. every night, " Kong Tienhua stated in one interview (while discussing the impact of World War II). "And the leather merchants would just be standing outside the tannery door, waiting to take the leather away immediately." Other tanners talked about the wars between India and Pakistan (in 1965 and 1971) as further instances of war-generated sales. And Qiao Tanming's son told me an ironic tale about the business opportunities provided by the Korean War. Tanming, the dependable tanner who journeyed through a soaking monsoon rain to pay a rawhide dealer, received extra financial help from the Bank of China during the war era. These loans were extremely useful in helping him expand his business and sell leather to Americans—who then used it to make army boots to fight the Chinese in Korea! (Of course, as far as the Calcutta Chinese were concerned, the Sino-Indian conflict in 1962 was an exception to this pattern of fortuitous wars.)

From Tenant to Owner

Whereas some individuals were able to begin tenant tanning businesses almost immediately upon immigration to India (because they had ready sources of funding and help from relatives or surname group members), others had to first put in as many as thirty-five years in different lines of work. Among my sample of eighteen first-generation tanners, the average number of working years an individual spent prior to starting a tenant tanning business was eleven. Once established as a tenant, a tanner would need to invest several years in his business before even contemplating the building or buying of a tannery of his own. Among the same sample of first-generation tannery owners, it took an average of twenty-three working years before an individual succeeded in building or buying his own tannery.

Since it costs a great deal more to build a tannery than to start a business as a tenant, the transition from tenant to owner could not and cannot be contemplated lightly. In the early 1980s, for instance, a tenant tanning business could be started for about 20,000 rupees— enough money to purchase chemicals, pay workers for two to three months, and buy a few batches of rawhides. On the other hand, building a tannery requires the purchase of land, the value of which is constantly escalating, and of complete sets of tanning machinery. Furthermore, the structure has to be built large enough to provide both factory space and living accommodations for the owner's family. In the early 1980s, it cost at least ten lakhs of rupees (slightly less than $100,000 at that time) to build even the smallest factory. Enormous amounts such as this cannot be raised with rotating credit associations, which were and are used in Dhapa for raising much smaller sums. Building a tannery therefore involves the outright borrowing of money, usually from other community members and usually at high interest rates, as well as the use of one's own savings. According to most people I interviewed in the early 1980s, one needed to have in hand at least one-third to one-half of the funds required for building a tannery. Given the lucrativeness of the tanning business, and the types of profits that people could earn, it was not impossible to come up with these amounts. But such sums could not be raised easily or quickly.

To build a tannery, one has to have a more solid business reputation than the person who wants to start out as a tenant. Because greater financial risks are involved in this case, potential lenders will be even more careful in determining who will receive loans. One can also use the strategy of pooling funds with partners. In this scenario, several partners, sometimes brothers and sometimes unrelated individuals, pool their funds and loans and construct a tannery together. Each then owns a share of the factory but runs a separate business within it. Once his factory is built, a tanner has the option of making further financial arrangements that will expedite the repaying of loans. For example, he can use funds earned from tenants' payments in order to increase his earnings and to help repay loans and interest. Or he can lease one-half of the tannery until his debts are repaid.

Those who are unable to build a tannery can purchase an existing tannery or buy a part of one. This procedure is considerably cheaper. Occasionally, individuals buy shares of tanneries first, and several years later build tanneries of their own.

A few examples will illustrate how the timing of becoming a tannery owner varied over the course of different men's lives. Yan Baoxia arrived in India in 1937, when he was nineteen. He first went around Calcutta by bike, selling items from house to house. "People looked down on me, I was poor," he remembered. Later, Yan worked as a shipfitter in the port of Calcutta, an occupation he continued for five years before joining an elder brother who was already working in Dhapa as a tenant. Yan married three years later. In 1949 a younger brother who had just migrated from China joined them. The eldest brother returned to Hong Kong in 1950. The two remaining younger brothers continued in business together as tenants for ten years. In 1960, one year after his eldest son had married, Yan Baoxia separated his business from that of the younger brother. He ran his own business as a tenant for another fourteen years with the help of his three sons, before building his own tannery in 1973, shortly after his second son's marriage.

Since he had been in Dhapa for so long a time, and since his sons were also deemed competent by others, Yan was able to obtain the funds necessary to build his tannery. It was known that even if he retired, his sons, who were themselves experienced and trustworthy, would be able to carry on the business. In fact, within one year of building this tannery, Baoxia retired from active participation in the business. He had ensured a continuing income for himself and his family through tenancy, which he had planned for by constructing a fairly large tannery. After his retirement, four tenant families continued to rent living quarters and machinery in the tannery. The income from these sources contributed to Yan Baoxia's success in repaying his loans.

It took almost an entire working lifetime before Yan could build a tannery of his own. In his case, the transition from tenancy to tannery ownership paralleled the transition from stem to joint family. His elder son had been married for many years before Yan built his tannery, but the second son married only shortly before the tannery was constructed.

Whereas Yan took in tenants as a means of generating additional funds to repay loans and interest, Ma Hongzhang utilized a partnership and a leasing arrangement. He built a tannery in partnership with his wife's brothers. It was their intention from the outset to conduct separate businesses inside the same tannery. Therefore, they built a tannery that was partitioned in half. For the first five years after the tannery was built, they shared one-half of the tannery and leased out the other half to a wealthy Indian tanner. Since this tanner paid them rent for an entire year in advance, they were able to use his funds to help pay back their loans. After five years, the Indian tanner built his own factory, and the two sections of the tannery were divided between Mr. Ma and his brothers-in-law.

In Jiang Yongzhi's case, he joined forces with a brother and an unrelated partner. They pooled their funds and purchased a tannery, which cost them less than building a tannery. Since the two brothers had put more money into this venture than the third partner, they owned a three-quarter share of the entire tannery. In this particular case, the two brothers ran one business together, a continuation of the business they had conducted together as tenants for almost twenty years. But after two years they began conducting separate businesses within their factory.

A final example is Tan Qiyun, who bought a share of a tannery after eleven years as a tenant. Three years later, at the time of his eldest son's marriage, he constructed a new tannery.

Exceptions to the General Pattern

In a few cases individuals did not follow the usual sequence from tenant to owner. Yuan Qide, for instance, came to Dhapa in 1913 when there was no possibility of being a tenant in someone else's factory, since he was one of the first tanners. Furthermore, during this period, building a tannery did not involve constructing permanent structures. In the early years, tanners simply put up bamboo sheds and did most of their tanning through sheer physical labor. It was only several years later, when Chinese tanners switched to chrome tanning, that it became necessary to acquire some rudimentary machinery.

There is also one instance of an individual who built his tannery without going through a period as a tenant. This case is unique because the individual in question, Song Yifu, had close connections with the leader of one of Dhapa's two tanning associations—a man who was extremely influential and powerful within one faction of the tanning community. Interestingly, however, Song Yifu's case illustrates why the institution of tenancy was necessary in most situations. Although he had good connections and was therefore able to get the funds necessary to build a new tannery, Song was ultimately unsuccessful in business. He was compelled to lease half his tannery to others, and even within his half, he had a tenant. In addition, he considered selling the part of his tannery that he leased, since he was unable to repay his loans. Had Song Yifu gone through a period of tenancy, people would have determined whether he was worthy of risk. Additionally, he would have had a chance to learn the essentials of the tanning process and gained critical on-the-job experience before constructing his own factory.

Indian Tanners, Some Critical Differences

Although most of the tanneries in Dhapa are owned and operated by Hakka Chinese, a few businesses are run by Indians. In 1982, Indians owned seven tanneries outright and another seven Indian tanners leased parts of Chinese tanneries. The Indian tanners belong to several ethnic groups. Most of them are Punjabi Hindus, a few are Punjabi Muslims, and a small minority are high-caste Bengalis. The Punjabis' original connection with tanning was through their role as leather traders—as buyers of the finished product. There are numerous Punjabi leather traders, but only a few have invested in tanning businesses. The Bengali tanners, however, chose a different route; they learned tanning as students at the College of Leather Technology in West Bengal.

Clearly, tanning as a polluting occupation would not seem a natural choice of occupation for high-caste Bengalis, so some comment is called for here. High-caste Bengalis constitute a majority of the workers in professional and white-collar jobs in Calcutta, gravitating toward occupations that require moderate to high educational levels. But many desirable occupations, such as medicine, are extremely difficult to enter; exams are very competitive, and only a small minority of aspirants succeed. Given these facts, some students choose to apply to technology institutes, one of which is the College of Leather Technology. Entry into these institutes is much less competitive than entry into medical or engineering programs, yet they still guarantee a good job afterward. Many of those who attend the College of Leather Technology, for instance, are later employed in the organized sector of India's leather industry, working in a technical capacity for large leather companies like Bata. A few, however, choose to strike out on their own and establish small businesses in Dhapa. Thus, the life course of these Indian tanners is quite different from that of the Chinese, who entered tanning without formal study or involvement in the leather trade.

[137]

Moreover, the Indian tanning enterprises themselves vary in significant ways from those of the Chinese. The Chinese tanneries function as both homes and factories. The Indian tanneries, on the other hand, are used strictly as factories. The families of Indian tanners reside away from the tanning district. One of the implications of this difference in the relationship between residence and factory is that whereas Chinese women often play an important role in the operation of their family tanning businesses, women in the families affiliated with Indian tanneries do not get involved in tanning operations. Their physical separation from the tanning district means that tannery operations are simply not a part of their daily lives.

On the other hand, the sons of Indian tanners sometimes do participate in the day-to-day operations of their tanning businesses. But both fathers and sons participate in their businesses in a substantially different way from their Chinese counterparts. Chinese tanners tend to wear rough clothes while working in their tanneries and often perform physical work. Most Chinese tanneries, except for the largest ones, do not even have formal offices. In contrast, Indian tanners tend to wear good clothes to their factories and oversee tannery operations from a distance.

Finally, since the Chinese live in their tanneries, they can keep their machinery running throughout the day and night. Conversely, Indian tanneries resemble nine-to-five operations, shutting down and locking up at the end of the workday. Some Indian tannery owners, however, have incorporated aspects of the Chinese system within their own tanning enterprises. They employ Chinese managers who are given living quarters within the tannery and who keep the factory operating even when both owners and workers have returned home.

The Apprenticeship Model: Only for Chinese Workers

Although the overwhelming majority of Chinese men in Dhapa presently operate their own tanning businesses, this is not true for all. Even those men who now run their own businesses, as I have shown in this chapter, achieved this position only after many years of working for others. Thus, in the early 1980s a few Chinese men in Dhapa still worked as factory managers or as ordinary workers. The role or status of these Chinese workers should not be confused with that of the Indian workers, who comprise the majority of laborers in Dhapa.

Therefore, before moving on to a more detailed discussion of the internal organization of Dhapa's Chinese tanning businesses, I must briefly delineate the very real differences between the economic opportunities of these Chinese and Indian workers.

The job of factory manager exists only in the very largest tanneries of Dhapa, where family members cannot assume all managerial roles. Most Chinese men have used this job as a stepping stone, as an opportunity to gain the requisite knowledge and experience of tanning before starting out in business on their own. As an acquaintance of mine in Dhapa said to me one day, "You can never keep a good manager for long," his assumption being that a good manager will ultimately attempt to start his own business. Like the position of factory manager, the job of tannery worker has served, for the Chinese, as an apprenticeship in which future entrepreneurs learn the technology of tanning and the intricacies of running a tanning business.

By contrast, the situation of the Indian workers, who, after all, comprise the bulk of the labor force in Dhapa, bears no resemblance to that of the Chinese. Indian workers are not viewed by the Chinese tanners as future tannery owners or as apprentices, and the strategies used within the Chinese community to help Chinese get started in business, such as rotating credit associations, are not available to them. Indian workers could not and cannot draw upon native-village, same-surname, or kin ties to get help either from the tannery owners for whom they work or from other tannery owners in the community.

The majority of Indian workers are male migrants of the Chamar caste, an untouchable caste traditionally associated with leather work, from the neighboring state of Bihar. Like a good number of Bihari migrants in other occupations within Calcutta, such as rickshaw wallahs, many have come alone to the city, leaving their family behind in their native villages, and sending remittances to them whenever they can. Although these Bihari migrants have not, by and large, been able to transcend their class position as workers, they are well organized into unions and have not hesitated to strike for higher wages or benefits.

In addition to the Biharis, Chinese employ male Nepalese workers who are not unionized, and during strikes they continue to work for the Chinese. These Nepalese occupy the most unskilled jobs in the tanneries. Even though they do not strike with the Bihari workers, the Nepalese have not yet posed a significant threat to the power of the union. Most of them are unskilled, and their numbers are also fewer than those of the Biharis. During strikes, therefore, productivity in the Chinese tanneries is still drastically reduced, and the tanneries can resume full capacity only when the Bihari employees return to work. The fact that the Nepalese act as strikebreakers has generated friction which sometimes boils over into physical attacks on Nepalese workers during strikes.

Interestingly, residential patterns also highlight the structurally different positions held by these two groups of workers, Biharis and Nepalese, vis-à-vis the Chinese tannery owners. Bihari workers live outside the tanning district and walk to work. Many Nepalese workers, however, actually live within the tanneries. The Chinese say that they find Nepalese workers more trustworthy and reliable, but there is no doubt that their lack of militancy has played a major role in endearing them to the Chinese owners. At the same time, the Chinese acknowledge that the Bihari workers have had much more experience in the tanning industry, and that only they can perform tasks requiring special skills. Indeed, the Nepalese are relatively new to the industry, having entered the work force only in the 1970s. The Biharis, on the other hand, have been employed by the Chinese since the first years of the tanning community.

A few tanneries also employ Muslim men from the north Indian state of Uttar Pradesh as well as Bengalis. Uttar Pradesh Muslims work as packers in large tanneries that have export businesses, and they produce leather bags in one tannery that has expanded from leather making into leather goods. Bengali men are employed only in the very largest tanneries in professional positions, for example, as accountants or as leather technologists.

What is most critical to remember, however, is that for the majority of these workers, who are not tied to the Chinese by ethnicity, kinship, surname, or village origin, there is little hope of climbing the economic ladder as was done by many first-generation tanners.

The First Generation: Drawing on Affines, Agnates, Matrilateral and Native-Place Ties

As this chapter has shown, Chinese men who founded the first generation of tanning businesses in Dhapa drew upon various social connections in their early years of immigration and in their attempts to found and expand their businesses.

We have seen examples in which siblings followed each other to India: Kong Tienhua immigrated to India a few years after his brother had done so; Fei Shengchan followed his sister to India and then used his connections with her to obtain a job, working for her father-in-law. Sometimes contacts were made with those whose origins were from the same native village in China, but who were related neither by descent nor through marriage.

As might be expected in a patrilineal, patrilocal kinship system, we have encountered cases in which brothers got together to start a business. But we have also seen instances in which affinal relations proved critical in both the formation and operation of tanning businesses. Ma Hongzhang went into business with his wife's brothers. Frequently, individuals became tenants in the tanneries of their affines. Qian Weigang, the individual who failed in his first attempt at starting a tanning enterprise, but who ultimately succeeded in setting up business as a tenant, spent most of his years of tenancy in his son-in-law's tannery before he built a factory of his own. Another acquaintance of mine leased a tannery from his maternal uncle. Finally, partnerships were also formed by individuals who were not related at all.

Despite the diverse social relationships used to establish this first generation of tanning businesses, the inheritance of these businesses has rarely diverged from the classic patrilineal pattern. That is, once established, businesses have usually been divided among adult sons. Ironically, many of the men who comprised the first generation of entrepreneurs, and who worked so hard and waited so long to build their own factories, did not have to wait much longer for this process of division to begin. By the time many first-generation tanners built factories of their own, they were often at the helm of large joint families with several married sons.

Such an outcome, of course, makes sense in terms of the general patterns described in this chapter. As we have seen, the average first-generation tanner spent two decades or more before building a tannery of his own, time in which he usually married and helped raise a family. Before long, his adult sons began to assert their own claims and personalities on the business. I examine the process of division and its implications in Chapters 7 and 8, but first I must take a closer look at the day-to-day operations of these tanning businesses. For although they were ultimately inherited by men, few would have gotten off the ground without the important contributions of women.

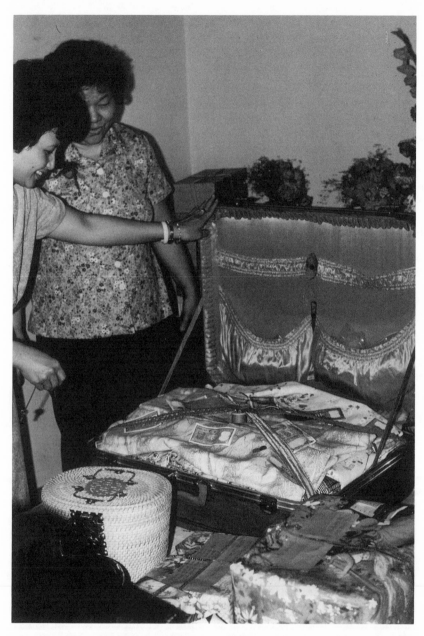

The suitcases a bride brings with her to her husband's home are opened by relatives at a specified time on the day of her wedding. Inside is revealed the cash her family has given her, as well as clothing and other items.

[6]

"Wife's Wealth": The Familial Division of Labor and Income

Lilan told me the story of Qin Liyue one evening over tea. "Qin Liyue was not very smart, so when it came time for marriage, no Chinese from Dhapa wanted their daughter to marry him. Finally, his family arranged a marriage with a Chinese woman from Darjeeling, and it turned out that she was extremely capable and worked very hard. Pretty soon the family was really prospering. So now people refer to Qin's good fortune as 'wife's wealth.'" Qin Liyue's is not really an unusual story for Dhapa. The Dhapa Chinese frequently cite the role played by women as one reason for their success, and as a means of favorably contrasting the Chinese tanneries with those run by Indians, in which female family members play no discernible role. That the community in question here is a community of Hakka Chinese may also be significant; scholars have frequently contrasted the Hakka with other ethnic groups in China in terms of the relatively greater role that their women play in productive tasks and economic life (see Blake 1981:51–59).

Indeed, the Dhapa Chinese emphasize that both men and women in their families are willing and able to perform tasks within their enterprises that upper- or middle-class Indians would consider unpleasant. They explain that although they employ Indian workers, they themselves do not hesitate to tackle even the most laborious chores in their factories.

This immersion in even the most unappealing chores within the family business is eased by the fact that Chinese tanneries function both as homes and as factories. Moreover, few tanneries have formal

[143]

offices. Women can oversee tannery operations even while engrossed in domestic tasks like cooking. And, instead of wearing office clothes and supervising work from a distance, most Chinese men plunge into the work themselves, toiling in baggy pajamas and torn T-shirts alongside their Indian employees. They revel in recounting stories about the confusion that their manner of work and style of dress cause among buyers from abroad who mistake them, the tannery owners, for the tannery workers.

But while both men and women in Dhapa participate in their family businesses, they do so in dissimilar ways, and they have differential access to the income and assets that their activities help generate. It is therefore important that I describe both the contributions and rewards that various family members give to and take from their enterprises. To accomplish this, I first examine the familial division of labor. I then turn to the distribution of income and assets within families, focusing solely on families that share a family economy. (The question of what happens to family assets upon family division is discussed in the next chapter.)

Not surprisingly, despite their pride in hard work, men move away from physical labor and toward managerial roles as their firms grow; married women, on the other hand, withdraw from business activity altogether. I explain these patterns in terms of the interaction of entrepreneurial ideology with familial roles.

The Sexual Division of Labor in Dhapa's Tanning Businesses

Relationship between Home and Factory

A typical day in Dhapa begins early. By 5:00 A.M., Hakka women fill the Chinese market in Dhapa, which is open for two hours every morning and is well stocked with pork, beef, good-quality fruits and vegetables, and an assortment of Chinese condiments. By 6:30 or 7:00 A.M., these women (with the help of their sisters-in-law or a mother-in-law if they live in joint families) have returned from their early-morning shopping, prepared breakfast, and awakened and readied their young children for school. Meanwhile, as Chinese women make their early-morning rounds to the market, the lanes and streets of Dhapa also begin to fill with delivery trucks and pushcarts piled high with rawhides. Upon reaching their destinations, these delivery trucks are unloaded by Bihari women who, though not employed within the tanneries as leather workers, do work outside the factories unloading supplies. By 8:30 A.M., the tannery employees themselves arrive to begin a day of work.

Around 9:30 or 10:00 A.M., however, one suddenly sees a procession of Chinese men exiting Dhapa astride their scooters. Where are they going, and why do they leave at this moment, just when the workday is getting under way? These men are on their way to the rawhide markets. In many conjugal families, where there are no other adult males, their departure means that for several hours of the working day, their wives oversee internal tannery operations.

Although the overlap of home and factory in Dhapa has facilitated the participation of Chinese women in the labor process, it has also created some clear-cut divisions between male and female economic domains. Business activities that are generally more "public"—or, to be more specific, involve a high degree of sustained interaction with unrelated males—are usually undertaken by men, whereas those activities that can be carried out in greater proximity to the domestic sphere may be carried out by either men or women.[1]

The delegation of responsibility for the purchase of rawhides is a good example of the prevalence of this principle in family business organization. Buying rawhides is a critical first step in a tanning business, since nothing can undo the damage created by the purchase of a substandard hide or the loss created by paying too much for this initial ingredient. Furthermore, tanners view other inputs (e.g., the cost of labor, which is set through negotiations with labor unions; and the cost of electricity) as factors over which they have little control. On the other hand, the cost of rawhides, set through bargaining with the rawhide merchants, is one expense over which a tanner may be able to exert some influence.

For these reasons, the purchase of rawhides is viewed as the key element in running a successful tanning business. Rawhide purchasers must spend a few hours in the hide market every morning, even if

---

[1] I use the words *domestic* and *public* with some misgivings, since recent scholarship has shown that women often form their own strong communities with ties that extend far beyond the household (see, e.g., Abu-Lughod 1985; Honig 1985). Therefore, in this case I use these terms only in reference to economic activities. Furthermore, *public* in this context implies activities that require long-term interchange with male outsiders, and *domestic* implies activities that take place in close proximity to the household.

[145]

they don't intend to buy on that day, for they have to follow trends in the market. Accordingly, the purchase of rawhides is considered so critical that it is delegated to the individual who has the most skill and experience in the business, commonly the family head (usually the eldest male of the senior generation) or a successor. Although widows may be viewed as family heads for certain ceremonial and social purposes, they are not allowed to take on this critical business role. A widow whose own sons are too young to manage the business on their own must rely on a male relative to buy rawhide for her, and if she is unable to do so, she may have to sell the business.

Why is rawhide purchase off-limits for women when, as will be shown in this chapter, women take part in many other activities during the various stages of leather processing? Perhaps one reason has to do with the location of the rawhide markets. Inasmuch as the hide merchants are primarily north Indian Muslims, rawhides are sold in two Muslim areas of Calcutta. In the areas surrounding the rawhide markets, one rarely sees a woman on the street, and certainly never one who is not fully covered in the traditional veil (*burkha*).

But it is unlikely that Chinese women would participate in this phase of the business in any case, for rawhide purchase draws one out into a public sphere of hard-core bargaining and business relations. Although Chinese women accompany one another on shopping trips, it is not considered proper for married women to spend considerable time away from home, especially in activities bringing them into prolonged contact with men. In this community, the sexes rarely mingle once they are out of school. At weddings and other social occasions, men and women don't mix, and banquet tables tend to be sex-segregated. The majority of marriages are still arranged, and women who depart from the prescribed norms by talking freely with men are gossiped about and frowned on as people who "show off" (*chu fengtou*).

As Esther Boserup points out: "Female home industries are often located in regions where women keep completely away from other remunerative activities. The social ban on other activities compel secluded women to take the only activity by which they can earn money without the loss of social esteem in the community" (1970:108). The women in this overseas Chinese community are certainly not secluded, but there are limits beyond which they may not venture without incurring social sanctions.

In addition to rawhide purchase, there are other tasks that only

Chinese men can perform. In the early afternoons, when most of the men who have gone out to the rawhide market are back at home, they are visited by Punjabi or north Indian leather merchants who come to inspect samples of and to negotiate contracts for purchasing the finished leather. Although bargaining with these leather merchants does not take an individual out of the home, it does involve continuous bargaining and interchange with male outsiders and, as such, it is also a male job. Additionally, the person who sells leather receives large cash payments and therefore tends to be the family head or a successor who holds an important role in managing the family's financial affairs.

But even when family financial control may belong to a woman, as in the case of a widow with young children, women never negotiate the sale of leather, relying instead on male relatives. Widows may sometimes resolve the problem of hide purchase and leather sale by doing what is called "job work" for a male relative. Under this arrangement, raw materials, including hides, are furnished to the tanner, who then sells the finished product back to the provider of raw materials at a price that has been negotiated in advance. This frees the producer of finished leather from having to negotiate with both rawhide merchants and individual leather buyers. A widow who owns a tannery may also form a business partnership with a male relative who has no business of his own. Both gain from the arrangement, since she is able to resolve the problems of purchasing the rawhide and selling the finished leather, while he receives a share of a tanning business without having to raise funds.

The problem with such an arrangement, however, is that the male relative may lose his position once the widow's own sons are old enough to participate in the business. In one such case, a widow teamed up with a cousin who bought rawhides and sold finished leather, while both of them supervised tannery operations. Once the sons of the widow were grown, however, the cousin had to establish his own separate business. In another case, a widow and her unmarried brother formed a business partnership.

Although women neither purchase hides nor sell finished leather, they do take an active role in the actual leather-manufacturing process. In the tannery, certain jobs are performed only by Indian workers, others by Indian workers or by male or female family members. No duty in the manufacturing process is handled exclusively by male family members. Women often oversee the preparation of tanning

[147]

chemicals, trim finished pieces of leather, pay workers, and keep attendance records; hired Indian laborers do much of the heavy physical work.

Indeed, in some tanneries female family members oversee the entire manufacturing process. They assume significant business responsibilities, but it should also be noted that none of the tasks in which they engage requires them to leave the home. Tables 3 and 4 summarize the tasks involved in the tanning process and the individuals who engage in them. They indicate that as far as family participation in production is concerned, a separation exists between a totally male sphere, which deals with the external world of the rawhide market and the leather buyer, and an internal sphere of factory production, in which both male and female family members participate. The tables also demonstrate that those duties that most directly affect business profits—the purchasing of rawhides, the measuring of finished leather (since a mistake in measuring can result in over- or underpayment), and the selling of the final product—are almost always delegated to male family members. Although women do occasionally measure leather, they virtually never purchase rawhides or sell the finished product. In short, the split between the relatively public realms of family business activity and those areas of business activity that allow a person to remain in close proximity to the domestic sphere is therefore the most salient feature of the sexual division of labor in these family businesses.

Table 3. The division of labor in leather production

Process	Type of worker
Purchasing rawhides	Chinese men (usually family heads)
Processing leather[a]	Indian workers, male or female Chinese family members
Finishing leather[b]	Chinese men, Indian workers (Chinese women participate only in packing)
Paying workers	Chinese family members (male or female), employed Chinese managers, or Indian clerks
Selling finished leather	Chinese men (usually family heads or successors)

[a]Steps 2–10 in Table 4.
[b]Steps 19–22 in Table 4.

Table 4. Sequence of procedures and division of labor in the production of leather

Step no.	Process	Performed by
1	Purchasing rawhides	Chinese family heads or successors (always male)
2	Soaking, liming, dehairing	Indian workers
3	Fleshing	Indian workers
4	Mixing tanning chemicals	Chinese family members (male or female), employed Chinese managers, or Indian foremen
5–7	Tanning, drying, shaving	Indian workers
8	Splitting	Indian workers (splitting machine found only in large tanneries)
9	Preparing for fat-liquoring	Chinese family members (male or female), employed Chinese managers, or Indian foremen
10	Fat-liquoring	Indian workers
11	Setting	Indian workers (setting machine found only in large tanneries)
12	Nailing	Indian workers
13	First trimming	Chinese family members (male or female) or Indian workers
14	Preparing "season" (polish)	Chinese family members (male or female), employed Chinese managers, or Indian foremen
15	Applying "season"	Indian workers
16–18	Staking, grazing	Indian workers
19	Second trimming	Chinese family members (usually male), or Indian workers
20	Selecting finished leather	Chinese family members (always male, usually family heads) or employed Chinese managers (in very large tanneries)
21	Measuring	Chinese family members (usually male, usually family heads) or Indian workers (in tanneries with measuring machines)
22	Packing	Chinese family members (male or female) or Indian workers (Bihari Chamars, north Indian Muslims, or Bengalis)
23	Paying workers	Chinese family members (male or female), employed Chinese managers, or Indian clerks
24	Selling finished leather	Chinese family heads or successors (always male)

Rawhides are unloaded outside a tannery.

Indian workers nail semifinished leather onto boards to dry under the sun.

Variations in the Sexual Division of Labor

Although it is safe to conclude that women tend to be involved in the more internal, less public sphere of economic activity, this by no means implies that all women throughout the community participate in the same way, or to the same degree, in their family businesses. For instance, a visit to Xi Taiguo's tannery, one of the largest in Dhapa, would reveal that none of the wives of his three brothers was involved in any aspect of the tanning process. However, a five-minute walk away, at Yan Baoxia's tannery, one would find both his daughters-in-law busy at work trimming finished leather pieces. Is this difference merely random, or is there an explanation for it?

First, it should be pointed out that unmarried daughters rarely spend any time on tannery work. Unlike women from working- and lower-middle-class families in Hong Kong and Taiwan (see Greenhalgh

[151]

1985b; Kung 1984; Salaff 1981), unmarried women in this community contribute neither labor nor funds to their natal families. It is not uncommon for young women to work for a few years after they have completed their schooling and before they get married, but they work primarily as hairdressers or teachers in local Chinese schools—and in order to earn personal spending money.[2] Perhaps the difference between these families and those analyzed in the aforementioned studies is the prosperous nature of the tanning community. Except in the least affluent families, the earnings of these young women make little dent in their family incomes, which are substantial. (For information on the important roles played by daughters in creating business connections and in strategies concerning emigration and familial division of assets, see the next chapter.)

But even married women do not participate in their family businesses to the same degree in all cases. In the summer of 1985 I conducted a survey of forty-six families in the Chinese tanning community where I had lived three years earlier. My purpose was to measure the connections between women's participation in their family firms and other variables, including firm size (measured by counting the number of nonfamily workers employed in the firm), family form (conjugal, stem and joint), and even the organization of space. The reader can turn to the appendix to this chapter for a more detailed explanation of my rationale for the categories and measurements. (And for a more in-depth analysis, see Basu 1991b.)

I found that women are much less likely to participate in firms employing sixteen or more workers. (This firm size is well above the median of nine workers and is considered large by almost all community members.) The forty-six family firms can be broken down as follows:

	Number of firms	
Size of firm	Women do not participate	Women participate
16 or more workers	7	5
Fewer than 16 workers	6	28
	13	33

[2] Interestingly, the Chinese own and operate the majority of beauty salons in the city of Calcutta. As in the case of tanning, the influence of the caste system is important here. Because hair is considered a bodily waste product, those who deal with it are considered polluted. Barbers are usually ranked quite low within a locality's caste

The Influence of Family Form

Although firm size clearly influences participation by women, my data also show a relationship between firm size and family type, with more complex families associated with larger firms:

	Number of firms by family type		
Size of firm	Joint	Stem	Conjugal
8 or more workers	10	8	10
Fewer than 8 workers	2	3	13
	12	11	23

This relationship can also be expressed in terms of the median number of workers employed by firms of each family type:

Famliy type	Median number of workers
Joint	17.5
"Complex" (stem and joint)	15
Stem	10
Conjugal	7

Noting how significant the correlation is between family form and firm size, one could reason that what looks like the impact of firm size on women's roles is really just a reflection of differences in family organization.[3] After all, as families grow from conjugal to joint, the responsibilities that once resided in the husband and wife alone come to be divided among several adult sons. When the husband in a conjugal family goes out to the rawhide market, the wife may be the only other adult family member who remains behind. Therefore, one

---

hierarchy. In opening up beauty salons, therefore, the Chinese have again hit upon an occupation that, though lucrative for them, has low status in the host society's stratification system.

[3] In this chapter I use the category of joint family to delineate families in which married brothers share assets, economic activities, *and* residence. Although coresidence is not always a necessary feature of joint families, the migration of married sons from Dhapa usually results in either family division (i.e., division of the family assets) or the removal of the migrants from active participation in a family's economic affairs.

would assume that supervision of factory work processes would automatically fall to her. On the other hand, one would expect that in a joint family adult sons would be available for work and that the demands made on female family members would consequently be far fewer.

However, no meaningful connections between family form and female participation can be found in my sample. This is true even when one uses the most inclusive measure of female participation (simply contrasting those families in which women contributed with those in which they did not, without measuring the intensity of this participation). Nevertheless, it is still important to explain why family organization and firm are connected, since the interaction of these two factors, though not related to the sexual division of labor, does affect other aspects of the division of labor, such as the distribution of chores between fathers and sons.

It makes sense that firm size is correlated with family form because of the manner in which the family developmental cycle works in this community. Brothers usually remain in business together as long as their father is alive, but split up after his death. The new enterprises are generally smaller than the original ones because the brothers divide their assets, including the number of workers held between them, and partition their factory space. Therefore, in many instances the conjugal families that result from the initial division of a joint family are associated with relatively smaller enterprises. Over time these enterprises often do expand, but by the time the expansion occurs, the conjugal units may have already grown into stem and joint families.

The pattern of migration through which this community was formed also contributes to a correlation between firm size and family type. Although migration to the community has decreased dramatically since its peak in the years before World War II, some of the smaller enterprises are still associated with people who have recently migrated to the community and are running fledgling businesses. Like the first generation of tanners discussed in Chapter 5, such individuals are usually single men who marry only when it is evident that their ventures are firmly established. Therefore, the formative years of the business, when it is still relatively small in size, coincide with the formative years of a family, when it is still a conjugal unit consisting of husband, wife, and young children.

Furthermore, in joint families in which several sons cooperate in one business, at least one of the sons has time to innovate. In Fei Shengchan's family, for instance, his middle son is in charge of sales, the youngest son oversees factory operations, while Fei still purchases rawhides, leaving his eldest son free to manage a new but related venture—a division that manufactures leather bags. In Yuan Dongtai's family, the fact that four of his five sons still cooperate in one business has enabled the second son to utilize his time to develop a new type of plasticized leather.

Finally, a small business that is only marginally successful cannot support all the members of a joint family. In such cases, it is likely that one or more sons will either emigrate or move to other cities in India to pursue different lines of work. Thus, through migration or emigration, such joint families will be divided, and new conjugal and stem families formed. Maurice Freedman's suggestion that different cycles take place within rich and poor Chinese families is relevant here. He points out that in many poor families, it is not possible for more than one adult son to remain at home (1966:44–45). Although I have not explicitly correlated firm size with wealth, because of the difficulties of getting accurate data on profits, it is obvious that a very small firm associated with a joint family would be at the lower end of the spectrum in terms of wealth. Joint families associated with such small businesses are inherently unstable and will tend to disintegrate.

I should note that my findings here are in perfect accord with the observations of most scholars who have studied the Chinese family.[4] Many of these scholars have linked joint families to relative wealth, although the proposed connections and reasons for this vary. Freedman, for instance, indicates that joint families are more likely to emerge among the elite classes, whose resources are more capable of sustaining them, whereas Greenhalgh asserts that it is the domestic cycle itself that changes a family's economic status, and contends that demographic differentiation is responsible for a significant component of income inequality in Taiwan (1985a). Harrell takes a sort of intermediate position, noting that in contemporary Taiwan, families "de-

---

[4] Sinologists have long been drawn to the type of questions that were asked first by A. V. Chayanov (1966) and later by Marshall Sahlins (1972) in their studies of the relationship of domestic cycles to a family's relative wealth and the organization of labor within it. In particular, scholarship on the domestic cycle in the Chinese family has long asked questions about family division: Why does it occur? When does it occur? And how does it affect the family economy (Cohen 1976; Freedman 1966; Lang 1946; Levy 1963)?

pendent on capital investment" are more likely to be joint than families of wage earners, because the capital sustains the joint family and, furthermore, the family's extra labor power makes it more likely that they will generate a surplus to invest as capital (Harrell 1982:159–160).

There are some who view family form as unrelated to wealth. Myron Cohen (1976) and Burton Pasternak (1972), for instance, attribute the prevalence of joint families in rural areas of Taiwan to such families' greater effectiveness in the use of family labor.[5] Nevertheless, most of these studies make a connection between family form and economic wherewithal. Of course, as I have said, my measure—firm size—is not the same as family wealth. In theory, the individual members of a joint family associated with a large firm may be no richer than the individual members of a conjugal family associated with a small firm. But the critical point is that affluence and ownership of a large firm may influence families in some similar ways, since both provide them with significant resources and flexibility.

Women's Roles and the Organization of Space

Whereas in most tanneries domestic space is closely intertwined with industrial space, in a few tanneries all domestic areas have been placed on floors separate from those devoted to industrial space. Do such differences in the arrangement of space have any connection with the other factors I have considered here, namely, family type, firm size, and the sexual division of labor?

To answer this question, I categorized the tanneries according to their organization of space. In some tanneries the living, eating, and cooking spaces were all adjacent to, or even within, the manufacturing area; in others the living space had been placed on a different floor, but the eating and cooking areas were still incorporated into the manufacturing area; and in still others the domestic space was completely separate from the manufacturing space. Indeed, when I correlated spatial organization with size of firm in my sample of forty-six firms, I found that a distinct separation of domestic and manufacturing space

[5] Recent work done on mainland China has resurrected the Chayanovian concern with the effect of the domestic cycle on a family's relative wealth. For instance, Mark Seldon has found that the most prosperous families in the agricultural villages he studied are those with favorable ratios of income earners to dependents (1985:195).

was clearly associated with larger firms (those with fourteen or more workers):

	Relationship of domestic space to factory area (number of firms)		
Size of firm	Totally separate	Kitchen adjacent	Kitchen and living/ sleeping area adjacent
14 or more workers	9	4	6
Fewer than 14 workers	4	4	19
	13	8	25

I also looked for a relationship between spatial organization and family type, and discovered that the separation of domestic from manufacturing space is associated with more complex families:

	Relationship of domestic space to factory area (number of firms)	
Family type	Totally separate	Kitchen or kitchen and living/ sleeping area adjacent
Joint	7	5
Stem	1	10
Conjugal	5	18
	13	33

Since differences in spatial organization appeared to be related to changes in family form and size of firm, I theorized that these differences would also be connected to changes in women's roles. As firms grew, I imagined, not only would women take a less active part, but the change in their status would be reflected in and facilitated by a more rigid division between domestic and manufacturing space. Unfortunately, things did not turn out that neatly. When I tried to correlate women's participation with spatial organization, I was unable to find significant connections, even when I used the broadest, most inclusive categories.

It appeared, therefore, that firm size was the major influence on women's roles in Dhapa's Chinese businesses. In the next section I try to explain why changes in firm size are so strongly connected to changes in the sexual division of labor and space.

[157]

Family Relationships, Entrepreneurial Goals, and Changing Roles

As discussed in Chapter 1, recent scholarship on Chinese folk ideology pays close attention to the influence of entrepreneurial thinking within Chinese culture (Gates 1987; Harrell 1985, 1987; Niehoff 1987; Stites 1985). But much of this recent work focuses primarily on the entrepreneurial strategies of men. Indeed, Harrell surmises that unmarried women "have little motivation to work hard" (1985:221) since they will marry out of the family, whereas married women employ "a variant of the entrepreneurial strategy" in which physical work is replaced by "manipulating . . . sons to work hard for the family's benefit" (1985:221).

Harrell's observations do not hold true in all cases. Recent research on Taiwan, for instance, suggests that unmarried daughters may work even harder than their brothers, the reason being that because they will marry out, they have less time to "pay back" their parents for earlier investments in their upbringing (see Greenhalgh 1985b).

But even if one grants that unmarried women may profit less than men from working hard to help their natal families achieve long-range economic goals, the question of married women's roles remains. Does it necessarily follow from the patrilocal and patrilineal family system of the Chinese that married women will always opt out of direct involvement in a family enterprise, relying primarily on their ability to motivate their sons, with whom they have close emotional ties, to work hard for the family? Or is it more likely that married women's activities vary with their economic situations, or with the composition of the households into which they have married?

Research on Chinese families in rural agricultural contexts suggests that family form and/or degree of wealth play an important role in the sexual division of labor. Thus, in his work on Hakka farm families in Taiwan, Myron Cohen (1976) notes that the division of labor between the sexes tends to be more pronounced in complex than in conjugal families. Says Cohen, "With a smaller work force sexual segregation can more readily be detrimental to efficiency, which can take priority; but as a family comes to comprise a larger number of adults, sexual discriminations are given greater latitude of expression" (1976:148). On the other hand, Clark Sorensen finds that among Korean villagers—who, like the Chinese, are patrilocal, patrilineal, and inspired by a Confucian ethos (1981)—a family's relative wealth is more significant than its structure in determining the sexual division of labor. In the village he discusses, women from wealthier families are more likely to engage solely in "inside" work (1981) as opposed to agricultural work, which takes them out into the fields.

But neither these studies nor others examines the issue of women's, and specifically married women's, contribution to a family enterprise in an urban entrepreneurial context such as that of the Calcutta Chinese. My data from this Calcutta Chinese community certainly demonstrate that although most women participate in their family businesses, this involvement decreases as the firms grow. Let me now try to explain why this is so.

Certainly, as Margery Wolf has so trenchantly demonstrated (1972), Chinese women have always used the strong emotional bonds they forge with their sons to ensure their own economic well-being. This strategy of forming a "uterine family" (Wolf 1972), of manipulating and motivating one's sons, is always an option. Through discipline and attention women can ensure that their sons grow up to be diligent and innovative. And their past sacrifices can motivate their sons to work hard in the present. Thus, one son tearfully remembered his mother's sale of her jewelry so that he could continue to attend school, a sacrifice which he said explained his present dedication to the business.

But such a strategy, in which one creates close bonds with one's sons, and utilizes these bonds to motivate them to work hard for the family, is not necessarily antithetical to participation in a family business. For working in the family firm is in fact one means of cementing bonds with one's children. In Chinese society, "work" has always been a primary symbol and medium through which people both talk about and create strong relationships. Sulamith Heins Potter comments in an article about Chinese villagers that when those villagers described a "wide variety of relationships . . . in every case the capacity to work, rather than the capacity to feel, was what was significant" (1988:203). She adds, "In speaking of child rearing, informants emphasized the importance, not of emotional ties, but of working to support their children and teaching them not to be lazy. Only by working for one another is the relationship between parents and children confirmed" (1988:204).

Of the adult men I knew, most were uncompromising and unashamedly fervent in their expressions of devotion to their mothers. "You can always get another wife," said my friend Mr. Wu, "but you have only one mother!" And this devotion was often enunciated within

[159]

a larger frame—a story crediting their prosperity to the hard work and sacrifices their mothers had endured. Women who labored assiduously for their family businesses were praised as those who had "toiled and endured hardship" (*ke ku nai lao*),[6] and "lost sweat and blood" (*chu han xue*).

The praise and devotion they receive from family members, and their enhanced reputation in the community, are surely strong motivating factors for women to participate in their family businesses. Indeed, community members attribute the wealth of certain families almost exclusively to the work of some of their female members, as in the story of Qin Liyue's wife which began this chapter.

Women themselves view their work as a necessary response to a need in the family and the enterprise. Indeed, many women talk about their contributions with pride, and I know of no case in which a woman attributed her involvement to overt pressure from other family members. On the other hand, women clearly do not want to impede—or appear to impede—the realization of goals cherished by their families and the community at large. Participation within the enterprise is accepted by married women as a role they automatically assume when their help is needed.

Given that participation in the business ensures high standing in the community and loyalty from the family, why do women opt out of such participation in larger firms? First, it should be noted that wealth is still the most critical measure of status in the community. All members of wealthy families are assured of a high status unless, of course, they flagrantly violate some social norm. Second, work within family enterprises *is* a burden added to other domestic chores, such as child care and cooking, which remain women's responsibility. Women in most Chinese families do employ Indian servants to wash clothes and to help watch over small children. But the bulk of child care and all of the cooking remain primarily the responsibility of female family members, even in the wealthiest families. (Chinese dishes are preferred, so Indian servants do not cook for their employers. At the same time, there are no longer any Chinese who are poor enough to seek work as cooks for individual families.)

Women can pull out of participation in a family enterprise, therefore, without being viewed as not working for the family. Unlike the work of men, their work in the business is an added responsibility. In a

[6] See Chapter 4, note 4.

small firm, the help of female family members may simply be viewed as necessary, but there are strong forces pulling women away from participation when they have the means. Indeed, married women from families associated with larger firms do not necessarily lose their power or influence in the family when they do not participate in the business. This becomes clear in the following section, where I analyze the allocation and control of income among Dhapa's Chinese families.

The Division of Income in a Family

In most ethnographies of the traditional Chinese family, the property of the *jia*, or family, has been viewed as a collective asset belonging to the family as a whole, which at the same time is controlled and managed by the family head, or if he is no longer capable, by one of his sons. Hsiao-t'ung Fei, for instance, describes the *jia* as "the basic social unit of production and consumption . . . the basis of the collective aspect of ownership" (1939:61). He adds, "The head of the *chia* [*jia*] has the final decision in any transaction concerning immovable property. It is also true for the produce of land and industry" (1939:61).

While the basically corporate nature of the Chinese family economy is always acknowledged in these ethnographies, it is also frequently pointed out that not all individuals utilize its resources to the same degree and that not all personal assets are rendered up to the collective entity. For instance, Fei states that "theoretically, according to the ideal system, other members, whenever they get money from other sources must hand it to the head; and when they need things must ask the head to buy them. It is a very centralized economy. *But, in practice, the earner usually reserves the whole or a part of his or her earnings* [italics mine]" (1939:62).

Myron Cohen has demonstrated that a family's economy may be either "inclusive" or "noninclusive" (1976:63). By this categorization he means that not all members of a family will necessarily participate in its economy (sons may migrate to the city, for instance, and hold a salaried job, but not contribute to or receive funds from the family). Furthermore, even those members of a family who do participate, do so to differing degrees. In a summary of Qing dynasty era (1662–1911) provisions concerning dowry and inheritance, John McCreery states, "Widows who did not remarry and unmarried daughters were customarily entitled to maintenance from their husband's or father's estate, but ordinarily they had no right to inherit" (1976:164). At the same time, he indicates that individuals could own personal property apart from the family. Writing about the historical present, for instance, Cohen points to the existence of "private money" for women (1976:190). In the case examined, such funds came primarily from cash gifts bestowed during the wedding ceremony, those presented during the New Year's celebrations from the family head, and income generated from women's private vegetable plots.

Fei also discusses women's money, stating that it might come from an allowance that a woman had saved or from income, earned in an outside job, that was not handed over to the family head (1939:62). Whereas for Fei the dowry was a form of women's money, scholars in general dispute the degree of control that women exercised over their dowries. As Rubie Watson notes in an article on women and property in Republican China, the control that women exercised over their dowries probably varied "from region to region and from class to class." This variation, she continues, "might be described as a continuum with some women holding a firm grasp on their dowries at one end and other women whose dowries are really family or *fang* property at the opposite extreme" (1984:7).

I should note here that when I talk about the degree to which women have access to or control over income or assets in the family, I am primarily talking about married women, since unmarried daughters are still very likely to be required to relinquish the whole or a part of their income to the family (see Greenhalgh 1985b; Salaff 1981). Among the Dhapa Chinese, however, even this pattern is not fully duplicated; as noted earlier in the chapter, unmarried Hakka girls from Dhapa who work as hairdressers or teachers usually retain their earnings for use as spending money.

Since the existing literature on the economic organization of Chinese families cannot necessarily predict the division of income within Dhapa's Chinese families, let us now take a closer look at this topic.

Who Controls Income?

In my discussion of the sexual division of labor, I mentioned the important role played by those who purchase rawhides and sell finished leather. I pointed out that these tasks are usually performed by the male head of the family or, if he is retired or deceased, by a son. I added that in the few cases where buying rawhides and selling finished leather are performed by different persons, it is the individual who sells the finished product who is most likely to manage finances within the family—since he is on the receiving end of large cash payments.

Myron Cohen's distinctions between a family's financial "redistributor" and a family's "financial manager" (1976:135) are useful here. According to Cohen, the redistributor is the individual to whom funds are transferred and who has the power to disperse them to other family members. But such an individual may not actually manage funds on a day-to-day basis, a task which is the province of the "financial manager."

A father's relinquishment of authority within the business and the family can therefore proceed in stages. He may first give up the role of financial manager and only later, when age or disability reduces his capacity to keep up with daily events, will he concede the role of redistributor. In Dhapa, outsiders may still call a particular individual the family head (*jiazhang*) even after he has relinquished both these roles. But at this point, the identification is merely ceremonial. For instance, invitations to the family for major social occasions will still be addressed to him in deference to his seniority in the family. The same holds for an elderly widow, who may retain the title of family head, although she performs neither the role of financial manager nor the role of redistributor.

Of course, in conjugal families both the managerial and redistributive functions are performed by the same individual, and it is only in complex families that it becomes possible to separate these roles. For instance, Yuan Dongtai, one of the first-generation tanners, has now retired from an active role in his family business. Although profits are still turned over to him, and funds are recycled back to the family through him, he no longer controls day-to-day financial decisions. These decisions are made by the second son, because it is this son who negotiates with buyers; he functions in the role of financial manager. The eldest son, on the other hand, is in charge of purchasing rawhides, a critical task but not necessarily the decisive one in terms of managing a firm's funds.

In the family of Mr. Wu, who talked so loyally of his devotion to his mother, economic relations reflected his statements about her importance. In Mr. Wu's family, his mother, who had been widowed for years, was the redistributor. It was she to whom funds were turned over, she who held the key to the safe, and she who dispensed the funds. When it came to running the business, however, it was her two

[163]

married sons who assumed total responsibility. Thus, they made the decisions about how to actually use the funds. Mr. Wu saw their arrangement as a device for preserving family unity. In his words, "If either of us two brothers controls the funds, there is bound to be conflict, but if my mother maintains control there will be peace in the family." And indeed, this arrangement worked for years. Only in 1989, upon a return visit to Dhapa, did I find that relationships between Mr. Wu and his brother had deteriorated to the point where they were seriously considering family division.

In some cases, however, elderly parents surrender both their redistributive and managerial roles. Kong Tienhua, for instance, was already in his early eighties by 1982. He was no longer interested in taking an active role in his business, and his eldest son by his second wife took charge of managing and redistributing all family funds. Kong Tienhua and his second wife now receive a monthly allowance from this son. (The children of Kong Tienhua's first wife had separated their economic activities from their father by the 1950s—a case I consider in detail in the next chapter.)

Owing to his very advanced age, Kong Tienhua relinquished his role as redistributor. Indeed, it is usually only because of very advanced age or infirmity that a father will renounce this role. Since the father is the unquestioned family head for several decades, his authority is secure. A widowed mother, however, is more likely than her husband to relinquish her role as redistributor. A mother's authority is much more contingent on her ability to manipulate her sons than is a father's. Some widows, such as Mr. Wu's mother, may exercise considerable authority over their grown sons; but it is not automatically assumed that they will do so.

The distinction between redistributor and financial manager is not always so clear-cut. For instance, in Fei Shengchan's family, Fei continues to buy the rawhides and sign the checks, while his eldest son negotiates sales and is responsible for the bulk of financial management. Fei is not merely a passive observer in whose name profits are made and through whom funds are redistributed. He is still actively involved in the business, although no longer its moving force. Thus, Fei and his eldest son share the roles of manager and redistributor.

Furthermore, whereas in some Chinese settings it is generally expected that the transfer of duties involving financial management and redistribution devolves from father to eldest son, this is certainly not the case in Dhapa. In Mr. Wu's case, it was his widowed mother who took over the redistributor's role from her husband. In other cases, a younger son may take over the role of financial manager in lieu of the eldest son.

In one joint family in Dhapa, all profits from sales go to the company, which is still represented by the father who remains the redistributor. But the second son is responsible for buying rawhides and selling finished leather, and the third son is charged with keeping the daily cash and making payments for daily operational expenses, including paying workers. Upon the death of the father, the role of redistributor will probably pass to either the second or third son or to their mother, and not to the eldest son. The second brother is already responsible for two key tasks in the tanning process, and the third brother has already been groomed in the management of family funds. If the mother assumed the role of redistributor, this would temporarily prevent conflict among the brothers, as in the case of Mr. Wu's family.

This lack of clear precedence for the eldest son to take charge is due partly to the emphasis that the Chinese of Dhapa place on achieving financial success. If one son possesses greater business acumen, it is then considered sensible for him to assume greater responsibility. For instance, in Qiao Tanming's family, his widow controls funds for domestic use while her younger son, who is in charge of sales, controls business expenses. The elder son, although he buys rawhides, is not considered quite as sharp as his younger sibling, and community members therefore assume that it is proper for the younger brother to control the business.

Of course, since all sons are entitled to equal shares in the business, but business sense and capability may ultimately bring one son to the fore in terms of the management and control of a particular family business, the differences that emerge among sons may ultimately lead to conflict among them and to family division, a topic I investigate in the next chapter. On the other hand, differences in the capabilities of brothers may sometimes postpone family division. For in situations of great imbalance between the brothers, the less capable brother may actually try to remain with the family, reasoning that breaking away would simply exacerbate his difficulties.

Xue Youcai faced such a situation when, several years after founding his tanning business in Dhapa, he lost his eyesight. At that point, he brought in his sister's husband to help, but when this man died, Xue asked his younger brother, who worked in town as an airplane mechanic, to come back to Dhapa to help with the business. This younger brother ultimately assumed the most dominant role in the enterprise, and even though Xue has complained about the treatment meted out to him by his younger brother, he is well aware that he is better off than if he had to conduct business on his own.

The control of resources within family firms is therefore much more variable in Dhapa than in some other overseas Chinese contexts. For instance, in Omohundro's study of Chinese family firms in the Philippines, he says, "Sons are apportioned profit (or allowance) and responsibilities according to their birth order as often as according to their ability. Income and expenses are monitored carefully by the family head, who is the father, his widow, or the eldest son" (1981:140).

Dhapa's entrepreneurial families, although still wedded to an essentially patrilineal, patrilocal system of kinship, are also much too devoted to the ideal of business success to bind the fate of their firms to the accidents of birth order. Indeed, as I show in the remainder of this chapter, the roles of redistributor and financial manager vary not only in terms of the possible individuals who might fill these slots, but also in terms of how much control they actually do exercise.

Allocating Funds

One might assume that only the redistributor in a given family has absolute freedom to dip into that family's funds. But although this is true in an ultimate sense, families in Dhapa vary in terms of the actual manner in which they allocate resources that pass through the redistributor.

For instance, in Yuan Dongtai's family, each of his four sons who work in the family business, as well their wives, receives a monthly salary. These salaries are used for pocket expenses, and little accounting is done on how they are spent. On the other hand, major expenses, such as tuition for the sons' children, travel, and food, come directly from Yuan Dongtai himself, who, as mentioned, is still the redistributor although he does not take an active role in the business. In Fei Shengchan's family, on the other hand, no salaries are given to any family member. Instead, petty cash is made readily available to each of his three sons and their wives. When withdrawals are made, the amounts are recorded. For Tan Qiyun's family, his retirement from active involvement in business affairs led to a change in the manner in which he fulfilled his redistributor's role. Tan Qiyun is still the ultimate authority in his family, but he no longer has exclusive control over the family safe and bank account. Any adult family member, including his daughter-in-law and his elderly mother, may either withdraw funds from the bank account or take possession of the key to the safe. But not all families are so lax. Mr. Zhou, the man who was constantly giving me advice on how to conduct business, gives his wife a set amount of spending money every month. But she does not have access to either the safe or his bank account.

In addition to allowances, salaries, and simple access to the safe, there are other forms of income that particular individuals within a family may receive and keep for themselves. For instance, Xue Youcai, the individual who became blind and was unable to continue working, receives a monthly allowance for himself and his family from the younger brother who is now in charge of the business. Xue has another source of funds as well. To cover machinery and electricity costs, his brother sets aside a certain sum of money for every piece of leather produced in the tannery. Periodically, the money that remains from this fund is divided among the two brothers and their sister, who continued to work in the business after the death of her husband. (This sister is in a highly unusual situation, since she has a share in her brothers' business, and shares are normally divided only among sons. This situation will have interesting implications if family division occurs.)

But not all monies are transferred to a common till and later distributed to family members. In Yan Baoxia's family, for instance, his married sons conduct separate tanning businesses from which they each derive separate incomes, but family division has not yet occurred. Although the sons conduct their own businesses in their father's tannery, the tannery's assets (the physical plant and capital) still belong to the family as a whole and are controlled by Yan Baoxia himself. Likewise, in Mr. Wu's case, while his mother served as the redistributor, and he and his brother worked together in one family business, his elder brother also ran a second business on the side. The income from this business was not handed over to the common family funds.

Such an arrangement between brothers is rare, because the involvement of a brother in a side business would usually take time away from his participation in the business he shares with other family members. This could ultimately lead to conflict and family dissolution, and indeed did so in the case of Mr. Wu and his brother.

Women's Access to Income and Wealth

Aside from the money that a young woman may earn prior to her marriage, usually as a hairdresser or teacher in a Chinese school, a woman's most important source of wealth is the gold jewelry and other gifts that she receives at marriage. As indicated earlier, there has been both historical and geographical variation in Chinese society in terms of the degree to which assets received at marriage are under a woman's control. However, most Dhapa Chinese believe that wedding gifts, including gold, are a woman's property. For instance, if a family fails in business and needs to raise funds to start over again, they may want to sell this jewelry. But this cannot be done without the wife's consent, and in at least one case in Dhapa, a woman refused to part with this asset.

Additional gifts that a woman receives when she marries include two red suitcases stuffed with clothes, personal items, and cash. The amount of cash varies, but it is usually a sum significant only as spending money. In some instances, however, a greater sum of money is presented, which may be used as seed money to start a young couple in business. This is especially likely to happen when the bride is marrying a man who has already separated from, or is not a part of, a larger family unit.

For instance, Deng Huilin, whose case I consider in detail in the next chapter, was descended from an extremely wealthy family in Dhapa whose members managed to dissipate their assets over three generations. He was reduced to finding a job as a laborer in another family's tannery. But fortunately, he became engaged to their daughter, and when they married, her family added enough cash to her trousseau for them to begin manufacturing leather as tenants.

It is important to keep in mind that none of the gifts a woman receives at marriage comes close to the value of a share of even a small tannery. The smallest tannery in Dhapa was worth at least ten lakhs of rupees (about $100,000) in 1982. So even a half share of such a tannery would have cost 500,000 rupees at that time, an amount much greater than the total worth of all the bridal presents given by the richest of families.

Furthermore, not everyone in Dhapa is unanimous about the degree to which a woman may exercise control over the gold she receives at marriage. For instance, most believe that if a woman leaves her husband (an extremely rare occurrence in Dhapa, but nonetheless a hypothetical possibility), she can take back with her only the gold she received from her natal family. And some people whom I asked indicated to me that even a woman's decision-making powers over whether or not her gold was sold were only theoretical. "How many wives will refuse a husband's request to sell their gold?" my friend Mr. Zhou asked rhetorically.

After marriage, women can gain access and control over some funds through the sale of leather shavings and trimmings. (Each piece of leather is shaved by machine until it reaches a uniform width and then trimmed by hand to smooth out the edges.) Indeed, among the forty-six families I surveyed in my division-of-labor study, thirty gave women the proceeds from the sale of these tanning by-products.

The income from these sales is often divided among the daughters-in-law and their mother-in-law in a complex family or taken by the wife in a conjugal one. In a small family associated with a small business, women are very likely to reinvest this income in family necessities. However, in joint families, where necessities may be paid for by the redistributor, women may have more leeway with this money. And in families associated with large businesses, funds from the sale of tanning by-products can amount to a significant amount. For instance, in 1982, the wives in one joint family associated with a large business earned between sixty and seventy rupees per day from this sale, or about 1,200 rupees per month (a middle-class salary in India at the time). Although these monies were divided among three sisters-in-laws, they still amounted to a significant source of cash which did not have to be immediately absorbed by family necessities. Indeed, many women in Dhapa take these funds and invest them in rotating credit associations, thus earning interest on their investments.

Women in tenant families are more limited in their ability to earn money from tanning by-products. Whereas leather trimmings are considered the property of the tenants in a factory, the shavings are considered the property of the tannery's owner, and the tenants therefore do not have the right to sell these. In Qian Weigang's family, this distinction between income from shavings and trimmings was used to decide how that income was to be allocated between his daughters-in-law and his wife. After Qian Weigang's death, his two sons each conducted a separate business within his tannery, and income from the sale of leather trimmings in each of these businesses was allocated to their wives. Qian's widow, however, took the income from the sale of leather shavings in the factory. She utilized this income to host Sunday lunches for her five married daughters and their families.

[169]

I found no clear relationship between the practice of generating women's income from the sale of tannery by-products and a particular type of family organization or division of labor. A majority of families of each family type, as well as a majority of women among both those who participated and those who did not participate in the family business, followed this practice, and it was also not distinctly connected to any particular category of firm size.

These findings are important because they indicate that women's access to funds in these businesses bears no relation to the degree of their participation in the business. Indeed, this conclusion is also borne out when one analyzes other mechanisms, in addition to the sale of scrap materials, by which women gain access to income or control over property in Dhapa. For instance, as indicated in the discussion of the redistributor's role in the family, an elderly widow may exercise considerable control over the disbursement of family funds, as in Mr. Wu's family. Yet these women frequently take no part in the daily activities of their family businesses.

But even though many women receive some income that need not be handed over to male members of the family, and even though some women may control the redistribution of income in businesses run by their sons, a woman has no opportunities to earn or control income that is totally unrelated to a husband's or a son's business. A woman's economic well-being is therefore ultimately tied to the family into which she marries. This fact, in addition to the good reputation that one attains through hard work, is most certainly a major motivating factor behind the high degree of participation of women in smaller enterprises. The benefits that accrue from the success and expansion of such enterprises form the basis of their future economic security. Likewise, women from larger enterprises are just as likely to decrease their participation in their family businesses. For, as this discussion has indicated, their access to the wealth these businesses produce is not contingent on their degree of participation.

The Influence of Firm Size on Men's Roles

What about men? As Margery Wolf (1972) points out, whereas the in-marrying Chinese wife has always gained her security through the emotional bonds she forges with her sons, her husband has always had the security of the patrilineal patrilocal structure to fall back on. He remains, after all, in the family in which he grew up. He has never felt the unease of the outsider. As his sons grow, therefore, a Chinese man is most concerned with maintaining his formal authority over his sons, a role that demands a certain emotional distance. This authority ensures that he will remain a family head and keep the family together. And the preservation of family unity is critical to the continued success of the family enterprise as well.

Although Chinese men, unlike Chinese women, do not have an alternative sphere in the family into which they can channel their energies, this does not mean that they do not alter their entrepreneurial strategies at all as family firms grow. Rather, they respond to these changes differently than women do. As businesses in the Calcutta Chinese community grow, for instance, nonfamily workers (Indians) tend to be employed in an increasing number of tasks. Technical tasks and even supervisory responsibilities that were formerly undertaken only by family members are increasingly delegated to workers. Family members in the largest tanneries, both men and women, have few specific responsibilities in the production of leather. Tasks like the mixing of chemicals, which are performed by family members in most tanneries, are delegated to skilled employees in these larger operations.

Whereas female family members in these large enterprises become less involved in the business in every way, male family members simply change the manner in which they participate. In the largest enterprises in the Calcutta Chinese tanning community, male family members have essentially become factory managers at the helm of a large work force that is varied in both role and ethnicity. (In addition to Bihari Chamars, the staff includes Nepalese workers, Bengali accountants, Muslim packers, and Chinese managers.) Such tanneries often have offices in which buyers come to negotiate with owners in private and comfortable surroundings, rather than on the factory floor.

Men also have the option of participating in a number of extrafamilial political structures that extend the range of their connections in the community and ultimately redound to the benefit of their businesses. I should emphasize that despite women's considerable participation and influence within families and family businesses, this *is* still a patriarchal society, and women *are* excluded from most of the political leadership roles that men occupy. These roles include high positions in surname and business associations, and, as in many Southeast Asian overseas Chinese communities (see Skinner 1968), such roles are primarily the domain of wealthy men.

[171]

The Xi Family—An Example of Changing Roles and Organization

One could argue that my data here are actually concerned not with transformations over time but with variations observed at one particular moment, that is, with synchronous variation. However, family histories illustrate that the variations I have found in the sexual division of labor as well as in family form, firm size, and spatial organization are variations not only within a slice of time but across time as well.

The family of Xi Taiguo, one of the more successful entrepreneurs in the community, exemplifies this kind of development. When his father (Xi Feiyuan) founded the business, the kitchen was located directly on the factory floor, adjacent to which were the bedrooms. Subsequently, Xi Taiguo relocated the bedrooms to a new second floor, and he enlarged the ground floor to create more manufacturing space. He later constructed additional manufacturing space in an area across the lane from the original factory, and he moved the kitchen there. Several years later, after Xi's two brothers and their families had returned from abroad to aid him in his expanding business, he enlarged the physical plant of the tannery for the third time. He built additional floors and removed all domestic space from manufacturing areas to a separate floor, which became the family's residence.

Xi's father and mother, the founders of the business, had both been involved and extremely active in the business while they were alive. But Xi and his two brothers do not share tannery work with their wives. Furthermore, during a period in which business was extremely bad, Xi's brothers dispersed to other locations, leaving Xi and his immediate family to carry on the business; when the business became successful again, the brothers reunited. Thus, changes in spatial arrangements, family composition, and the sexual division of labor all reflected changes in the size and success of Xi's enterprise.

As we have seen in this chapter, there is a clear sexual division of labor in this community. Yet married women's contributions to their family enterprises are not confined to manipulating other family members to work hard; the majority of these women participate directly in their family businesses. Furthermore, neither men's nor women's roles in this entrepreneurial community are fixed and unchanging, but vary with transformations in the size of family businesses. As their firms grow, men move away from physical labor and toward managerial roles, while married women withdraw from business activity altogether. I have explained these trends by relating them to the variable strategies available to men and women in pursuing the goals of a shared entrepreneurial ideology.

The studies by Sorensen (1981) and Cohen (1976), which examine the sexual division of labor in Korean and Taiwanese agricultural villages, serve to highlight what is distinctive about my findings. Cohen, for instance, argues that it is family form that is most salient in determining women's roles in rural Taiwanese families. Why is that not the case with the community I examined? I have already discussed the cultural, ideological, and economic forces that deter Calcutta Hakka women from contributing to larger family enterprises and that spur them to contribute to smaller ones. But it is also important to note the very real differences between the rural agricultural setting of Cohen's study and the urban industrial setting of mine.

The families described in Cohen's study attempt to cut costs by using as much family labor and hiring as little outside labor as possible. Small conjugal families, therefore, are stretched to the utmost, since they are trying to employ as many family members in the fields as possible. But at the same time, there is a limit to the number of workers needed on what is, for most families, a finite amount of land. In joint families, with their greater number of adult family members, therefore, female family members are able to engage exclusively in domestic tasks, since there are always enough male family members to do all the necessary agricultural chores.

In the industrial context of Hakka Chinese firms, however, the intrinsic limits to expansion are fewer. If an enterprise is doing well, the owners will do everything possible to maintain and increase its profitability. Space can be added by constructing more floors in the factory, or by purchasing empty land, which at the time of my field-work was still available in this marshy neglected area of Calcutta. Furthermore, as enterprises increase their profitability, more machinery can be added and more workers hired—for these constitute investments, not drains on family resources. In this setting, therefore, it is the size of the enterprise rather than the size of the family that determines whether female family members will participate.

Comparing the Calcutta Hakka with the Korean villagers Sorensen studied is also illuminating. The patrilineal, patrilocal, patriarchal, and Confucian-oriented Korean villagers whom he studied divide space and labor into "inner" (female) and "outer" (male) domains. Furthermore, poor village women are much more likely to participate in

[173]

field labor and other "outside" tasks than the wives of wealthier men. But among these villagers increased wealth exacerbates the differences between husband and wife, not only in terms of the division of labor but also in terms of their relative power in the family. The wealthier men tend to get out and about, while their wives are increasingly confined to "inside" work and ultimately have less influence on family decision making than the more active wives of poorer men (Sorensen 1981).

Hakka women, in a situation analogous to that of Sorensen's villagers, play a smaller role in income-producing activities when their families operate larger firms. But my data suggest that their power and influence in the family do not diminish accordingly.[7] For instance, as I have shown, a woman's control of property bears no necessary relationship to her participation in the family firm. Thus, at least in terms of access to and control of material resources, women who do not participate in their family businesses are not necessarily at a disadvantage. One reason for this situation may be that through formation of the "uterine family" and through work in the domestic sphere, women continue to earn the loyalty and respect of family members. As with the Taiwanese investigated by Wolf (1972), the uterine family remains a significant source of informal power.

Furthermore, although they do not participate in the business, women from larger enterprises continue to attend the same weddings, funerals, and other social functions as women from smaller enterprises. Indeed, their status in the community rises along with that of other family members, because in this community a family's overall status is closely tied to its wealth. Business success, therefore, does not necessarily exaggerate or change the nature of the differences between husband and wife.

Paradoxically, participation in the business can serve to enhance the familial power and community status of those women whose families run smaller firms. As I have shown, in Chinese culture hard work is an idiom for emotional connectedness, and it is one way in which family members create bonds with one another and help ensure subsequent loyalty and assistance. In addition, the community values hard work,

---

[7] Obviously, how one measures and defines *power* in the family is a complicated question. For my purposes here, I accept the definition that Michelle Rosaldo draws from M. G. Smith: "Power . . . is the ability to act effectively on persons or things, to make or secure favourable decisions" (Rosaldo 1980:21).

and women who "toil and endure hardship" for a family firm gain esteem in the community as well as in their own families. After all, the community as a whole shares and approves their goals—prosperity and economic security.

Women in Calcutta's Hakka families have therefore fashioned a number of different responses to an overarching set of goals shared by most community members. Rather than being passive spectators in a family's entrepreneurial drama, they pursue a variety of direct and indirect strategies to increase their families' economic well-being.

Appendix
Basis for Measurement in Tabulations

Relating Participation by Women to Firm Size

At the outset, it was necessary to find a suitable means of categorizing participation by women in the family firms in my survey. I began by counting the specific number of tasks for which each woman in a family was responsible, but this degree of specificity proved a bit unwieldy when I started to look for correlations. So I abandoned it for a more general measure: I simply compared those businesses in which women participated with those in which they did not.

As a measure of firm size, for the reasons discussed in Chapter 2, I settled on the number of nonfamily workers employed in the business. Establishing categories of firm size proved difficult, however. The firms in my sample varied from a small business with only 4 nonfamily workers to a large one with 150 workers (the median was 9 nonfamily workers). I finally decided to look for "threshold" numbers—that is, to look through the data and see where the meaningful breaks themselves occurred. In other words, I tried to determine whether certain firm sizes were associated with certain patterns in the sexual division of labor.

Indeed, I did find a meaningful threshold when I compared firms employing sixteen or more workers with those employing fewer than sixteen. The differences between these two groups of firms in regard to participation by women were greater than those between any other categories of size that I chose. In firms employing 16 or more workers, women were less likely to participate in business tasks.

[175]

Relating Family Form to Firm Size

Here I used the categories of conjugal, stem, and joint families as described in Chapter 1, with the further stipulation that families categorized as joint had to have two or more married brothers (and a parent or parents if still alive) sharing a residence as well as assets. Although coresidence is not always a feature of a joint family, I decided to make it a requirement for the purposes of categorizing for my sample. For even when sons who have migrated have not taken their share of the family assets, they usually make no economic contributions to their families, and more important, they cannot take part in the labor process.

In this case, I found a threshold of eight: firms employing fewer than eight nonfamily workers clearly differed in family form from those employing eight or more workers, with larger firms associated with larger, more "complex" families.

Relating the Organization of Space to Firm Size and Family Form

As far as the organization of space was concerned, I found a threshold when I compared firms employing fourteen or more workers with those employing fewer than this number. In general, the larger the firm, the greater the separation of domestic and manufacturing space.

Only by dividing spatial arrangement into two categories—tanneries in which living space was completely separate from manufacturing space, and tanneries in which manufacturing space was adjacent to either living areas or eating and cooking areas—did I find a clear relationship between family form and spatial organization. Complex families were associated with a more rigid segregation of domestic and manufacturing areas.

[7]

"Branches of a Tree":
Family and Firm in the
Second and Third Generations

It was a significant day in Mr. Zhou's life. Early on a June morning of 1982, a small procession left his tannery. Mr. Zhou's youngest brother, Zhou Hongmin, his three young children following behind him, walked out of the home and factory that the two brothers and their families had previously shared. They were setting off for their new tannery and home, where construction had recently been completed, and where they would officially celebrate their move on that day. At exactly 6:00 A.M., with the sound of firecrackers exploding in the background, Hongmin and his three children, each carrying a red lamp symbolizing their membership in a common line of descent, crossed the threshold of the entrance to their tannery. They proceeded to the main factory floor, where they hung their lamps above a table laden with offerings of meat, fruit, sweets, and wine.

Hongmin's wife, not being in the line of descent, did not participate in this morning procession. But she had gone to the new factory even earlier that morning to get things ready for the day's events. Hongmin, his children, and his wife then spent the rest of the morning making offerings not only to their ancestors but also to the spirits of the tannery doors and factory machines, to the spirit of prosperity, and to Tudigong, the spirit of the locality. Meanwhile, Mr. Zhou performed a few final rituals of his own to ensure that his brother had not taken the wealth out of the house with him when he left!

By noon of the same day it was time to celebrate. The main factory floor of the new tannery had been cleared to accommodate forty tables (400 guests). After the guests were seated, and another round of fire-

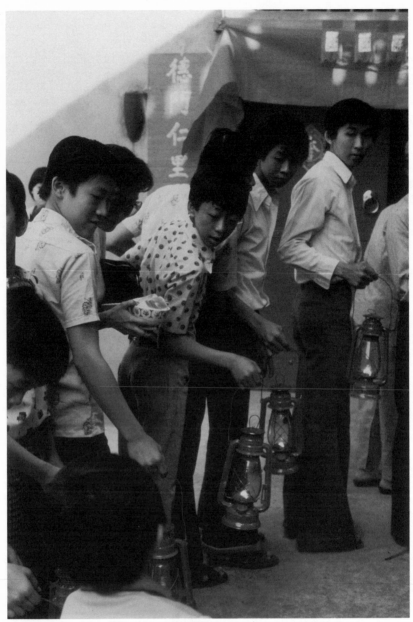

During the ceremony that marks the opening of a new tannery, the male descendants of its owners carry red lanterns and walk in a procession to the new factory.

Members of a family pose for a photographer on the day their new tannery opens.

crackers set off to clear the way for the commencement of the feast, it was time for Mr. Zhou to offer the first toast. Sounding a magnanimous note, he wished his brother's family well in their new tannery, and quoting an adage frequently written on family partition contracts, he acknowledged that their move was part of a natural process of family growth and ultimate fission: "Just as a tree sprouts many branches when it grows large, so, too, when sons grow up they will establish separate households [*shu da fen zhih, zi da fen zhu*]."

This house-moving ceremony and celebration, with as many guests as would attend a typical wedding in Dhapa, marked an important milestone in the history of the relationship between these two Zhou brothers, as well as in the development of their businesses. Each brother now owned a tannery of his own, and this day confirmed their mutual success. But such a happy outcome came only after many years in which Mr. Zhou, his youngest brother, and two older brothers (who

[179]

subsequently emigrated to Canada) struggled intensely over the terms of their family division.

In this chapter, I examine the development of Dhapa Chinese families in the second and third generations. Unless a business is founded by two or more brothers and subsequently divided by them, a sequence of events described in Chapter 5 for some first-generation tanners, family division in Dhapa assumes a preceding generation of tanners, because it involves the division of a business by a tanner's sons. (Obviously, if there is only one son, he will inherit.) Therefore, the various effects of family division on Dhapa's families can serve as a lens through which to analyze the course of family and business in the second and third generations. A crucially important aspect to this story is that of migration. Many Chinese in Dhapa today must make the difficult decision between staying in Calcutta, or moving to another Indian city, or emigrating to another country. In few families do all members remain in India.

Indeed, the pathways of Dhapa's tanning families have gone in several directions. In many cases, such as that of the Zhou brothers, new factories have been built as brothers who separate strike out on their own. However, family division sometimes results merely in the partitioning of a single business into several small shares. Migration is a complicating factor, for it may play into the scenario of family division in more than one way. Brothers may leave Dhapa as the end result of family division and be compensated for their share of the family business in cash or valuables. Or they may emigrate abroad without going through the formalities of family division, so that they have the option of returning home to continue in business with their brothers if their experience abroad proves less than satisfactory. Of course, during this interval they are not automatically entitled to income from the current operation of the tanning business, although brothers on either side may help each other if they deem it necessary.

The General Pattern

As discussed in Chapter 1, the family or *jia* group is united not only by blood and kin ties but also by their sharing of a common budget or property. *Fenjia*, or family division, therefore refers to the process by which these commonly held assets are divided among the smaller constituents of the *jia*, usually among each of the sons, and most

[180]

typically, after the death of one or more members of the senior generation. The establishment of separate kitchens by the new family units is a common feature of family division. But family division is much more complicated than this, since it involves a decision about the dispensation of a multitude of assets. In Dhapa, brothers need to agree not only on the apportionment of funds but also on the division of machinery and factory space. In a family that runs a tenant tanning business instead of owning a factory, division will be slightly less involved. Cash assets and household articles will be divided, and after that each brother and his respective family will rent living space and machinery on his own, rather than with a brother or brothers.

Although this general pattern sounds simple and straightforward, it is often a highly disputed and emotional experience. Sometimes brothers are able to settle the terms of division amicably among themselves, but some settlements are preceded by bitter disputes. In such cases, representatives from the surname group to which the disputing parties belong, or from one of the two Chinese tanning associations, must intervene and adjudicate a solution. Because they are so suspicious of the Indian community, the Calcutta Chinese never refer these matters to an Indian lawyer (there are no Chinese lawyers). Rather, the informal institutions of the Chinese community are almost always the last resort (see Chapter 3). Furthermore, although daughters are usually not shareholders in the family estate, they have a say, as I show in this chapter, in both family division and decisions about emigration.

The best way to understand the dynamics of family division in Dhapa is to consider particular cases. In the text that follows, I describe the effects of family division on several families in Dhapa. Each serves as an example of a distinct pattern that I found among the family histories I collected.

Diminishing Shares

When Mr. Wu's sister, Aifang, reached marriageable age in 1974, the family began to send discrete feelers out into the community. But Aifang insisted that she already knew whom she wanted to marry. This was Deng Huilin, a young Chinese man who was employed as a worker in their tannery. Mr. Wu, his mother, and younger brother were all surprised. Why marry a mere laborer, when we can arrange your

[181]

marriage to someone from a prosperous family? Upon further consideration, however, they began to appreciate Deng's good qualities, especially his capacity for unstinting hard work. They not only approved the marriage but placed enough cash in the two red suitcases that the bride customarily takes with her to her husband's home for the newly wedded couple to begin a tenant tanning business. For Deng Huilin, this was the chance to reverse what had been a sharp economic decline in his family over three generations.

How had this come about? Deng's grandfather, Deng Wenzhi, was the owner of one of the first established tanneries in Dhapa. But Wenzhi had two wives, and each wife had five sons. When Wenzhi died and the sons decided to separate their assets, the tannery had to be divided into ten parts, for each son was entitled to a share.

Since each share of this tannery was too small to be of any use in leather production, the Deng family leased the entire tannery to another tanner and divided the monthly rental income among the shareholders. Although these monthly stipends were useful, they were certainly not enough to serve as sole support for any of the shareholders or their families. Accordingly, in order to earn a living, many family members either migrated to other parts of India or emigrated overseas. Six of Wenzhi's sons now own and manage Chinese restaurants, three of them in India, two in the United States, and one in Bangladesh. Yet another son has emigrated to Taiwan (Figure 1).

The diminishment of the Deng family's wealth over three generations recalls a pattern that existed in rural China where the maintenance of a family's wealth over several generations was always being challenged by the inherent logic of partible inheritance (J. Potter 1970:129). The division of family land into equal shares for all sons meant that a family's fortunes would almost certainly decline over time, unless they could get access to more land. Under such a system, the same piece of land was continuously divided by succeeding generations and therefore had to support more and more people.

In Deng Huilin's case, however, the logic of family division was only one element of his economically straitened circumstances. After all, several of his father's brothers had migrated to new places where they did ultimately prosper, despite the impossibility of relying on income generated by their tannery. Huilin's father, on the other hand, was a habitual drunkard who was unable to hold any kind of job, and who relied for subsistence on his share of the tannery's rental income. Huilin was therefore forced to seek employment as an ordinary tan-

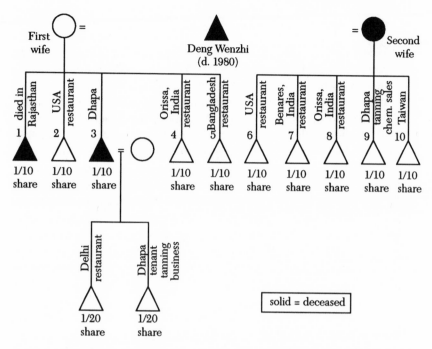

Figure 1. Distribution of assets from Deng Wenzhi's tannery

nery laborer at a young age, and he continued to work in tanneries for fourteen years, ultimately securing a job in Mr. Wu's tannery.

But family division in Dhapa often turns out much better than it did in the case of Deng Huilin's family. In many instances, brothers are dividing growing businesses, and one or more brothers may buy out shares of the other brothers and take control of an entire factory. Meanwhile, those who have sold out their shares will use the funds so gained to build or buy an entirely new factory. This was the ultimate outcome of family division in Mr. Zhou's family, and it is a case I consider later in this chapter.

Emigration usually moderates the effects of partible inheritance. At the very least, emigration enables a son or sons to find new sources of income outside Dhapa. In many cases (although not in the case of the Deng family), it also means that the sons who are left behind have a viable productive unit at their disposal. Occasionally, those who remain in Dhapa actually buy out the share of the emigrant. In other cases, family-partition matters are left up in the air. For instance,

Stephen Kong, the immigrant living in Toronto (see Chapter 1), has not yet gone through the process of family division with his brothers who remain in Dhapa. Yet the fact that Stephen is away and has his own job in Canada obviously lessens the economic pressure on his brothers in India, since their business has fewer people to support. According to Myron Cohen's terminology, in cases like Stephen's, emigration can be viewed as part of a process by which the emigrant diversifies the family economy and decreases the burden on those left behind. Such a situation, in which brothers in two different countries earn their own living but have neither gone through family division nor contributed funds to a common pool, can be understood as what Myron Cohen calls a "noninclusive" economy and a "dispersed" *jia* group (1970:27–28).

In the next section I consider in more detail the manner in which emigration and family division have interacted with both economic and political strategies among second- and third-generation Dhapa Chinese.

"Three Brothers Together Is Really Unlucky": Deciding to Emigrate

For "K. C." Yan, the youngest son of Yan Baoxia, the decision to emigrate was clear-cut. First, there was the situation in his family. Two elder brothers were already married, living in his father's tannery, and conducting separate businesses. As K. C. stated in a 1986 interview in Toronto, "three brothers all doing the same thing is really unlucky [*daomei*]. Suppose the tannery business goes down, then all of us will suffer. If I do my own business, then I can help them. . . . If I have problems, my older brothers can help me." Second, there was the situation in India. Said K. C., "India's environment is not very stable. . . . After the war [the Sino-Indian conflict of 1962], the situation for Chinese was not very good."

Although K. C.'s decision was made with an eye to his family's overall situation, it did not immediately meet with unanimous approval. In fact, K. C.'s father objected strenuously. Discussing his father's attitude, K. C. explained, "Even now he wants me to come back. He says, 'I have such a big tannery, three brothers, even ten brothers, could work together here.'" Indeed, K. C. fought with his father for four or five years before he received his approval to emigrate.

Unlike K. C. Yan, Stephen Kong's decision to emigrate was not solely the result of his own initiative. In fact, Stephen admitted, his father "came up with the idea first." But in deciding that some of his sons should leave, Stephen's father reasoned along lines similar to K. C.'s. Both familial economic factors as well as the larger situation of the Chinese in India were critical components in Mr. Kong's appraisal of the situation and his conviction that some of his sons should emigrate from India, and others should remain.

Emigration is not confined to poor families like Deng Huilin's or even moderately successful ones such as K. C. Yan's. Many of Dhapa's most successful entrepreneurs have also decided to emigrate. For instance, Fei Shengchan's eldest son, Kenneth, was the guiding force in the family tanning business for years. He expanded the operation by adding the manufacture of leather bags and had lucrative contracts with firms in Europe and the United States. I was therefore surprised when in the summer of 1989 he told me that his family had decided to emigrate to Canada.

"What is the use of money?" he sighed. He went on to lament what he perceived as the lack of security for the Chinese community in India, and explained that he had gotten a job as the manager of a leather goods factory in Canada. Of course, Kenneth would be immigrating to Canada with the assurance of a much better job than most Calcutta Chinese in Toronto are able to secure (a topic I consider in greater detail in the Epilogue). His export-oriented business had already brought him into contact with many in the leather business abroad, and these contacts had opened up fruitful employment prospects. Furthermore, for successful businessmen like Kenneth, emigration does not necessarily mean abandoning their businesses. In Kenneth's case, his two younger brothers and his father would continue to run the tannery and the bag-making section of the factory. Furthermore, Kenneth planned to continue his work by interesting importers in the factory's products.

Therefore, while the insecurity of being a Chinese in India was certainly crucial in Kenneth's decision to leave, and while he himself expressed the view that security was even more important than economic success, emigration also helped diversify the family's economic base. Since his two younger brothers had no intention of going through family partition, Kenneth was not cutting his ties to the prosperous business he had helped to create.

From the point of view of economic strategies, both emigration abroad and migration to other Indian cities lessen the pressure on families that must share businesses. Young men who move to other Indian cities often work as waiters or cooks in Chinese restaurants, which have become a fixture in recent years in the luxury hotels of Bombay and New Delhi. Many who work in these restaurants intend to open a small restaurant of their own someday. And indeed, the restaurant business has proved an increasingly profitable niche for Chinese in Calcutta and in other Indian cities.

But although diversification within India may offer economic benefits, it does not offer political and ethnic security. Hence, there are few families in Dhapa today in which at least one member has not emigrated. In Table 5, I summarize residence patterns in 1982 among 43 families in which all children had reached adulthood (over age eighteen), and in which all were descended from first- or second-generation tanners. This sample is based on the genealogies I collected at that time, and it should be kept in mind that in the last decade, Chinese emigration from Calcutta has proceeded steadily. As can be seen from this table, in forty-one of the forty-three families, at least one offspring had left Dhapa to live in another Indian city or to emigrate abroad. And in thirty-nine of these families, at least one of these individuals had emigrated abroad.

The table also indicates that both brothers and sisters have played an important role in the geographical dispersal of families through emigration. It should be pointed out that married couples, accompanied by their children, as well as younger as yet unmarried men and women have contributed to this flow of emigration. But when single men and women emigrate, they tend to leave under different circumstances. Unmarried men, like K. C. Yan and Stephen Kong, emigrate by themselves and stay with relatives or friends when they arrive in Canada. They may remain unmarried for several years after emigration. Unmarried women, however, usually leave home in order to marry a Hakka Chinese who has already emigrated from India. In some cases these are arranged marriages; in others, women marry Calcutta Hakka men of their own choice whom they knew prior to their emigration, or whom they met while visiting relatives abroad. Indeed, all the Calcutta Chinese women whom I met in Toronto, and who had left India while still single, said that they had emigrated in order to marry.

Although the emigration of unmarried women has little bearing on the problems created by partible inheritance of their families' busi-

Table 5. Residence patterns of adult sons and daughters (over age 18) in 43 families in 1982

Residence pattern	Number of families
All sons and daughters remain in Dhapa	2
All sons remain in Dhapa, but at least one daughter leaves Dhapa	10
All daughters remain in Dhapa, but at least one son leaves Dhapa	5
At least one son and at least one daughter leave Dhapa	26
	43

Note: In 30 of the 36 families in which at least one daughter left Dhapa, a daughter emigrated abroad. In 26 of the 31 families in which at least one son left Dhapa, at least one son emigrated abroad.

nesses (since daughters customarily do not inherit), it does address the issue of political and ethnic insecurity by creating connections abroad. A daughter who becomes a citizen of Canada, for instance, may choose to sponsor a parent or sibling from India for immigration at a later date.

Educational choices have also played a role in emigration strategies. Since most Dhapa Chinese emigrate to Canada, the overwhelming majority of parents now place their children, both sons and daughters, in English medium private schools, many of which are fairly exclusive boarding schools. This choice is directly influenced by the perception that fluency in English is a necessity for those who emigrate abroad. Few Dhapa Chinese go on to study at the university level, however, largely because of their perception that college education will have no bearing on their ability to conduct their businesses in India. (Nor does a college education figure into emigration strategies, since community members do not think it will greatly improve one's employment opportunities abroad.)

When the elderly emigrate, it is usually to live with sons or daughters who have already established themselves abroad. Thus, their emigration rarely serves as a link in a chain in which other family members will be sponsored. Unlike their children, many of these elderly family members know no English and have difficulty adjusting to life in Canada. However, they are usually welcomed by their children in Canada, for, among other things, they take care of their grandchildren when the parents go out to work.

[187]

The lives of these Calcutta Chinese emigrants in Toronto—men and women, young and old—are considered in the Epilogue. Here, the emphasis is on the impact of this emigration on families in Dhapa, who must deal with its immediate organizational and economic effects. The most pressing question, when the emigrant is a male, is whether his brothers and he should go through a process of family division, in which case the remaining brothers will buy out the emigrant's share. Let us now see how a variety of families have dealt with this question.

Migration, Emigration, and Family Division

When a son leaves Dhapa, either to work or to establish a new business in Calcutta or in another Indian city, or to leave India altogether, it is not a foregone conclusion that family division will occur. In many cases, the migrant will support himself, and if he is married he will support his immediate conjugal family, but he will leave open the possibility of returning one day and rejoining his brothers.

In K. C. Yan's case, each of his two elder brothers already conducts a separate tanning business (an arrangement discussed in Chapter 6). The tannery's assets, however, still remain the joint property of the entire family, under the control of their father. When, and if, the sons decide to divide these jointly held assets, K. C. will still be entitled to a share. If he prefers, he can sell his share to his older brothers at that time. But this action prevents his returning to do business in his father's tannery, an option he might want to exercise if life in Canada takes a downward turn for him.

Accordingly, many emigrants prefer to keep the issue of family division at bay, in case they need to return to India. For instance, during the recession of the early 1990s, a number of Calcutta Chinese immigrants in Toronto lost their jobs when the factories in which they worked closed down. Some of them returned to Dhapa and now work in their family tanning businesses. In one such case, Tan Qiyun's eldest son, William, returned from Canada and rejoined a younger brother in running their tanning business. William was one of the most highly educated emigrants from Dhapa, and he had secured a lucrative engineering job in Toronto. When the engineering company he worked for in Toronto hit hard times, William was laid off. His situation was further complicated by the fact that he had just been divorced from his wife, a circumstance which is still quite rare among Calcutta Chinese immigrants in Canada. William, who told me that he was "always too busy working to have time to meet people," hoped that his family in Calcutta would be able to arrange a new marriage for him with a Hakka woman there.[1]

In addition to economic difficulties in Canada, a sudden improvement in the economic condition of family members in India might prompt a sibling to return to Calcutta. For instance, when Xi Taiguo's tanning business suddenly took a remarkably successful turn, a younger brother returned from Canada to join in business with him.

In most cases, however, the prospect of rejoining brothers in India to do business is viewed both by emigrants and by those who remain as unlikely, and it is. In Stephen Kong's words, "I think I can work with them [his brothers in India], but I have been here thirteen years. I have established my roots over here, you have to think about it . . . the chances of going back there are getting slimmer." And as Thomas Liang, another Dhapa emigrant in Toronto whose family runs a very prosperous business in Calcutta, put it: "I could take part in the family business [if he returned], but whether I will continue to have the same kind of say in the family business is the question."

For Thomas Liang and Stephen Kong, and for many others, returning to India as anything more than a visitor is unlikely and impractical. But since they have not yet gone through a process of family division with their brothers, it is not impossible. In other cases, however, emigration is the final step in a process of family partition, one in which brothers divide their assets and buy out the emigrant's share. In such circumstances, emigration closes the door on economic reunion of the family. The case of Mr. Zhou's family, with which I started this chapter, serves as a very good example of this, and I will now consider it in more detail.

A Contested Division: The Zhou Family

When Mr. Zhou's father, Zhou Xianfeng, immigrated to Calcutta in 1919, he certainly could not have foreseen that the business he would labor so hard to build would one day cause an extremely bitter dispute among his sons. Like many other first-generation tanners, Zhou Xian-

---

[1] Interestingly, they did succeed in finding a bride, though not a Hakka from India. Age, and the fact that he was divorced, made William a rather undesirable marriage partner. Hence, the family made contacts with relatives in Mei Xian (their ancestral county in Guangdong, China) through whom they were able to find a bride.

feng spent many years in other lines of work before moving to Dhapa and becoming involved in tanning. He started out as a schoolteacher in one of Calcutta's Chinese schools, and he continued as its principal for twenty years. Later, he moved to Dhapa and began a tenant tanning business, ultimately purchasing a tannery of his own in 1948.

But Xianfeng died in 1954, when three of his four sons were still of school age (for simplicity's sake, I will refer to the four Zhou brothers as Zhou One, Zhou Two, Zhou Three [Mr. Zhou], and Zhou Four). Only the eldest son, Zhou One, was old enough to get involved with the business before his father died, and he was therefore entrusted with the responsibility of running and expanding the family business while his three younger brothers completed their schooling. In this endeavor he succeeded rather admirably. In fact, by 1960 he had built an additional tannery.

By 1960, however, Zhou One's three younger brothers had also begun to get involved in their family business, and Zhou One now wanted to divide the family assets and continue in business on his own. Perhaps, as the eldest son with the most experience in the business, and one who had expanded it considerably at that, Zhou One thought he would be better off without the others, who had less knowledge and would be more of a liability than an asset to the business. In any case, by 1963 Zhou One was able to convince his younger brothers to sign a separation agreement in the presence of surname elders.

Zhou One's timing was unusual since none of his younger brothers had married yet, and therefore they had not even created conjugal families of their own, family units whose interests might conflict with the joint family of which they were a part. Moreover, their agreement was unconventional in that it did not apply immediately, but instead specified a series of steps that would lead to family division in five years. Finally, several particular circumstances of the Zhou family's case complicated the terms of the agreement. To fully appreciate the decisions they wrestled with, we must consider two important distinctions. The first is whether brothers engaged in different economic activities have or have not agreed to a division of family assets. The second distinction is between acquired and inherited property.

Separate Businesses versus Family Division

In the families of K. C. Yan and Stephen Kong, brothers are engaged in different economic activities, but the family estate has not yet been divided. This state of affairs may occur when one brother emigrates and can even take place when siblings remain in tanning. As we have seen, each of K. C.'s brothers conducts separate businesses within their father's tannery, but the assets of this tannery belong to the family as a whole and are under control of their father. Furthermore, the two brothers and their families still eat together with their parents, and the rental income from the tannery's tenants goes to the father, who sets it aside for communal expenses such as food and factory maintenance.

Such a situation may exist in relation to sons and fathers as well as between brothers. In one Dhapa family, for instance, the eldest of three sons decided to run a separate business in the early 1980s. He became a tenant in his father's tannery, and he no longer eats with his brothers or parents. Yet his brothers and he have not yet gone through a process of family division, and it is unlikely that they will do so as long as their father is alive, or at least active in the business. As with K. C.'s brothers, the eldest son's business in this situation is simply a separate source of income. He still retains rights in the family's jointly held assets.

Such arrangements may continue for protracted periods. Although they may be a prelude to family division, they may also forestall ultimate decisions about the dispensation of property (which can involve heated family arguments). One Dhapa emigrant, Susan Qin, who is now living in Toronto with her husband and mother-in-law, explained this to me very clearly. Susan told me that five of her husband's brothers live in India and conduct separate tanning businesses. But the tannery still belongs to their mother, even though she now lives in Canada with Susan and her husband. None of the brothers, Susan asserted, is looking forward to dividing the estate, and they hope to postpone this as long as possible, because "then the whole family will fight."

Lung-sheng Sung has analyzed similar processes among families in rural Taiwan (1981:369). He points out that in rural Taiwan, sons may establish separate households but not go through the process of dividing the family estate until after the father's death, or until the various households composed of his sons and their families grow so "large and ambitious" that the father no longer retains any real control (1981:371).

Inherited and Acquired Property

In theory, the principle of partible inheritance sounds simple— simply divide an estate and assets among all sons. In fact, problems crop up because sons may have contributed unequally to the growth of this estate. Hence, it becomes necessary to distinguish between property that can be rightfully inherited from the family head and property that has been added to the estate by different brothers, to which the same rules of partible inheritance do not apply so neatly.

According to Lung-sheng Sung, the second type of property is considered to be acquired property, and the son who is most directly responsible for its acquisition receives extra compensation at the time of family division (1981:373–75). But distinguishing between property that rightfully belongs to all descendants and that which has been acquired by the efforts of particular individuals is not always easy. As Sung reminds us, "The greater right of brothers who contribute most to an estate tends to be forgotten by those who contribute least, particularly when it comes time to divide the income from the estate. Quarrels . . . are the usual result" (1981:376).

The Argument among the Zhous

The Zhou family was a perfect candidate for the eruption of such quarrels during family division. Over the course of six years following his father's death, Zhou One had expanded the business while his younger brothers played no role in it at all. Inevitably, the brothers would argue about whether and how much Zhou One should be compensated for the value he had added to the family estate.

Perhaps it was in an attempt to forestall such conflicts that the Zhou brothers signed their agreement in 1963. According to this agreement, which was ratified in the presence of surname group elders, the Zhou brothers would divide the family assets in 1968. At that time, Zhou One would receive a two-fifths share of all family assets, and each of the three younger brothers would receive a one-fifth share. The three younger brothers now claim that they thought this was a fair solution, because their eldest brother had added to the family business while the three of them were still in school. Further, by the terms of this agreement, Zhou One also consented to help each of his three younger brothers establish separate businesses by giving them seed money to buy their first batch of rawhides and tanning materials.

When the brothers signed the agreement, they also assumed that by the time the tannery's assets were to be divided in 1968, each brother would be married and running a business of his own. Until that time, as with several other families already described, their family economy would gradually become more "noninclusive," but they would not divide their jointly held assets. During this interim period, Zhou One agreed to share the manufacturing space and machinery in his new tannery with Zhou Two. Mr. Zhou, who was the third in line, agreed to share the older tannery with Zhou Four. Since the Zhou brothers viewed the care of their mother as a joint responsibility, they agreed that she would live in the new tannery and spend one week of each month dining with each son. In keeping with the formula for division of family assets (two-fifths for the eldest, one-fifth each for the rest), she received an allotment of 240 rupees a month from her eldest son, and 120 rupees from each of the younger sons (a comfortable sum at that time).

Unfortunately, despite their attempt to almost ease their way into family division, disputes soon erupted in the Zhou household. Before the five years of the interim period had passed, Zhou One's wife and Zhou Two started quarreling. The immediate cause of the dispute was a disagreement over the management of water tanks within the factory they shared. But, as in many such situations, the quarrel was really an expression of tensions that had been building for some time. Although the three younger brothers had agreed with Zhou One about the ultimate division of shares in the factory, they believed that he had not lived up to all the preliminary terms of the agreement. For instance, Mr. Zhou felt that Zhou One had not provided him with enough seed money to start his own business (this amount had been specified in the 1963 agreement, but Zhou One later delayed giving the entire amount, stating that he would give some of it at the time his third brother started his business and the remainder when he married). Moreover, although the four brothers had agreed to a two-fifths share for Zhou One, it is probable that they were beginning to smart over the terms of this agreement, realizing that each of them would ultimately get considerably less than their eldest brother.

The crisis in the Zhou household came to a head in 1966 when Zhou One began to insist that his second brother move out of the factory they were sharing. As discussed in Chapter 2, when disputes between family members get out of hand, it is customary for surname group representatives to try to intervene. Accordingly, Zhou surname group elders attempted to mediate the dispute that was brewing among the Zhous. Seeing the breakdown in relationships among the brothers, the Zhou elders insisted that the brothers not wait until 1968 for family division, but that they immediately divide family assets by the terms of the 1963 agreement.

But now a further complication arose. In their 1963 agreement the brothers had agreed to a two-fifths share for Zhou One, but what was to constitute two-fifths of the family's assets? Moreover, the breakdown in communication among all the brothers was more serious than the elders had realized. Under normal circumstances, the surname committee members who are adjudicating a dispute among brothers will consult all the parties. Then, on a specified date, they will announce the final settlement. In this case, the surname committee simply accepted Zhou One's contention that his new tannery was equivalent to a two-fifths share and that the old tannery constituted the remaining three-fifths. The other three brothers felt that they had not been given an adequate opportunity to tell their side of the story, and when the announcement of the final settlement was made, they were furious.

Usually, when a settlement is announced, the surname committee will ask if anyone objects. Committee members will then be invited to a feast by the contending parties. Since these committee members customarily consult with all the disputants beforehand, these last steps are generally taken for granted. Indeed, asking whether anyone objects to the settlement is about as serious as the statement "speak now or forever hold your peace" at American weddings.

But on this day, to the apparent surprise of the surname committee and Zhou One, the third brother responded. To the question "Does anyone have any objections?" Mr. Zhou answered flatly, "Yes, I object. We have been given too much!"

Too much? Everyone was shocked. How could the three brothers be complaining that their shares were too large? But Mr. Zhou soon continued, "Let us take the two-fifths you have given our eldest brother, and give him the three-fifths."

His point, obviously, was that the younger brothers believed the three-fifths that they would divide among themselves was actually smaller than the two-fifths allocated to Zhou One. The three younger brothers thought that Zhou One's new tannery was so valuable because it had modern machines, which the older tannery did not have. Most important was a hydraulic press, an expensive machine which very few tanneries had at the time, and which they contended was worth more than all the other machines combined. Owners of a hydraulic press not only can produce superior quality leather but can also earn additional income by renting the use of the machine to others.

The Zhou elders therefore were obliged to mediate several more sessions among the Zhou brothers, but they made no headway in creating a consensus about what was to constitute the eldest brother's two-fifths share. As a last resort, they called in the chairman of one of the two tanning associations.

This man, Jia Lanpo, proposed that the eldest brother rectify the seeming imbalance between his share and that of his younger brothers by giving them additional cash compensation. When the youngest brothers expressed their doubts that Zhou One would actually turn over the money, Jia Lanpo promised to put up his own money for the amount owed as a bond. Zhou One agreed to this solution, but whether through greed and dishonesty (as claimed by the younger brothers) or inability (as he himself claimed), he never did compensate them with extra funds. Instead, Jia Lanpo paid the brothers back with the money he had guaranteed them. Worst of all, and unbeknownst to the three younger Zhou brothers, their own mother was repaying Jia by giving him monthly payments, taken from her own monthly allowance, for a rotating credit association.

The Zhous' mother previously had used part of her allowance to purchase live chickens, which she would take to be cooked at the home of whichever son she was eating with during a particular week. The Dhapa Chinese cook a number of chicken dishes that they believe are particularly nourishing for the elderly and the sick, and the chickens that their mother brought for cooking played a significant role, in the estimation of the Zhou brothers, in maintaining their mother's health. Mr. Zhou therefore thought it odd when his mother came to eat with his family one week without bringing any chicken. Then, after another month went by, when she returned to eat with his family, Mr. Zhou was sure he could detect a considerable decline in his mother's health. He asked her what was going on, and she finally disclosed the story about her payments to Jia Lanpo.

Furious, Mr. Zhou stormed over to Jia's tanning association headquarters. Shouting, "How could you do this to my mother!" he insisted that Jia Lanpo accept no more payments from his mother. Instead, the three younger Zhou brothers completed the monthly payments, thereby returning most of the extra money that they had received through the settlement negotiated by Jia Lanpo.

Thus, as specified in the surname association's original decision, the three youngest brothers ultimately divided the older tannery. Zhou One took possession of the new tannery, but within a few years he had sold it to a nonfamily member and emigrated to Canada. This outcome demonstrates the limits of the community's informal institutions and sanctions. For reasons specified in Chapter 3, few Chinese are willing to take matters out of the Chinese community to the Indian courts. Thus, if an individual is willing to ignore everyone and risk the consequent social stigma, not much can be done about it. Of course, most people are unwilling to risk this outcome, knowing that they may need help from community members at some future date. But in Zhou One's case, emigration was the final outcome. The knowledge that he was leaving the community no doubt lessened his interest in going along with the agreements that had been hammered out so tediously.

In the meantime, the three younger brothers had settled into a fairly amicable arrangement in the factory they shared. Each conducted a separate business within it and paid a set fee to a jointly managed fund for each piece of leather produced. This money was then utilized to pay for overhead expenses in the factory, such as maintenance and electricity.

By 1975, Zhou Two had also emigrated to Canada. Since he was not interested in returning to India, he sold his share of the tannery to the two youngest brothers, who expanded their businesses considerably over the next four years. Indeed, the demand for their finished leather was more than their two businesses could produce in one small factory. After considerable discussion between them as to who would be the "outpartner," Mr. Zhou's younger brother, Zhou Four, decided that he would be the one to leave their old tannery and build a new one (I consider these events in more detail in the next chapter). He sold his share of the old tannery to Mr. Zhou and utilized these funds, along with loans from other sources, to help with construction costs for his new tannery. For the next few years, while his new tannery was under construction, Zhou Four leased tannery space from Mr. Zhou, since he had already sold his share. Finally, when construction was completed in 1982, the new factory was dedicated in the series of rituals described at the beginning of this chapter. (See Figure 2 for a visual representation of the division of assets in the Zhou family.)

Despite the bitterness of the dispute between the Zhou brothers, family division did not lead them down a path of increasing poverty, as in the case of Deng Huilin's family. Rather, the two youngest brothers ultimately were left with tanneries of their own, and the two oldest brothers were each able to emigrate with a nest egg by selling their assets either to family outsiders, as in the case of the oldest brother, or to family members, as in the case of the second brother.

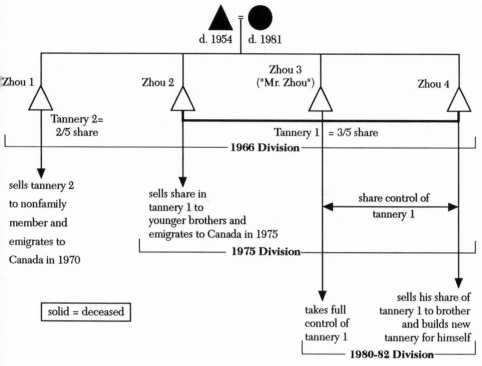

Figure 2. A contested division: Distribution of assets among the Zhou brothers

The Role of Surviving Parents

The story of family division in Mr. Zhou's family also reveals another problem commonly encountered by second- and third-generation tanners, namely the dilemma of what role a parent or parents should play in a family in which the brothers have divided up assets and live in separate residences. Mr. Zhou's mother moved in with the eldest son for a time, but she ate alternately with all four sons and received allowances from each of them in proportion to their shares. For other families in Dhapa, the problem may be resolved in another fashion. For example, if a son initiates family division when his parents are still active in the business, the parents will probably choose to live with the sons who did not initiate the split. In Qian Weigang's family, his eldest son decided to go into business on his own and go through the process

[197]

of family partition, even though Qian not only was still alive but was intimately involved in the family business. Qian's younger son, who was already married, continued in business with his father, who also continued to eat with the younger son's family.

Emigration is another alternative for surviving parents. They can live with married children abroad, many of whom need child care and are only too happy to rely on their parents for this service. This arrangement, however, is not without its difficulties for both generations, a topic I consider in the Epilogue.

Special Circumstances

Family division in certain Chinese families in Dhapa is made more difficult by the existence of complicating circumstances. When sons are adopted or when they are the offspring of their father's second marriage, a special set of problems may arise.

Adopted Sons and Daughters

In Dhapa, both sons and daughters are adopted, though for different reasons. In a later section of this chapter I discuss the important roles of daughters in family dynamics and the reasons families desire daughters enough to adopt them. For now what is important to know is that both sons and daughters are adopted, but that the implications for family division are not the same in each case.

When daughters are adopted in Dhapa, they do not create special problems at the time of family division. They normally marry out, and though they receive some wealth at the time of their marriage, they are not considered shareholders in the family estate. Moreover, I know of no case in the community in which the wealth transferred to an adopted daughter upon her marriage was different from that transferred to a daughter born into the family.

On the other hand, when the family estate is divided, adopted sons do not always fare as well as sons born into the family. This might at first seem curious, given that the logic of adopting sons within Chinese families seems more obvious than that for adopting daughters. Sons are necessary to carry on the family line and are important to parents' support in their later years. In families in which no son has been conceived or survived, adoption is usually an economic necessity. In fact, when one or more sons has been adopted and no natural sons have been born into the family, the adopted sons will inherit as if they were natural sons at the time of family division. But sometimes a natural son is born into a family after an adoption has taken place. Whereas some families make no distinction in inheritance between their natural and adopted sons, others not only force the adoptees to depart from home but also disinherit them.

Before such ruptures occur, mothers typically quarrel with their adopted sons. In several instances, reputed misbehavior by the adopted son or failure to assume responsibility within the business is the pretext for a final break. Yet although mothers have maneuvered to move out adopted sons so that a natural son could inherit everything, such deeds are generally frowned upon by the community. In Qiao Tanming's family, for instance, a natural son was severely injured in a tanning accident shortly after his adopted older brother was compelled to leave home. This incident occurred several years after Qiao's death, and many in the community thought it was divine retribution against his wife, who they felt had been unfair and unduly harsh to her adopted son.

Even if he is maneuvered out of a tanning business, an adopted son may still have some recourse. He may bring his grievances to his surname association, and its officers may demand that he be given some cash compensation for his share. This was the outcome for Qiao Tanming's adopted son. On the other hand, if the son has thereby lost his claim to a business, and if this business is expanding and profitable, he may rightly believe that cash compensation will never equal the profits that would have been gained by continued association with the business.

Sons of Second Wives

Like adopted sons, sons of second wives have not always fared as well as their brothers during family division. The problems associated with the sons of second wives occur under two different sets of circumstances. The first occurs when a man remarries after his first wife's death; the other, when a man actually takes a second wife while the first wife is still alive. A few cases of the latter type do exist in Dhapa, involving men who are now in their seventies and eighties. The public role and ritual status of a second wife is inferior to that of a first wife. Dhapa Chinese refer to the first wife as *da laopo*, or "senior wife," as opposed to the second wife, who is referred to as *xiao laopo*, or "junior wife." (The word *concubine* should *not* be used in this context, since one of its meanings in English is "a woman who cohabits with a man without marrying," and this definition does not apply to the Dhapa Chinese.)

Whether a man remarries after his wife's death, or whether he actually takes a second wife while his first is still living, there is likely to be a large age gap between the sons of each wife. The first wife's sons are likely to have worked in the business for many years before their brothers join them. Therefore, the sons of the first wife may be interested in partitioning the family assets long before it is in the interests of the younger brothers to do so. Furthermore, if a father has married a second wife while the first wife is still living, the sons of the first wife may be anxious to partition the family for other reasons as well. They may resent their father for rejecting their mother, and this may lead to increased friction between them.

Stephen Kong's family presents a good example of the problems encountered in such a situation. Stephen's grandfather, Kong Tienhua, went back to China in the late 1940s, where he married a second wife with whom he ultimately returned to Dhapa in 1953. By this time, however, two of Tienhua's eldest sons by the first wife were already conducting separate businesses within their father's tannery, although they had not gone through the process of family division. Hence, Tienhua had one set of sons who were already conducting businesses of their own and another set of sons who were in early childhood.

Tienhua's eldest sons, including Stephen's father, Mr. Kong, continued to conduct separate businesses for more than twenty years. Finally, in 1971, they agreed to draw up a family partition agreement. By this time, a whole host of complicating factors had crept into the situation. Not only were there offspring from two different wives, but there were also sons who had returned to China, and one son who had emigrated to Canada, all of whom had valid claims on the estate. In addition, both wives were still alive, as was Kong Tienhua. Simply dividing the estate among all the sons would leave open the tricky question of which son Tienhua and his second wife, not to mention his first wife, would reside with.

As with Mr. Zhou's family, this case was one that needed outside intervention. With the help of the Kong surname association elders, a settlement was finally agreed to and signed by the Kong family. Ac-

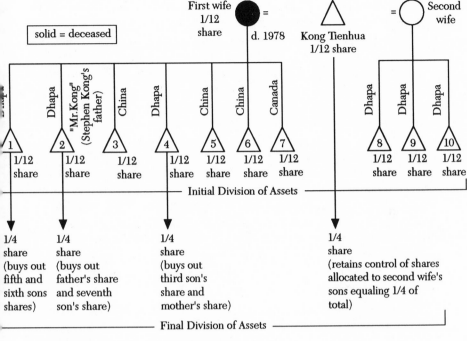

Figure 3. Division of property in the Kong family

cording to this agreement, each son was entitled to one-twelfth of the total estate. In addition, Kong Tienhua and his first wife were each allocated a one-twelfth share. Setting aside a share for the first wife was atypical, since women may have considerable input in decisions about how family property or funds are allocated, but do not usually receive property or assets themselves through the processes of family division.

This initial allocation of shares was really just a mechanism by which the first wife's three sons, who still remained in India, could consolidate larger shares. As Figure 3 shows, these three sons bought out their mother's share, as well as the shares of those brothers residing abroad and the share directly allocated to their father. This gave each of them a quarter share. (Ultimately, each of these sons built a factory of his own.) Meanwhile, Kong Tienhua also retained one-fourth of prepartition assets through his continued control of the shares apportioned to his second wife's three sons.

The sons of the second wife, therefore, ultimately received much less than their brothers. When all the buying and selling of shares was over, the amount allocated to all of them together was equal only to that held by each of the first wife's three sons who still resided in India.

There are cases in Dhapa in which sons of different wives have partitioned the family property equally. Deng Huilin's family (see Figure 1) divided their assets in such a manner, though they were hindered by the small size of the total pool they were dividing. Nevertheless, such a situation is often fraught with danger. The age difference alone means that sons of a first wife are likely to have invested much more time and energy into a family business than their younger brothers. Thus, some second wives have taken steps of their own to secure a better financial future for their sons. For instance, one woman who was in such a situation started her own illicit liquor business after her husband's death (women's role in this activity is discussed in Chapter 6). With her income from this business, this woman eventually launched her sons in a tanning business of their own.

The Role of Daughters

Although family division and inheritance normally proceed along patrilineal lines, daughters—particularly married daughters—have played critical roles in their natal families over the second and third generations. Indeed, I found that the roles played by daughters within their natal families in Dhapa were at some variance with the roles often described in both Chinese works and Western sources.

Views about the role of daughters in the Chinese family are articulated in a variety of Chinese works and traditions. For example, Mencius admonishes that there is no greater unfiliality than to have no heirs, that is, no sons (Baker 1979:46), and there is documentary evidence of such practices as female infanticide and the giving out of female infants (see page 236) as "little daughter-in-laws" (Wolf and Huang 1980). In fact, in the wake of China's One-Child Policy there has been a disastrous rise in female infanticide and violence against women who bear female children (Wasserstrom 1984). It is often hard to find a vision of daughters in the Chinese family as anything much better than "small happiness," the words used by an old peasant in Carma Hinton's film of the same title to describe his attitudes toward the birth of a daughter.

In Western scholarship on the Chinese family, emphasis on the dynamics of patrilineality and patrilocality has also usually underscored the importance of sons (see Baker 1979 for a good synthesis of work on the Chinese family). But as pointed out in Chapter 1, some scholars acknowledge the importance of patrilineality yet insist that other dynamics are also at work within the Chinese family, thereby providing us with a slightly altered view of the role of daughters. These scholars emphasize the importance of affinal and matrilateral ties (see Ahern 1975; Freedman 1970; Gallin 1960; Watson 1985, 1981; Wolf 1970), the significance of unmarried daughters' contributions to the family as wage earners (Salaff 1981; Kung 1984; Greenhalgh 1985b), and the role of the "uterine family," the personal ties that mothers forge with their own children within larger patrilineal units.

But none of these approaches really challenges the notion that sons are of primary value. A daughter's value, insofar as she has value, is at best portrayed as her usefulness in supporting her brothers and enriching the patriline. When scholars stress the importance of affinal ties, for instance, they focus not solely on the role of daughter but on the important benefits that families can reap through ties to their affines, ties which are established because of a woman's marriage, but which are frequently pursued by males. As Bernard Gallin states in an article on affinal and matrilateral ties, many of the contacts between *ch'in ch'i* [*qinqi*], or affines, are "limited to the male members of the family. . . . If . . . the woman does accompany the men back to her native home, she usually dresses up and spends most of her time talking and helping in the kitchen and back rooms with her female relatives. The men, on the other hand, are warmly entertained in the main room of the house and introduced to other guests, usually the host's *ch'in ch'i* [*qinqi*] through other relatives. Often such meetings also lead to new contacts and friendships" (1960:639).

Likewise, Margery Wolf's account of the uterine family makes clear that it is a woman's ties to her son that are most critical and long-lasting. As Wolf states, there comes a time when a little girl discovers that "when the mother speaks of the future, she speaks of her son's future"(1972:34).

Finally, the analyses of the impact of wage labor on the status of daughters in Hong Kong and Taiwan emphasize that working daughters can be a real asset to their families, but their worth is precisely the sort that reemphasizes the primary importance of sons. Indeed, Susan Greenhalgh suggests that by working and remitting their wages to their elders, daughters both repay the cost of their upbringing and finance the education and career development of their brothers. All of this is done within a relatively short time span, before daughters marry and leave the family forever. Greenhalgh therefore suggests that parents are more "selfish" when it comes to daughters. Parents expect daughters to repay the cost of their upbringing in a relatively short span of time. But sons can stretch this repayment out over the course of their entire adult lifetime, during which they dispense care, concern, and support to their aging parents (1985a:270). This model of filial daughters increases the emphasis on their secondary status in the family—they are not only an added expense ("goods on which one loses one's capital" [Baker 1979:41]) but must now return this expense before they depart the family for marriage.

In Dhapa, however, although unmarried daughters may work, they rarely remit their earnings to their natal families and usually use their earnings on personal spending money. This phenomenon can in part be explained by the current prosperity of the community. Nonetheless, comments made to me over the years in which I lived in the community, and a careful analysis of patterns of interaction and adoption, reveal that both mothers and fathers in Dhapa do place a high value on daughters, one that goes beyond an interest in what daughters can do to further the interests of the patriline or the life-chances of their brothers.

First, mothers often stated that they experienced an emotional closeness and intimacy with their daughters that was important to them. Daughters were seen as people you could talk to. Second, both mothers and fathers emphasized the added zest that married daughters and their families added to their lives—family gatherings without the participation of these daughters and their families were imagined as dull and lifeless.

In addition, an analysis of the relationships between married daughters and their natal families indicates that though affinal ties are critical in this community, as in many other Chinese settings, married daughters are not simply the medium through which ties are enacted, but active agents—they help their natal families achieve important family goals, and at the same time they utilize these ties to advance their own interests. Therefore, affinal ties are not simply the work of men who are affiliated with different patrilineal entities, and who utilize and pursue such connections to better their own political and economic positions in the community.

These values ascribed to daughters—the intimacy that parents, particularly mothers, experience with them, the festive nature of occasions on which they return to their natal homes with their families, and the importance of connections made by and through them—create strong desires for daughters as well as sons. Interestingly, all these positive values come to full realization only *after* a daughter's marriage, the period when, according to many of the other models I have considered (the patrilineal family, the uterine family, and the filial daughter), a daughter's worth to her family is already exhausted.

Before considering these positive valuations in more detail, I must establish that families really do want daughters. In the following section, therefore, I examine both ideas about family size, as well as patterns of adoption and sterilization.

The "Ideal" Family

Simlien was visiting her brother in Toronto, Canada. It was the first time she had visited Canada, and she sardonically complained about her "boring" life in India. The majority of Calcutta Hakka who have emigrated to Canada are not in businesses of their own but work in wage labor. Simlien, noticing the many Hakka women in Toronto who were employed, and therefore working outside the house, remarked, "For us, all we do is get married, have two boys and two girls, and that's it."

While her comment revealed dissatisfaction with the roles of women in her home community, or perhaps the fact that having just arrived in Canada she was still in the thralls of a "honeymoon" period attending her first encounters with a new and different society, her statement also articulated a common theme that emerged in my discussions with many other Calcutta Hakka. For most, the ideal family includes several daughters and sons—not sons exclusively. Patterns of adoption, the timing of sterilization (which is always performed on the woman in this community), and the recognition of daughterlike relationships are clearly in accordance with this ideal.

An analysis of the timing of sterilization is particularly revealing. Whereas earlier generations practiced virtually no form of birth control, hysterectomy has been utilized as a means of ending a woman's fertility since at least the early 1960s, and almost all married women in this community undergo this operation when they wish to put an end to childbearing. But from an examination of family size and composition in the community, it is apparent that women wait until the birth of

[205]

at least one daughter before taking such a step. There are few sibling sets born since the early 1960s in which there are no daughters.

While I was in the field in the early 1980s, most women in their childbearing years underwent hysterectomies after the birth of a third or fourth child. But many based their decision on the birth of a daughter. Typical of the attitudes articulated was that of a friend of mine. Aifang was sterilized after the birth of her third child, a daughter. But she was emphatic in her insistence that she would not have undergone the operation if her third child, like the first two, had been a son.

What happens to families with no daughters? Some decide on adoption. In a few cases these are "lead in" adoptions, that is, a daughter is adopted before any children are born in the hope that she will "lead in" a son (see Wolf and Huang 1980:246). In other cases, adoption occurs after a succession of sons has been born, revealing that there are other reasons for adopting daughters besides their role in bringing in sons.

In a few instances a woman who is not actually a daughter is recognized as one. For example, in a rather unusual, but still very revealing, case a woman remarried after her husband died. She had been a second wife, and at that time, her dead husband's first wife was still alive and had a daughter who continued to reside with her. Several years later, after the first wife had died, and this daughter had married, the second wife's new husband recognized this daughter as his own. From that time on, the "daughter" returned to their home on festival days, such as during the New Year celebrations, just as a "real" daughter would have done. The reason given for this arrangement was that the couple had no daughters of their own but had fervently desired one.

These examples demonstrate that daughters are far from unwanted; indeed, they are actively wished for. Why is this so? I believe that the answers can be found through an examination of the roles played by married daughters in the lives of their natal families.

Intimacy and Festivity

There is no doubt that women see their daughters as individuals whom they can talk with, and several young women articulated this view to me when I asked them why they wanted to have daughters. Daughters can and do establish emotionally satisfying relationships with their mothers which endure long after their marriages. Daughters in the Calcutta Hakka community are frequent visitors to their parents' homes. In addition to the festival days when they show up with entire families in tow, they may come alone, or with one or two small children, on ordinary days.

Elderly women often utilize the power they have slowly built up in their families to ensure that they have contact with their daughters on many occasions. One particularly interesting case was that of an elderly mother whose five daughters were all married, and all resided in the tanning community. Among families involved in tanning, it is customary for wives or mothers-in-law to pocket funds that are earned from the sale of waste products created by the tanning process. In this family, the two married sons controlled the profits from the leather business, but their mother had complete control over the funds she gathered from the sale of these waste products. She used these funds to pay for a weekly gathering, in which each of her five daughters and their families would return to their natal home for Sunday lunch.

Nor are fathers indifferent to events and crises in their daughters' lives. Married daughters may chat more with their mothers. But if trouble strikes, their fathers may also become involved. This is most common in the case of family division, or potential family division. One woman told me of the difficulties she used to have with her in-laws. It was her father, she said, who had encouraged her and her husband to divide the family and establish a separate business.

Despite this fairly regular contact, it is on the annual festival days and during important life-cycle crises and celebrations that the presence and contributions of married daughters are felt most significantly. One middle-aged woman in the community summed up this feeling well when she told me, "The best of times are when your daughter returns with her family [*hui niang jia*]. There is a lot of hustle and bustle [*renao*]. If you don't have daughters you can never experience this kind of happiness. Everyday will be the same as any other." In addition to the return of a married daughter and her family during the New Year celebration and on other important days in the annual ritual cycle, the presence of married daughters is critical during the weddings of their brothers, birthday celebrations for their parents (celebrated every ten years starting with age sixty-one), house-moving ceremonies, and most significantly, during their parents' funeral proceedings.

As the title of a paper by Bernard and Rita Gallin so succinctly states, "daughters cry at your funeral" (1988). But, in addition, daughters are more responsible in following through on the entire host of obligations that ensue after a parent's death. During the seven weeks that follow the death of an individual, for instance, his or her soul is said to wander until, at the conclusion of this period, it is reincarnated in another being. The offerings that one makes during this period can have a critical effect on the nature of the soul's new incarnation. Many families, therefore, stage a small ritual every week for seven weeks after the death of a parent. But whereas sons usually participate in the last of the seven ceremonies, it is married daughters who perform the rest and who are responsible for all of the planning. Hence, it seems reasonable to conclude that sons are still primarily responsible for their parents' material welfare, married daughters for their spiritual welfare.

Connections

A married daughter does not necessarily confine her connections and bonds with her natal family to the emotional and spiritual realms. Indeed, in certain cases, a daughter may step in where a son or sons have failed to fulfill their duties through either negligence or misfortune. Thus, Xue Youcai, whose case was discussed in the preceding chapter, asked his sister and her husband to manage the business when he went blind. Later, this sister's husband died, and one of her younger brothers left his job as an airplane mechanic to join the business. Though another brother ultimately stepped into the situation, the Xues' sister has continued to play an extremely active role in the business. Although they have not yet gone through a process of family partition, family members insist that this sister will be treated as a full shareholder when partition does occur.

Brothers may also rely on contacts with sisters during periods of crisis. When brothers are in the throes of family division, for instance, they may move their businesses out of the family's factory until the proper allocation of space, money, and machinery is finally resolved. During these periods, they may rent space from a sister and her husband in another tannery. And when brothers emigrate, they are just as likely to initially reside with a sister's family as with a brother's family (as discussed earlier, both brothers and sisters play important roles in sponsoring the immigration of other family members).

In some situations, the conflict between a married sister and a brother or brothers may be mentioned as a prominent cause of family division, and as a factor that is as significant as the frictions between brothers or between sisters-in-law. This is most likely to occur when a woman's natal family is renting or leasing factory space in her husband's tannery. What is interesting about these cases, however, is that they reveal that after marriage, sisters are not always disinterested spectators in the business affairs of their brothers.

In the second and third generations of Dhapa Chinese families, not only mothers and wives but also sisters and daughters have played critical roles. In Chapter 6, I concentrated on the roles of mothers and wives in the division of labor in the family business. Here I have illustrated the ways in which daughters and sisters are also valued, not only for the emotional intimacy they provide their parents, and not only for their role in protecting their parents' welfare in the afterlife, but also for the active roles they play in family partition and emigration.

Cooperation

In this chapter I have emphasized the fissive quality of businesses and families among second- and third-generation Dhapa Chinese. This fission has sometimes led to diminution in the size of businesses, but more often, through a combination of emigration, the buying out of shares, and the continual expansion of business opportunities, Dhapa's tanners have been able to utilize the processes of family division in ways that have maintained or enhanced their economic viability. This has been true even for families like Mr. Zhou's, in which family division has been rife with dispute and discord. It is important to point out that the structures of patriliny, patrilocality, and partible inheritance are continuously reproduced by community members as they apply them to their daily lives. The existence of disputes or discord should not blind us to the fact that these elements of family structure have often been manipulated to the economic and political benefit of many Dhapa Chinese. (Whether these underlying principles of family structure will continue to be reproduced among community members who have emigrated is a separate topic which I consider in the Epilogue.)

Although family division may be inevitable, it can be postponed for long periods. Several of the cases examined here involve brothers who

operated separate businesses for many years before actually partitioning the family estate. In addition, as I have shown, brothers often
emigrate long before family partition, thereby retaining their claim on
their family's business in India. Some brothers continue to work together profitably in a joint family—indeed, joint families are associated with Dhapa's largest businesses. In such joint families, there is
little impetus to go through family division, and one would expect that
such families would be likely to follow the normative pattern, partitioning only after the death of one or more members of the senior
generation.

Finally, family division does not end the ongoing relationships
among siblings, and family members still make use of connections to
both their brothers and sisters. Whether or not a family has partitioned its estate, for instance, has no bearing on the use of familial ties
in emigration. Indeed, as we have seen, not only brothers, but also
sisters, are likely to play a role in sponsoring the newcomer.

Brothers who remain in Dhapa may also continue to cooperate in
various ways after family division. They may pool their funds to buy a
tannery, even though they plan to run separate businesses within it. In
Qian Weigang's family, for instance, the two sons cooperated in building a tannery, despite the fact that they had gone through the process
of family partition, and the fact that the older brother had been running a separate business for many years. Each brother runs a separate
business within the new tannery, eats separately, and lives in separate
quarters. However, had they not cooperated, it is doubtful that either
of them would have succeeded in building an entire factory of his own.

At the very least, it is usually assumed that if an individual wishes to
sell his share of a tannery, he will first offer it to one of his brothers. In
Mr. Zhou's family, for instance, the second brother sold out his share
to brothers three and four in order to take cash with him when he
emigrated, and the fourth brother sold his share to the third brother in
order to gather funds to build a new tannery. Thus, a spirit of cooperation among siblings is not necessarily confined to the period in which
they share economic resources.

On the other hand, relationships that are bitter prior to family
partition often continue that way long after the split. For example, the
decision of Mr. Zhou's eldest brother, when he emigrated, to sell his
tannery to an outsider and not to his brothers was a reflection of bad
relations that had begun long before family division. As I reveal in the
next chapter, it was a harbinger of more trouble to come.

[8]

Individualism, Holism, and the
Profit Motive: Mr. Zhou's Story

"So, in 1955, that time I was very young. . . . Nineteen or twenty like that. When my mother fell sick . . . she is very sick lying nearly half dead. Then she told me that, see I don't think I can pass this time. . . . So I heard it, then I cry, then I pray to God, even if I die, let the sickness fall upon me. . . . So I fell sick, I was down for a week's time . . . it is so hot, I am so thirsty also, because of high fever. But in my mind I was very happy because I see my mother getting better. . . . And then, after a week or ten days, so I recovered from my sickness. . . . So, since then, I can absolutely very proudly say I have never felt sick. So I think that is my return, my boon. Boon means the return. . . . Nowadays I told quite a lot of persons . . . you have to *xiao shun nide muqin, fuqin* [show filial devotion to your mother and father], then you will get this type of return!"

It was the end of July 1989, a muggy monsoon afternoon in Calcutta. Tears welled up in Mr. Zhou's eyes as he recalled this pivotal incident in his life. As Mr. Zhou spoke about his past experiences and relationships that afternoon, new complexities in the entrepreneurial ideology of the Dhapa community were revealed to me.

Throughout this book, I have emphasized the interaction among entrepreneurial ideology, family relationships, and the constraints of the host society. In Chapters 5 and 7, I discussed how, with an eye to such constraints, the Dhapa Chinese manipulate family relationships in order to attain both political and entrepreneurial goals. And in Chapter 4 I described how in Dhapa the entrepreneurial ethic itself is neither a straightforward nor internally unambiguous set of beliefs and practices, but is riddled with simultaneously held and seemingly contradictory ideas about fate and individual power, calculation and risk.

But Mr. Zhou's recollections exemplified in vivid fashion the ways in which the entrepreneurial ethic, as it existed in Dhapa and as it was influenced by both family and host society, contained complex views not only about fate and control, but also about the self and its relationship to others.

In the United States we are barraged every day with the autobiographies and biographies of "self-made" men, a cultural form which has changed and evolved along with transformations in the structure of American capitalism (see Traube 1989). But few published works are devoted to such a character type in "non-Western" cultures and within capitalist contexts.[1] Mr. Zhou's story, I began to realize, might not only help me to understand the interaction between ideologies of the self and entrepreneurship in the context of the Dhapa community, but also shed light on larger questions concerning the relationship of entrepreneurship to views of the self in different cultural contexts.

If I was searching for individuals who most closely approximated the American "rags to riches" stereotype, Mr. Zhou would not be an ideal choice. With an old factory, employing some thirty workers, he stood squarely in the middle of the community's status hierarchy—a hierarchy almost directly determined by one's wealth relative to other community members. There were certainly larger businesses. A few even employed more than one hundred workers each and carried on extensive export operations. But on the other hand, Mr. Zhou employed far more than the community's median number of nine workers per firm. In addition, the income of even the smallest Chinese tanning enterprises far exceeded that of the average middle-class Indian, and Mr. Zhou often proudly referred to the fact that he had a great deal more cash on hand than those whose earnings were limited to their salary.

I therefore encouraged Mr. Zhou to delve more deeply into his recollections. For many hours, over the course of several days, we sat together as he recounted those incidents in his life that he regarded as

---

[1] A notable exception is John Kelly's fascinating work on Gujarati merchants in Fiji (see Kelly 1989). In addition, autobiographies of some of Japan's most powerful industrialists have recently started to be marketed in the United States. They have yet to be analyzed in terms of their self-presentations or the reactions of the varied audiences to whom they are aimed.

significant. Indeed, once he began to speak, his story flowed out with few hesitations, and I had the eerie feeling that I was listening not to a spontaneous verbal response but to a completed text with chapters. Mr. Zhou told his story in several distinct parts—each associated with a subplot involving his relationship with a particular family member: most important were those with his older brother, his younger brother, and his mother.

This organization should not have surprised me, for one of the most prevalent scholarly paradigms about Chinese notions of selfhood and personhood[2] contends that "sociocentric" or "familial" orientations dominate over egocentric or individualistic ones. In this paradigm, which I discuss more fully later in the chapter, it is generally held that within Chinese cultural contexts—whether one is focusing on the experiences of a self, characterizations of self and other, or notions about selfhood and personhood—identity is primarily experienced and conceptualized in terms of relationships with others. Such a view of personhood is often contrasted with a model of personhood that is said to dominate in the modern West. These "Western" notions of personhood and selfhood are described as being *relatively* more individualistic than those of the "non-West," catering to a penchant for thinking of both the self and others as almost context-free and distinctive personalities who exist prior to particular relationships and status categories. Those who hold such constructions of personhood are said to conceive of individuals as entering into relationships that are largely self-generated and contractual, rather than obligatory and embedded in preexisting social roles.

But Mr. Zhou's account was too varied and complex to be pigeonholed so easily. First, while he saw himself and others as enmeshed in a web of social and familial obligations and hierarchies, he

---

[2] In this chapter, I use both the terms *personhood* and *selfhood*, for they refer to distinct but inextricably related concepts. Grace Harris characterizes the distinction in this way: self can be characterized as "the human being as a locus of experience" (1989:601), whereas person involves consideration of a human being as an "agent." She states, "In this sense, to be a person means to have a certain standing (not 'status') in a social order, as agent-in-society. Consequently, it is not sufficient to a discussion of personhood to talk about people as centers of experience, selves. To be a person means to be a 'somebody' who authors conduct construed as action" (1989:602). Clearly, both concepts emerge in the course of considering a life history. One considers, on the one hand, the subject's articulation of personal thoughts and feelings at a particular time, and of the meaning of personal actions as well as the actions of others, and, on the other, the subject's description of his or her relationship to others.

sometimes assessed these obligatory hierarchical relationships in terms of their benefits for the individual, particularly through the use of entrepreneurial metaphors such as "returns" on investments (as in the quotation that begins this chapter). Furthermore, while he acknowledged that the profit motive sometimes harmonized with familial role obligations, he also saw circumstances in which the two worked at cross purposes. Indeed, in his description of family relationships, he alternated between an emphasis on the critical importance of obligation and love, and a feeling that there is an almost natural, irrepressible urge to profit oneself, even at the expense of other family members, through the application of individual cunning, intelligence, and quickwittedness. In particular, it is in his descriptions of economic transactions among his brothers that Mr. Zhou expressed the greatest ambivalence about human motivation.

In this chapter, therefore, I describe and then attempt to account for the particular ambivalences and seeming contradictions in Mr. Zhou's account, focusing on the relationship between his internal formulations and the contradictions of the surrounding context. I also ask what scenarios and relationships brought his inner conflicts to the fore and why. In the process, I closely inspect the relationship between the micropolitics of the family economy and the values and imperatives of the larger economic, political, and ethnic context in which it is embedded.

Before I turn to Mr. Zhou's story, however, I must briefly summarize several current theoretical debates that are raging within anthropological and sinological circles. These debates will provide a context that can help the reader to make connections between the particularities of Mr. Zhou's story and the Dhapa Chinese community, and larger questions about the construction of selfhood within both Chinese culture and market economies in general. A consideration of these general issues can, in turn, provide a deeper understanding of processes within Dhapa Chinese entrepreneurial families in particular.

The remainder of this chapter is therefore organized as follows. In the first section I summarize existing literature on concepts of selfhood and personhood in Chinese settings. In the second section I suggest that an examination of the aforementioned scholarship on personhood indicates that cultural constructions of personhood may vary within one culture according to the domain of action or the social identities of the transactors. But my data go farther, suggesting that in a given cultural context, individuals may not only bring variable understandings of personhood to bear on different domains of action, but actually *hold conflicting and contesting models of personhood with reference to even one transactional realm.* Relevant literature on "heteroglossia" and the "dialogical" nature of thought is considered here. Then, in the third section, Mr. Zhou's life story serves as a case study illustrating the preceding points. In the final section, I attempt to ground this analysis within a larger context, arguing that Mr. Zhou's contesting visions are not merely personal or idiosyncratic, but derive from real conflicts inherent in the cultural, social, and economic context of his life.

Theorists in Search of the Chinese "Person"

As noted earlier, within the literature on notions of personhood in Chinese society, one approach emphasizes the relative predominance of holistic, hierarchical, and sociocentric orientations as opposed to individualistic and contractual ones. A second approach seeks to modify this view and emphasizes that both individualism and holism exist within Chinese culture, contending that these orientations vary according to the realm of action and/or period of history and context that one is investigating. Others question the dichotomy between holism and individualism itself. In this section, I summarize the arguments of those who underscore the predominance of holism in Chinese orientations; then, I briefly review the arguments of those who dissent from this position. This synopsis is obviously not meant to be exhaustive, but to give a sense of the parameters in which the discussion has taken place.

I should point out here that I do not wish to create "straw men" to demolish. Certainly, no scholar contends that Chinese culture is so completely holistic as to exclude all individualistic or egocentric outlooks. But there *is* a serious debate about the degree to which holistic orientations dominate in Chinese contexts and about which social situations and relationships are most conducive to such orientations (see Oxfeld 1992 for a summary of a parallel debate among Indianists).

Orientation A: Holism Predominates

Marcel Mauss was probably the first, and certainly one of the most influential scholars, to argue that the concept of a person as a unique individual who existed prior to and before the development of any

[215]

particular social relation, was a Western one. In China, according to Mauss, "birth-order, rank and the interplay of the social classes settle the names and life style of the individual, his 'face'. . . . His individuality is his *ming*, his name. China has preserved these archaic notions, yet at the same time has removed from individuality every trace of its being eternal and indissoluble. The name, the *ming*, represents a collective noun, something springing from elsewhere: one's corresponding ancestor bore it, just as it will fall to the descendant of its present bearer. . . . Other nations have known or adopted ideas of the same kind. Those who have made of the human person a complete entity, independent of all others save God, are rare" (1985:14).

Mauss was not a professional sinologist, yet many of these sinologists also find a holistic, rather than an individualistic, model of personhood predominating within Chinese culture. Thus, Donald Munro writes that values like uniqueness, privacy, autonomy, and the notion that "each individual person possesses key traits independent of any social relations" are undeveloped in China (1985:16). And he goes on to state that "some Western accounts of individual rights and of autonomy rationalize or even celebrate competition. One does not find in these Chinese writings any counterpart of the 'hidden hand' which, for the Westerner, presumably ensures that social competition will be constructive" (1985:21).[3]

Likewise, though Wei-ming Tu's discussions of Confucianism emphasize the notion of self-development, he is quick to point out that self-development for the Confucian is eminently social. Says Tu, "The living Confucian is also aware that the idea of learning for the sake of the self could not have meant a quest for one's individuality. . . . Self, in the classical Confucian sense, referred to a center of relationships" (1985:53). He continues, "The cultivated self is not private property that we carefully guard against intrusion from outside. The ego that has to be protected against submersion in the waves of social demand is what the Confucians refer to as *ssu* (the privatized self, the small self, the self that is a closed system). The true self, on the contrary, is public-spirited, and the great self is the self that is an open system" (1985:57).

Chad Hansen elaborates on the notion that holism, rather than individualism, dominates Chinese thought. The dichotomy of "part/ whole" rather than "one/many" characterizes Chinese linguistic forms,

---

[3] Munro does acknowledge, however, that until the eighteenth century, holistic values were also an important aspect of Western thought (1985:22).

Hansen states, and therefore predisposes Chinese to describe the world as a set of interrelated, dependent parts, rather than interchangeable individualistic units. So whereas Western thought is atomistic, Chinese thought is holistic (Hansen 1985:47).

This holistic mode of thought, according to Hansen and others, is characteristic of descriptions of the human world as well as of nature. Thus, desirable attributes like *ren* (perfect virtue) and *xiao* (filiality) can be achieved only in a social context, through interaction with others, particularly in the familial setting (King 1985:59). This point is echoed by Francis Hsu, who asserts that Chinese virtues tend to be conceived as relational rather than individualistic, and that Chinese art and fiction tend to be situation-centered whereas Western art and fiction are individual-centered (1983:280). Indeed, almost all of Hsu's works (1968, 1971, 1973, 1983) emphasize and contrast different aspects of Western individualism with the more situation-centered, holistic, and kinship-oriented Chinese.

Hsu's orientation has influenced a number of motivational studies as well. For instance, Anne Pusey and Richard Wilson, in a comparative study of "achievement motivation" among Chinese and Americans, found strong "achievement motivation" in both groups. But the Chinese, they argue, wanted to achieve for different reasons than the Americans. Whereas the Americans in their sample scored higher on achievement motivation as "the result of independence training" (1982:197), the Chinese scored higher on achievement motivation for reasons of "face consciousness and group orientedness" (1982:197). Quoting Pusey's earlier work, they contend that Chinese who achieve "tend to explain their motive for achievement in group terms and attribute their success to their groups, teachers and parents" (1982:199). This outlook is a result of "training [in] identifying one's self with [the] group and the pressure on conforming to the group's values" (1982:199).

The social orientation of the Chinese has also been emphasized in a recent anthropological study of emotion among rural Chinese villagers. Sulamith Heins Potter, the author of this study, contends that in the United States individual emotions are viewed as the building blocks of all social relationships. Thus, "it is assumed that social relationships are continuously created by individuals and maintained by individual feeling and individual enactment. Relationships are derived from and affirmed by feeling, and feelings are direct expressions of the self" (1988:18). On the other hand, Potter states, in rural China emotion is viewed as almost epiphenomenal. That is, while rural Chinese

[217]

villagers do not deny the existence of emotion, and indeed, with the exception of romantic love, they express emotions like rage, sorrow, and happiness quite openly, they do not view individual emotional experience as constitutive of social order. In her words, "An emotion is never the legitimizing rationale for any socially significant action and there is no cultural theory that social structure rests on emotional ties. Thus, social relationships persist legitimately without an emotional basis, either real or fictive" (1988:185). Social relationships in rural China, insists Potter, need only be affirmed by outward behavior, particularly through the willingness to work for one another, rather than through "inner emotional response" (1988:185). Thus, "the Chinese believe that a person derives social meaning primarily from social context, rather than from within; they are, in a word, sociocentric" (1988:186). Indeed, says Potter, it is precisely because of its ability to undermine social structure, since it can create relationships "whether they have structural significance or not" (1988:199), that romantic love is viewed with great suspicion by rural Chinese villagers.

Orientation B: Holism and Individualism in Complex Combinations

In a recent paper Arthur and Joan Kleinman make a case for going beyond the simple dichotomy of "non-Western" sociocentrism versus "Western" individual-centeredness. The Kleinmans cite Potter's essay as an example of this dichotomization, and they go on to state that her position exemplifies "one of the basic orientations of contemporary psychological anthropology" (1989:18). Those who follow this approach, they argue, are falling into the trap described by Edward Said in *Orientalism* (1978). For "what evidence is adduced must (1) portray homogeneous, unidimensional stereotypes, not real people, (2) it must discount examples to the opposite . . . and (3) above all it must leave out any shared human qualities that suggest there is an obdurately panhuman grain to human conditions" (1989:19).

Likewise, Mark Elvin, in a sweeping historical review of conceptions of the self in China as revealed in literature and philosophical texts, also dissents from the view that the notion of the individual was not an important category in China. As he points out, Mauss was simply mistaken in his description of the "re-use of personal names by descendants" since "this practice had died out [by the third-century B.C. and] . . . ever since, Chinese personal names have been almost unique to the individual, a stock of perhaps several million appellations. By comparison, our limited repetoire of 'Johns' and 'Marys' is meagre" (1985:157). Indeed, in Elvin's survey of Chinese philosophical thought over the millennia, he stresses the great variety of schools of thought. Some, like Mencius, emphasized that the individual was "a microcosm" of all things in the world (1985:166), whereas the Taoists strove for individual immortality, though paradoxically, this was ultimately achieved through "absorption [of the individual] into the workings of nature" (1985:167). The same sort of paradox can be found, according to Elvin, in many neo-Confucian thinkers, who, like Mencius, saw the individual as a "microcosm reflecting a macrocosm." But, at the same time, "while this gave the self an irremovable centrality as the carrier of moral action, it also meant that any distinctive individuality . . . was for the same reason morally somewhat suspect" (1985:174).

Elvin's main point, however, is that Chinese thought is too vast, and has too long a history, to simply state that the self is either a central category or an unimportant one. Furthermore, in many of the schools of thought that he discusses, it is through individuals that more cosmic aims are achieved, and it is through these cosmic aims that individuals perfect themselves. To call such thought either "individualistic" or "holistic" is to simplify its import. The Kleinmans make a parallel point in their discussion of the Chinese word *renqing*, which they define as "the emotional response of an individual who confronts various concrete situations in daily life" (1989:22). *Renqing* can be thought of as understanding and empathy, but it is can also be repaid and exchanged between persons. In this sense, the Kleinmans argue, it is "both social and deeply personal" (1989:24).

In fact, it is noteworthy that several recent works by Chinese scholars also challenge the holistic/individualistic dichotomy. Nan Lin, for instance, in an exhaustive treatment of the Chinese family system, points to a characterization made by many indigenous Chinese writers, who portray individual Chinese as considerate and caring while describing Chinese as a group as "selfish, careless, cruel, morally decadent, lacking in public morals and respect for laws and incapable of cooperation for the common good" (1988:66).

Admitting that this dichotomy is overdrawn, Lin nevertheless goes on to ask if particular features of the Chinese kinship system, specifically the rules of resource transfers, affect Chinese attitudes and behavior. Resource transfers, he states, can be of two types—transfers of authority and transfers of property. But different kinship systems place different priorities on these types of transfers. In the Chinese kinship system, greater emphasis is placed on the transfer of authority than the transfer of property, thereby stressing the importance of sentiment and loyalty, rather than skills, as "transfer criteria" (1988:81). This contrasts with the Japanese system in which both authority and property transfer are equally valued. Hence, in the Japanese system an eldest son can be bypassed by the father and replaced by a son-in-law, or even a nonrelative, if the father thinks that this individual will manage the property or firm in a more efficient manner than the son.

The rules of resource transfer, states Lin, can explain a great deal about behavior. On the one hand, "because of its emphasis on authority rather than property relations and its insistence on bloodline demarcation" the Chinese family "strongly promotes loyalty through filial piety and discourages the desire and opportunity to form other entities with outsiders" (1988:89). Lin concludes that "while the family is the reference point for the self, once outside the family, Chinese become totally self-centered. . . . When it comes to familial matters, Chinese are very group oriented and group conscious [but]. . . Relationships with the larger entity and other individuals are maintained and promoted so long as they help maintain and promote self interest and, therefore, family interests" (1988:92).

However, Lin admits that even though the Chinese kinship system emphasizes sentiment and loyalty between the generations, problems crop up in relations between the brothers, for Chinese resource transfer criteria are also "heterogeneous"—that is, authority is transferred to the eldest son, but property is inherited by all sons. Hence, once the father dies, the bonds of sentiment and loyalty weaken. The eldest brother, unlike the father, does not have a say in resource transfers to his younger siblings. Hence, they "have nothing much to gain by being subservient to him" (1988:81).

Through such an examination of the rules of resource transfer, Lin attempts to explain what appear to be contradictory elements of Chinese behavior in terms of the context of action. The family is viewed as creating a context in which actions are holistic and sociocentric. Once outside the family, however, actions and even justifying ideologies become much more egocentric and individualistic. This is an advance over those theories that posit oversimplified holistic actors. But *the variety of orientations that exist within the family itself are not devel-*

oped. Thus, while the contradictions between brothers are alluded to, they are not elaborated upon.

Likewise, in another recent treatment of the Chinese family by Kwang-kuo Hwang, different *spheres* of Chinese social life are described as entailing different rules of exchange. Among family, kin, and close friends, says Hwang, the "expressive component always claims precedence over [the] . . . instrumental component" (1987:949). So even when one utilizes such personal ties to gain temporary access to a social or material resource, these relationships cannot be characterized as fundamentally instrumental in nature. Hence, states Hwang, "with a view to attaining his material goals, an individual must establish instrumental ties with other people outside his family . . . when one attempts to establish an instrumental tie, the relationship serves only as a means or an instrument to attain other goals" (1987:95). Hwang also acknowledges that some relationships entail what he calls "mixed ties." These involve some expressive components but are also deeply influenced by norms of reciprocity in which status, face, and connections (*guanxi*) can be traded for both material and affective advantages.

Like Lin, therefore, Hwang describes a much more complex Chinese social world and orientation than that described by many of the social theorists discussed in this chapter. But also, like Lin, Hwang does not investigate the possible combinations of holistic and individualistic motivations and justifying ideologies that are utilized to understand relationships within the family itself, particularly relationships among brothers. In my discussion of Mr. Zhou's life story, I will pay close attention to the latter, for as I hope to demonstrate, it is in relationships among brothers that the greatest potential for such conflicting motivations and ideologies occurs.

I should point out here that what Margery Wolf calls the "brittle relationship between adult brothers" (1970:61) has been elaborated at length in the literature on Chinese kinship (see, e.g., Cohen 1976; Freedman 1966; Potter and Potter 1990:253–254; Watson 1985; A. Wolf 1970:199; and M. Wolf 1970:61). Maurice Freedman, for instance, states that "the fraternal relationship was one of competition" and that brothers "were entitled to equal shares in the family estate, and they anticipated their individual shares of this property by showing jealousy for their separate rights" (1966:46). He goes on to claim that whereas the father could usually keep the lid on fraternal competition, "without him they are liable to be at one another's throats" (1966:54). Rubie Watson (1985) and Sulamith Heins Potter and Jack Potter (1990) elaborate on the fact that such competition among brothers often extended beyond individual families to all male agnates. As the Potters state, the Chinese lineage combined "hierarchical order and competitive struggle" (1990:252). They note that the ideology of lineage solidarity, which applied to one's own brothers as well as one's lineage brothers, might take precedence in a situation where the lineage was endangered by outside threats. But in other situations, competition among lineage brothers was the order of the day (1990:254).

What has not been addressed, however, is the implications of such competitive and conflicting relationships for the outlooks of the participants themselves. Given the conflict inherent in fraternal relationships, might not this relationship also serve as a focal point for the expression of the greatest internal ambiguity, ambivalence, and contradiction as well?

As we will see, this is certainly so in Mr. Zhou's case.

The Inner Dialogue

The aforementioned works suggest that holistic and individualistic outlooks may be applied to different spheres of exchange in a given society. But as I have suggested, we must be open to the possibility that considerable ambivalence may occur even in the interpretation of one realm of action.

Such a possibility has been suggested by the Russian literary theorist M. M. Bakhtin as well as by several scholars who worked closely with him during his early years. Thus, in an essay attributed to V. N. Voloshinov, but thought to have been largely written by Bakhtin, the notion of differing "voices" within a "monologue" is discussed. Says Voloshinov [Bakhtin]: "As soon as we begin meditating about some question, as soon as we start to think it over carefully our inner speech . . . immediately assumes the form of questions and answers, assertions and subsequent denials, or to put it more simply, our speech is broken down into separate repliques of varying size; it takes the form of a *dialogue*" (1983:119).

But Voloshinov is equally clear that such inner dialogues are socially implicated. Early essays by Voloshinov [Bakhtin] directly link such internal monologues to differing ideologies representative of competing class interests. But later on, Bakhtin writes in a less deterministic vein. Still, however, he insists on the social character of all speech and thought: "Any utterance, in addition to its own theme, always responds . . . in one form or another to others' utterances that precede it" (1986:94). Internal dialogues, therefore, can never be purely idiosyncratic. They always exist in some relationship to their social context.

Dorinne Kondo makes a similar point in her study of workers in a Tokyo sweets factory. We must discard the concept of a self divorced from historical, political, and cultural contexts, and the notion that a "self" in a particular culture is never "contradictory" or "multiple", asserts Kondo (1990:42).[4] In an exploration of the life story of one of the factory's chief artisans, for instance, Kondo finds "not a single 'self,' but different selves, alive with complexities and deeply felt, subtly nuanced, often contradictory emotions" (1990:257). As Kondo suggests, we must begin to investigate the self as a site for multiple discourses (1990:44).

In an American setting such a "dialogical" approach has been utilized by Claudia Strauss, who has investigated the various ways in which American workers may integrate seemingly contradictory notions about success (1990). Strauss suggests that when individuals hold apparently contradictory views, these differing "voices" may actually be integrated by a deeper theme. Another possibility is that such differing voices will be compartmentalized in various ways, so that they do not necessarily conflict with one another at a conscious level. Strauss's focus, however, is on the various ways in which such contending voices are conceptually organized within individuals, rather than on the social-structural, cultural, or economic contexts that give rise to them and on which they reflect.

In the account that follows, I hope to clarify the nature of Mr. Zhou's ambivalences as well as the cultural, social, and economic contexts out of which they arise.

---

[4] Kondo's suggestion is also important in light of the discussion by other authors on the relationship of subjectivity and ideological hegemony. Louis Althusser, for instance, has suggested that the creation of subjects who see themselves as free agents is essential if ideological systems are to attain the compliance of these subjects. Ideological systems that *subject* individuals, says Althusser, are paradoxically able to do so by creating in them the feeling that they are in command of their own beliefs (1971:181–183). Althusser does not, however, discuss the possibility that subjects may be internally divided and *subject to* competing ideological demands.

Mr. Zhou's Story

Mr. Zhou organized the telling of his life story into several sections, each associated with his relationship to a particularly significant individual in his life. I follow the same organization here, summarizing several important incidents he recounted to me in the order in which he told them.[5] I then analyze his account in terms of the implicit and explicit notions he articulates about self and personhood. Finally, I examine the relation of these notions to their political, economic, and historical contexts.

I should add, however, that this is very much an investigation of male ideology. Because of their very different roles in family and in economic action, I would expect a rather different constellation of ideas about selfhood and personhood to characterize women in Dhapa—although I believe they would also combine both individualistic and holistic themes.

To Forego Profit: Gaining the Respect of a Younger Brother

Most of the incidents used by Mr. Zhou to illuminate aspects of his own character, or of his brothers', revolved around the buying and selling of shares in what was once a joint family estate. As discussed in Chapter 7, Mr. Zhou was the third of four brothers (for simplicity's sake, I again refer to them as Zhou One, Zhou Two, Zhou Three, and Zhou Four). The Zhou brothers divided their family assets only after the death of their father, in that sense following the expected pattern. But, Zhou One received a larger share than each of the younger brothers, since he was allocated an entire factory whereas the three younger brothers had to divide among themselves the space and machinery in one factory. By the mid-1970s, Zhou One had emigrated to Canada, though he retained ownership of his factory, which he leased to another family. Zhou Two had also emigrated to Canada by this time, leaving the two younger brothers to share one factory in which each conducted a separate business. But the terms of the original separation had a continuing impact on the brothers' relationships.

---

[5] Mr. Zhou's interviews were conducted in English, sometimes punctuated by Mandarin phrases and/or expressions common to Indian English. I have transcribed his remarks verbatim and quote from them as transcribed, without altering the word choice or sentence structure.

[224]

In his account, Zhou Three portrayed his relationship with his youngest brother as exceptionally close: "I and my younger brother are . . . . very close friends, *though we are brothers*, we treat each other as friends." The statement that they are close "though" they are brothers is interesting. As we will see, Mr. Zhou waffled on the point of whether siblings are under any special obligation when it comes to economic transactions. He usually spoke as if familial relationship does entail some kind of suspension of the search for profit which characterizes the marketplace. But since there were plenty of exceptions in his own family, and in the community at large, to such brotherly consideration, he viewed the good relationship between himself and his younger brother as exceptional rather than as the norm.

In this particular case, his portrayal of closeness between the two brothers was primarily exemplified by descriptions of honesty during business transactions, and by a willingness to suspend the quest for profit in order to help each other out. It is interesting to note here that Donald DeGlopper, in his description of business relationships in the Taiwanese town of Lukang, also indicates that the fraternal relationship in and of itself was not viewed as sufficient for the establishment of good business relationships. Says DeGlopper, "In Lukang cooperation or special help in business affairs is not considered one of a brother's axiomatic obligations. Any use of one's brothers in business is a function of the personal relation, the *kan-ch'ing* [ganqing], that exists" (1972:318).

One of the most pivotal incidents for Zhou Three centered on his attempts to sell land to this younger brother. Although he stated that an outside buyer would have paid him 25,000 rupees more than he was asking of his younger brother, Zhou Three asserted that he continued to hold this buyer at bay, while attempting to convince his younger brother to purchase the land, at reduced cost.

What was the context of this attempt to sell land to his younger brother? At that time, the two brothers shared one factory, but both were also experiencing business expansion and success. They had come to the conclusion that one of them should move out and build a new tannery, so that each would have his own factory. Whoever moved out would be compensated for his half of the old factory by the other. One might reasonably conclude, therefore, that it was in Zhou Three's interest to sell his land to Zhou Four, thereby ensuring that Zhou Four would vacate the original factory, and enabling Zhou Three to use some of the funds earned from the sale to buy his younger brother's share.

[225]

But Zhou Three presented this story not in terms of good business sense for himself, as he might if the transaction involved a stranger, but as an altruistic effort on behalf of his younger brother. In fact, Zhou Four needed quite a bit of convincing before he agreed to buy Zhou Three's land, yet his recalcitrance is described by his older brother as a failure to act in his own best interests. Why did Zhou Three continue to hold the outside buyer off while he continued to pressure Zhou Four to buy his land?

Because, in his words (with my emphasis), "I am so much *in love with my brother*, so it is not that I am going to *push* him out of my factory. So, I advised him that he should buy my land to build a tannery." And, "no matter how poor you are. The best way is that you should own a tannery by yourself. . . . So I advised my brother that if he is interested to buy my land, I will forego that 25,000. . . . That means I will not get any single profit . . . because I don't like in the future to see that I have a tannery and he doesn't have. So *as a matter of fact, I am the elder brother, I have to look after him as much as I can.*" He continued, "Because I really *love him* . . . he is my younger brother, how can I see by my eyes that he takes a bad decision. . . . If one things goes back, then you will go backward, if one things goes good, so you will be prosperous, and richer and richer and more safety. . . . if you are to become poorer and don't own a tannery, I want to satisfy myself and to satisfy God that I have been *so kind* to you."

At the same time, Zhou Three also acknowledged that in a world in which the profit motive is dominant, it is natural that such "kind" actions may be misconstrued. Even with one's brothers, one must be on guard. Rather than initially feeling gratified at his brother's concern, Zhou Four suspected him of "bluffing. . . . He thought that if I couldn't sell the land, then I couldn't buy his share. Actually he is mistaken. The reality is there *is* a buyer."

Indeed, when Zhou Four continued to hesitate, Zhou Three gave him additional time to decide. In the following passage we can see Zhou Three's acknowledgment of his brother's independence and autonomy conflicting with a sense of his responsibilities, obligations, and love toward his younger brother (again, my emphasis): "So I said okay, since you are not agreed, it looks like I *force* you to buy my land . . . it looks not very good. So I said . . . we must give up our hope to convince him. After all, he is not a fool. *He can decide his future himself*, so let him do accordingly." But then he added, "As a matter of fact, I am *so kind* to my brother, I gave him one week more to decide."

In the end, Zhou Four did buy Zhou Three's land, and Zhou Three went to the other buyer's house to inform him that he could not go through with the sale. Despite this missed opportunity, this buyer, as portrayed by Zhou Three, was understanding and approving of his decision to sell his land to his brother. At the same time, in Zhou Three's account of the dialogue between himself and the buyer, it is also clear that the buyer considered Zhou Three's decision to be an exception to the normal operation of the profit motive—an exception made on account of a family member.

In Zhou Three's words, he went to the buyer and said, "I am very sorry, but today is, actually I am not going to sell my land to you. Most probably my brother will buy it." Then, commenting on the buyer's reaction to this news, Zhou Three added, "So Mr. ——, he also is very nice, a gentleman. He says, 'Yes, this is the best way you have done. I do wish that your family will have a good addition, and then one of your brothers will build a tannery. This is my hope also. Before this moment, you said you wanted to sell the land, so therefore I helped you to sell the land by giving you some profit.'"

In telling me this story, Zhou Three also confirmed the reasonableness of his initial motive for selling to the buyer: "Because we are the businessmen, *whatever you engage in you have to get the profit, na?*" (my emphasis).

The search for profit, therefore, is a perfectly normal and defensible principle of action. But familial obligations and love justify and explain the suspension of this ordinary principle.

In a later episode, when the youngest brother faced possible demolition of his factory, because it was constructed without proper permits, Zhou Three invited him back to the old tannery. This incident, and the earlier one involving the sale of land, were presented by Zhou Three as the reasons that Zhou Four had continued respect for him. Interestingly, a younger brother's respect for his elder brother is not presented presented as just a function of the age difference between them. Indeed, Zhou Three asserted that other community members could not understand why his younger brother held him in such high esteem, especially since his younger brother was "richer" than he was. Only after Zhou Three gave examples of his sacrifices on behalf of his brother did community members say, "Oh, no wonder he has so much respect for you."

Middleman and Greedy Fellow: Brothers One and Two

Whereas love, friendship, and responsibility—symbolized by the ultimate sacrifice of a profit—marked Zhou Three's portrayal of his feelings and actions toward his younger brother, suspicion and the constant need to be on guard, to use every bit of intelligence and cunning at his disposal, marked his characterization of his relationship with Zhou One. According to Zhou Three, Zhou One was consumed with a runaway urge for profit, an urge untempered by any feelings of familial responsibility and obligation. Zhou Two, on the other hand, balanced kindness with cleverness. He was basically good, but as with most ordinary actors in the marketplace, one could not always take him at his word. Zhou Three's characterizations of his elder brothers were revealed in his account of their role in a pivotal series of incidents in his life. Again, these critical incidents all revolved around property transactions.

This story began in 1980, shortly after the death of the Zhous' mother. Zhous One and Two were returning to India for the funeral, and in Zhou Three's imaginative reconstruction of what occurred, they had a talk in the airplane about the disposition of Zhou One's factory. In this account, Zhou Two, displaying his basic regard for his younger siblings, suggested to the eldest brother, "Why don't you give your tannery to our younger brothers by means of selling [to] them?" Zhou One apparently indicated his willingness to go along with such a sale, and set a price.

In his discussions of the ensuing transactions, Zhou Three portrayed Zhou Two as a middleman or mediator who shuttled between his two younger brothers, who wanted to buy the tannery, and Zhou One. Here is how Zhou Three described Zhou Two's role at the beginning of the negotiations (my emphasis throughout): "Of course my second brother *is quite good to us*, then he is very kind to us also. But he *is also a very clever man*. So he has not let me know that he has been deciding with my elder brother. . . . They have decided, but he is not letting me know these things." Although basically a decent fellow, Zhou Two was still capable of playing games with his younger brothers. One still had to be on guard.

Zhou One, on the other hand, was described in much more negative terms. During the negotiations, Zhou Three explained to Zhou Two that the eldest brother would never stick to his price: *"He is such a greedy fellow.* Whatever you agree, again he will jump. Whatever you agree, again he will jump." According to Zhou Three, such selfishness could only be countered by cunning. Thus, he told his brother, "You should buy his tannery by your refusal, not by your agreement! Your agreed conditions he will refuse . . . [if] you . . . reject it, then he will force you to buy."

Negotiations went on for years, long after the two elder brothers had returned to Canada, but the sale did not take place. Later, Zhou One returned again to India, this time with the express intention of selling his tannery. This time, Zhou Four went to negotiate a sale with him. But despite his better opinion of this youngest brother, Zhou Three explained that he knew that no solution would result from these discussions. Why? "Because these two are absolutely the same type of man. *They are clever, intelligent, they want to kill others.* They want to take advantage for himself, not to give advantage to others. So in this way how to compromise the sales?" As Zhou Three saw the situation, cleverness, greed, and cunning in the service of individual advantage here taking precedence over brotherly relations. In fact, the sale never materialized, and Zhou One eventually sold his tannery to an outsider.

Interestingly, this sour relationship may have been set off years earlier when the initial terms of the brothers' separation agreement were set. As I indicated, the three younger Zhou brothers were left sharing one factory while Zhou One had another factory to himself. (Of course, Zhou One had supported his younger brothers for several years after his father's death and he had purchased this second factory himself.) Each side could argue its case with reference to customary practice within Chinese families: the three younger brothers could argue that all brothers were entitled to equal inheritance; the eldest brother could argue that this principle of equal inheritance applied only to assets and property of ascendants and therefore did not include the assets he had acquired after the father's death.

In any event, though Zhou Three made it clear that he harbored no affection for, indeed he detested, his eldest brother, he was not as clear about the degree to which his brother violated social norms in these later rounds of conflict. He seemed torn between the expectation that family ties should alter the nature of economic transactions, and a naturalist/realist shrugging of the shoulders—acknowledging that many people will simply try to get the better of others, and there is no force that can prevent them. Our exchange on this topic follows (my emphasis).

EO: Should he [Zhou One] sell to his brothers first?

Z: Practice is, it depends, it depends, if the brother is more active, more like strong, and then, if we are weak, *if the buyer is stronger than me, then how can I stop him?*

EO: So he is not bound?

Z: Usually it's this, usually most of the people do this. When you want to sell off your property, maybe your brother will have the first choice. But it is not absolutely that you are bound to do it, but most people do it in this way.

EO: But he didn't . . .

Z: *He* will not do. He will not do that, he only looks for the money, who will offer more, he will sell out. Suppose you want something, of course you will ask your sister, as a sisterly relation . . . [6]

EO: Maybe I'll get less from her, but still . . .

Z: Yeah, maybe you will sell to others also, that is your own business, *nobody can stop you* . . .

The Returns on Filial Piety: Mother, Father, and Son

In Mr. Zhou's discussion of his relationships with his brothers, obligation and love were portrayed as forces that might restrain the profit motive in certain circumstances. By way of contrast, it is as independent, autonomous individuals that people pursue the profit motive. For when profit is the object of action, hierarchical reciprocal role relationships are ignored. This set of concepts is revealed most strikingly when one compares Mr. Zhou's portrayal of his eldest brother with his characterization of his relationship to the youngest one. But in Mr. Zhou's stories about his parents, particularly his mother, it becomes clear that this is not the only possible configuration of these themes. As in the quotation with which I began this chapter, Mr. Zhou holds out the possibility that by acting according to one's role within the familial hierarchy, one may actually ensure some later return.

---

[6] This example was aimed specifically at me, since Mr. Zhou knew that I had one sister and no brothers. Otherwise, given the marginality of sisters to this account, it is unlikely he would have picked this as an example.

Furthermore, when parents work hard in pursuit of profit, there is no contradiction, as with brothers, between this work and their familial connections. Indeed, stories about the sacrifices made by hardworking mothers for their families are widespread among the Calcutta Chinese. In Mr. Zhou's account, he detailed the travails of his mother as she cooked foodstuffs, made wine, washed clothes for other families, and engaged in numerous other activities in order to add to her family's meager income, slowly pulling them out of their initially difficult circumstances.

Indeed, from the standpoint of individual women, there are obvious "returns" for their labors. As discussed in earlier chapters, creating strong bonds between themselves and their sons is an important means by which Chinese women build up future security in a patrilineal, patrilocal family system (see Wolf 1972), and work is a critical means of affirming relationships within the Chinese context (see Potter 1988). Likewise, when sons repay their parents for their labors, by working hard and trying to prosper, they are acting in a filial manner. The profit motive, the urge to accumulate wealth, is filial when it is directed toward parents.

Interestingly, Mr. Zhou's account contained much less information about and description of his father than his mother. In part, this may reflect the type of Chinese family dynamics described by Margery Wolf, in which mothers gain informal power through the forging of close emotional connections with their children, but fathers retain formal authority through a more distant and authoritarian stance (1970, 1972). But there may also be reasons more specific to Mr. Zhou's family.

Mr. Zhou's father, who emigrated to India in 1919, did not establish a tanning business until 1944, with much of the initial investment coming out of money saved by the mother from her various enterprises. He was a schoolteacher who founded the local Chinese school and served for years as its principal, an honorable but unprofitable job. One day, according to Mr. Zhou, his father sat him down and said, "I really am very sorry for a man being a teacher . . . a teacher is poor. Because what can a teacher earn? What can they give you? It is not like a monk or priest. They have no children, their food is supplied by the church, on and on, so they have no worry. . . . But . . . if you are teaching, how much can you earn for your family, wife and children?"

Thus, it appears that one of the most important "lessons" that Mr.

Zhou learned from his father was not to follow in his footsteps. Again, in this anecdote about his father, the profit motive is a necessary component of parental responsibility, not a force undermining familial relationships. Only monks and nuns, those without families, can afford to dispense with it.

Nevertheless, one of Mr. Zhou's stories about his mother included the theme that familial love may sometimes require the sacrifice of material advantage. In this story, Mr. Zhou relates how when he was a small child, a woman from a wealthy family made the following proposition to his mother: "I want to buy your son, as my son." Pointing to the economic difficulties faced by his family, this woman listed all the advantages he would reap by being adopted into a relatively prosperous family. Mr. Zhou's mother refused the offer.

The Familial Self in a World of Commodity Exchange

Double-Voiced Discourse

In Mr. Zhou's world, the instincts of individual competitiveness exist side by side with those of familial devotion, love, and duty. Despite his claims of financial sacrifices made on behalf of his younger brother, he also considered himself to be an excellent businessman who knew how to look out for his own interests and to make a profit when the opportunity arose. On the other hand, he made it clear that, in his view, the eldest brother *never* suspended his quest for gain.

This is not a world of relationship-resistant monads in search of individual gain, nor a world of perfectly attuned holistic actors sensitively fulfilling their role obligations. Rather, it is a world of varied and sometimes contending impulses, and it is among brothers—who begin life together, but almost always eventually split owing to the system of partible inheritance—that such contending impulses are most likely to come into direct competition.

Bakhtin's ideas about heteroglossia and dialogism can help us to understand the form of Mr. Zhou's account. Earlier in the chapter, I referred to the ideas of Bakhtin-school theorists concerning "internal dialogues,"—the conflicting values often exhibited even within monologic discourse. Bakhtin pointed out that one method by which such internal dialogue is exhibited by a single speaker is through "double-voiced discourse" (1981:324).

Heteroglossia . . . is *another's speech in another's language,* serving to express authorial intentions but in a refracted way. Such speech constitutes a special type of *double- voiced discourse.* It serves two speakers at the same time and expresses simultaneously two different intentions: the direct intention of the character who is speaking, and the refracted intention of the author. In such discourse there are two voices, two meanings and two expressions. And all the while these two voices are dialogically interrelated. . . . Examples of this would be comic, ironic or parodic discourse, the refracting discourse of a narrator, refracting discourse in the language of a narrator, refracting discourse in the language of a character and finally the discourse of a whole incorporated genre— all of these discourses are double-voiced and internally dialogized. A potential dialogue is embedded in them, one as yet unfolded, a concentrated dialogue of two voices, two world views, two languages. (1983:324)

Thus, while Mr. Zhou's descriptions of Zhou One's machinations served in part to characterize his brother's actions as an unbrotherly quest for gain that compared unfavorably with Mr. Zhou's own actions, it is not quite so simple. For in some ways, Mr. Zhou's characterizations of his eldest brother were a commentary on the potential of all brothers, including himself. Remember Mr. Zhou's comment about his youngest brother to the effect that they were friends *even though they were brothers?* This statement and others belie to some extent the easy conclusion that the eldest brother was merely a deviant from more acceptable and expected norms.

Indeed, one might consider the representation of Zhou One to be a case of "triple-voiced" discourse, for he not only expressed his own intentions but also refracted two conflicting outlooks of his "author." For, as the author of the account, Mr. Zhou's voice spoke through the character of Zhou One, but this voice expressed two contrasting judgments—a negative judgment about his eldest brother, and an admission that the potential for placing self-interest above family hierarchy and solidarity is inherent in all brotherly interactions. The author, in this case Mr. Zhou, expressed both a negative judgment and an ultimate acceptance of profit-seeking competition among brothers through the "triple-voiced" character of Zhou One.

I have heard such ambivalent feelings and expectations about the relationships among brothers expressed in everyday conversation among other community members as well. For instance, one man who

[233]

treated his brothers ruthlessly during a partition dispute was later injured in a motorcycle accident. Many community members expressed the sentiment that he was being punished for his overly aggressive attitude toward his brothers. But on the other hand, community members do not always express negative judgments about the enhancement of one brother's control over a family's assets at the expense of the others. Indeed, they may remark that when partition takes place, however equal the agreement looks on paper, it is to be expected that the more talented brother in a family will have already stashed some extra assets away for himself.

When he reached adulthood, Mr. Zhou often joked with the son of the woman who attempted to adopt him as a child. Though meant in jest, these remarks clearly indicate the very real fear, and even expectation, that market relationships, even those of the most predatory character, will eventually characterize the relationship among brothers: "If I am your brother you will have had it. *I will get all your tannery and your shoeshop, they will all be owned by me, I will not spare you* [laughs]. . . . you are very lucky that I am not your brother now, if it will be so I think I will be pulling you off [laughs]!" Notice that in the joke, Mr. Zhou cast *himself* in the role of the predatory, profit-oriented sibling.

The Contexts of Inner Dialogue

I began this chapter by suggesting that notions of personhood be investigated in particular economic, social, and cultural contexts. As Arthur Kleinman has pointed out, "Persons and families exist in local worlds of experience, moral worlds where macro-social pressures are refracted (or concentrated)." And, he goes on to assert that "*experience is constituted and negotiated as an intersubjective flow of lived engagement with that which is culturally constituted as most at stake*" (1990:1).

We must therefore ask, what are the "macro-social pressures" in Mr. Zhou's local moral world? And, what is most at issue for him and why? Certainly, one of the most immediate social and economic contexts within which Mr. Zhou's attitudes must be understood is the Chinese system of partible inheritance among brothers, and the inevitability of conflict contained within it. But at the same time, these inheritance rules are themselves reproduced in this particular context because family members can manipulate them successfully to respond to both

[234]

the political and economic exigencies of their situation. As we have seen, brothers in the community who emigrate, such as Zhou One and Zhou Two, often sell their shares to brothers who remain. This allows family members who stay in India to work with larger shares than if all brothers stayed at home. Emigration also gives family members a link with someone who is living abroad, a connection which Calcutta Chinese, as members of a politically insecure minority group, can activate if circumstances get worse and they need to flee the country.

The fact that patrilineal partible inheritance is utilized in many different Chinese contexts, therefore, does not mean that it represents an immutable and unchanging essence. Rather, the endurance of such an inheritance rule must also be explained with reference to the particular situation in which it is found. In the case of the Calcutta Chinese, it is a rule that is susceptible to successful manipulation by family members in their attempts to gain greater economic and political security.

But are there other levels of explanation as well? In addition to the influence of a specific inheritance rule, and its conditions of reproduction, are there additional economic, social, or cultural contexts in which Mr. Zhou's ideas are situated? One easy response is that he is a member of an entrepreneurial community, so naturally, entrepreneurial metaphors slip into his characterization of human relationships, and he sees a world in which individuals are advised to be on guard against cunning schemes for profit, even—or perhaps especially—among one's own siblings.

It should also be pointed out that unlike certain Indian merchant communities (see Bayly 1983), the Calcutta Chinese have not tried to convert their wealth into "higher" status by undertaking other economic activities that would be considered "purer" within the caste hierarchy. As pariah entrepreneurs, the Chinese have succeeded economically precisely because they have *not* assimilated caste ideology.

And let us not forget that in the case of Chinese society, both on the mainland and overseas, we are dealing with a society in which monetary thinking and commoditization have a long history. As Hill Gates points out, late imperial Chinese society "included important capitalist elements. . . . The Chinese treated the major factors of production— land, labor, and capital—as commodities, with well-developed markets for each" (1987:260). Gates states that capitalism did *not* play a "hegemonic" role in late imperial China, because "capitalist elements were always subordinated to state control" (1987:260). Nevertheless, "a constrained but powerful capitalist worldview was reproduced constantly by the Chinese populace as an alternative to the bureaucratic/feudal vision enshrined in the formal structure and practice of the state" (Gates 1987:261). That is, capitalism appeared as an attractive alternative for working people, since it "offered a social model of upward mobility based directly on wealth rather than on connection with the state through the highly limited channels of degree- and office-holding" (Gates 1987:261).

Further, says Gates, the commoditization of Chinese society was so intense that money was used not only "for the purchase of everyday commodities" but also for gifts and for the "purchase of persons" (1987:262). For instance, the sale of young girls in adoption as "little daughters-in-law" was quite common. In such instances, an infant girl was sold by her family to another family. Her foster family would raise her, and when she came of age, she would marry one of their sons (Gates 1987:264; also see Wolf 1968, and Wolf and Huang 1980). The family into which she was sold would thereby avoid the tensions of incorporating an adult bride into a strange household, as well as the expensive ceremonies that were expected when a woman joined a household as an adult bride. Gates also notes that the sale of young girls into prostitution by their relatives was another form of this market in human beings, and she points out that this market has not vanished completely in contemporary Taiwan, despite the fact that it "persists on a scale much reduced by the expanding economic opportunities of the past half-century and by changing values" (1987:264).

Indeed, Chinese society has been monetized to increasing degrees since the eleventh century (Elvin 1973:149). It is a society in which even rural areas have been linked with a national market in some items for almost one thousand years (Elvin 1973:106) and in which "increased contact with the market made the Chinese peasantry into a class of adaptable, rational, profit-oriented petty entrepreneurs" (Elvin 1973:167). As such, as pointed out in Chapter 1, Stevan Harrell argues that there has long been a "Chinese entrepreneurial ethic, a cultural value that requires one to invest one's resources . . . in a long-term quest to improve the material well-being and security of some group to which one belongs and with which one identifies closely" (1987:94), and, as explained in Chapter 4, even popular Chinese religious practice reflects a worldview thoroughly influenced by monetary thinking.

Thus, for the Calcutta Chinese, a high priority is placed on entrepreneurial thinking as a result of their ethnic role in India and the cultural ethos carried with them from their country of origin and perpetuated in their overseas environment. And as the above examples demonstrate, a whole range of human relationships, and even relationships with spiritual beings, have long been encompassed by monetary transactions in the Chinese context. It should not be surprising to find such transactions serving as a focal point in Mr. Zhou's description and assessment of family relationships.[7]

Monetary Transactions as an Idiom for and Creator of Social Relationships

The aforementioned discussion reveals that entrepreneurship and the attainment of wealth are important community values and form an important context for Mr. Zhou's assessment of relationships. Furthermore, as I have shown, monetary exchange has long been an important symbolic idiom in the Chinese context, and it has frequently been used to express the nature of relationships among people, and between humans and spiritual beings. Indeed, money not only serves as a symbolic idiom but has very real power to create and forge such relationships, not to mention destroy them.

But we must not assume that as an idiom for, or as a means of shaping, human relationships, money and economic transactions are one-dimensional, or that they imply an internally consistent worldview. Indeed, as we have seen, this is certainly not the case with Mr. Zhou. In his story, the description of monetary transactions among his siblings encompassed a range of human motivations and affects.

It is important to keep in mind that for many earlier theorists, the

---

[7] My observation that monetary or business transactions are important idioms for human relationships in the Calcutta Chinese context curiously complements Arthur Kleinman's analyses of bodily idioms in contemporary mainland China. In both cases, an analysis of idioms for self/society relationships hinges on an understanding of the relationship between what Kleinman terms *macrosocial forces* and *local systems* (1986:181).

Kleinman's work in contemporary mainland China revealed that "somatized affect—feeling as physical pain and bodily, not psychic suffering" is the "appropriate liminal state" (1986:178). Among the Chinese patients whom Kleinman interviewed, somatization was more frequently expressed than psychological depression. Kleinman concluded that this pattern existed because physical pain does not carry with it the same implications as "depression"—withdrawal from the social order—and it was therefore a less threatening "liminal state" under the present political regime.

existence of money in itself implied a universally individualistic orientation. As Jonathan Parry and Maurice Bloch remind us, for theorists like Karl Marx, Georg Simmel, and Karl Polanyi, "money is associated with, and promotes, the growth of individualism and the destruction of solidary communities" (1989:4). Therefore, as economies become increasingly monetized, one would expect, according to these theorists, a growth of individualism. But as with the old dichotomies of holism and individualism themselves, recent research suggests that the existence of money in itself does not necessarily imply a uniform or internally consistent orientation.

Thus, Parry and Bloch point out that the equation of money with individualism derives from our own cultural orientation: "*for us* money signifies a sphere of 'economic' relationships which are inherently impersonal, transitory, amoral and calculating" (1989:9). In fact, they contend, in some cultural contexts money may not be viewed as "the antithesis of bonds of kinship and friendship, and there is consequently nothing inappropriate about making gifts of money to cement such bonds" (1989:9).

Indeed, Parry and Bloch emphasize that money may take on many different meanings and has the power to affect social relationships in many different ways, in even a single culture, depending on the context in which it is used. It may cement or undermine social relations. It may be used in "short-term exchanges associated with individual appropriation, competition, sensuous enjoyment, luxury and youthful vitality" (1989:24) in which exchange is primarily between strangers, or it may be utilized in "transactions concerned with the reproduction of the long-term social or cosmic order" (1989:24). Illustrations of the latter might include donations to a ritual specialist, for instance, or the funds utilized in a Chinese context for worship and propitiation of the ancestors, including cash used to purchase the symbolic spirit money which will be subsequently burned as offerings, as in the cases discussed earlier in this book.

But even when religious or transcendent uses of money are excluded from analytical purview, monetary transactions, even those that appear strictly commercial, can have many shades of meaning and social purposes. In his study of south Indian bankers, David Rudner noticed that they established different sorts of deposits depending on the social bonds that existed between them and their clients. For instance, some types of deposits were only made available to caste mates (1989:449). Even in a study of a public produce market in the

American Midwest, Stuart Plattner found that particular customers and vendors had established ongoing business relationships and that these customary relationships were an important aspect of market transactions (1983).

From the long-term investment in heavenly "credit" to impersonal market transactions with strangers to cash transactions among relatives, lineage mates, and friends—which transactions of the Chinese are short-term and imply no continuing obligations? And which transactions contain an implicit demand for reciprocity? It may not be easy to answer these questions. For as soon as we admit the possibility of multiple uses and meanings for monetary exchange, we must also admit that the possibility of misunderstanding or contention about meanings arises. It is unrealistic to expect that what is multifaceted in the social world will be represented in completely unambivalent terms within a given participant's understanding.

In the case of the Calcutta Chinese, such confusion is most likely to crop up when attempts are made to reconcile entrepreneurial goals with the equally compelling demands on role obligations that exist within a hierarchical familial context. In theory there need be no conflict. After all, earning huge profits can be an expression of filiality, a means of repaying one's parents for their sacrifices, or a fulfillment of parental responsibility. As Harrell points out, Chinese usually dedicate their entrepreneurial efforts to a group, and this group is customarily the family (1985:219). Likewise, Skinner states that the Chinese peasant was "not only grateful to his ancestors for what his immediate family had, but was responsible to them for what he did to further the fortunes of his family and lineage" (1957:92). However, partible inheritance means that former shareholders in a joint estate may later be pursuing their entrepreneurial quests at cross-purposes. Brothers who see themselves as working for the benefit of their conjugal families may also perceive themselves to be locked in competition with each other. These factors help explain why Mr. Zhou's accounts of relationships with his brothers, rather than his stories about his mother, exhibited the greatest ambivalence.

Analysts of Chinese kinship have long pointed to conflicts created by what Hugh D. R. Baker terms the *structural paradox* of equal inheritance for all brothers combined with hierarchical superiority based on age (1979:18). The most likely outcome of such tensions is usually taken to be the fission of the family, particularly after the death

[239]

of the father. But the ramifications of these structural conflicts for conceptions of selfhood and personhood have not been spelled out.

In this chapter, I have tried to address some of these issues and to analyze some of the implications of these kinship structures on conceptions of selfhood and personhood in one particular case. However, to understand Mr. Zhou's case, I have gone beyond the microcosm of family structure, important though it is, and asked how these familial dynamics have combined with larger cultural, economic, and social imperatives to create the context in which his specific ideas about personhood have developed.

What happens when these family dynamics exist within a culture and society in which money has long expressed and shaped a great variety of relationships and values? And how are they further influenced by a specific social context in which one's ethnic role limits one's possible economic options to specific entrepreneurial pursuits? Such a situation engenders a complex view of personhood, one in which sociocentric, holistic, and familial orientations both coexist and contend with individual quests for profit and gain.

Epilogue: Immigrants and Visitors in Toronto

"In 1978, just a few years before she died, my mother decided she wanted to visit my two brothers in Canada," Mr. Zhou told me one day. "She was already quite elderly, and she did not know English, so we arranged for another woman on the plane to keep an eye on my mother. Halfway through the trip, when they arrived in England, all the passengers left the plane to walk around the airport, and somehow that woman forgot about my mother. Well, my mother became disoriented and somehow, I don't know how, she walked right out of the airport!

"She started to walk and walk, and she didn't know where she was. It was raining on the road too, and she was getting more and more confused. Suddenly an elderly Sikh gentleman passed by. Recognizing someone from India, my mother turned to him and asked him in Hindi, 'Where is Canada?' Realizing that something was wrong, the gentleman began to talk with her in Hindi. When he found out that she came from the airport, he was very nice, and he brought her back there."

Mr. Zhou's mother ultimately did make it to Canada. She stayed for a few months, alternating between her eldest son's and second son's households. But as the summer months passed, she could feel a chill in the air long before it bothered anyone else. And she began to miss the familiar and closely knit Dhapa community, where one only had to walk out the door to find a number of other elderly Hakka women with whom one could talk and gossip. So, having finally seen for herself what life in Canada was like, Mr. Zhou's mother returned to India.

A "Calcutta Chinese" wedding in Toronto. The bride and groom pose here with close family members, some of whom have traveled from India for the occasion.

Although it was not Mrs. Zhou's definitive plan to leave India permanently, many other elderly Dhapa Chinese have actually immigrated to Canada in the past several years, and the flow of younger and middle-aged individuals has continued unabated. Even family members who have no intention of emigrating from India, like Mrs. Zhou, have visited their relatives abroad. Families are spread across continents, and family members move back and forth in an uninterrupted stream.

In this Epilogue I focus on some of these families, primarily those living in Toronto, the destination of the greatest number of Calcutta

Hakka emigrants, in an effort to ascertain how they have responded to and been affected by their new surroundings. But in examining the lives of Calcutta Chinese immigrants in Toronto, I must also refer back to their families in Calcutta, for news and people continuously travel between both countries, community members and families in both cities remain inextricably linked.

This movement between Calcutta and Toronto brings to mind Arjun Appadurai's recent admonition to anthropologists that "as groups migrate [and] regroup in new locations . . . the *ethno* in ethnography takes on a slippery, nonlocalized quality" (1991:191). Appadurai goes on to coin the word *ethnoscape*, by which he means "the landscape of persons who make up the shifting world in which we live" (1991:192). He continues, this "is not to say that nowhere are there relatively stable communities and networks of kinship, friendship, work, and leisure, as well as birth, residence, and other filiative forms. But it is to say that the warp of these stabilities is everywhere shot through with the woof of human motion, as more persons and groups deal with the realities of having to move or the fantasies of wanting to move" (1991:192).

Of course, the Calcutta Hakka were already part of a diaspora community when they resided in India. And even as "guest people" in Guangdong, China, the Hakka were considered migrants from another area of the country. In immigrating to Toronto, therefore, their status as migrants has not changed. Movement for them is not merely a recent phenomenon. On the other hand, air travel and the relative prosperity of the community in India has meant that family members in both countries can visit each other with regularity, a phenomenon which was certainly not possible in the early part of the twentieth century, when the first Chinese tanneries were established in Calcutta.

This changed nature of space does have implications for Calcutta Chinese immigrants in Toronto, since it makes it easier for them to maintain links with their relatives in Calcutta. Yet what exactly is the nature of these connections between Calcutta Chinese in Canada and in India? Does the fact that Chinese in the two cities live very different lives weaken the links between them? Or do the ongoing processes of family division and dispersion, and the relative ease of communication and travel, form the basis of continued connections between Calcutta Chinese in both India and Canada? Can one talk about individuals residing in both places as if they form a single community, and if so, what kind of community is it? Finally, what impact, if any, do economic and political forces (at the local, national, and international levels) have on these connections?

The movement of populations in the modern world has caused many people to comment on the phenomenon of deterritorialization, the break in what was once regarded as an inherent link between place and culture. One can no longer look at a map of France, for instance, and assume that the physical area represented there is in any way coterminous with French culture. Versions of French culture might be found in many other areas of the world. However, in a recent article, Akhil Gupta and James Ferguson argue that the deterritorialization does not mean that subjects are created who are "free-floating monads" (1992:19). Rather, cultural difference in the contemporary world can be mapped to several grids, not just that of physical distance or proximity. For example, they state, the rich in Bombay and London may in some ways be less distant from each other than they are from those of different classes in the same city (1992:20).

Gupta goes on to argue in another article that "citizenship ought to be theorized as one of the multiple subject positions occupied by people as members of diversely spatialized, partially overlapping or non-overlapping collectivities" (1992:73). Other identities, such as ethnic group membership, he asserts, may bind people not only from within but also *across* national boundaries.

Gupta's and Ferguson's insights about the lack of fit between physical proximity and cultural or social nearness are certainly applicable to Calcutta Chinese immigrants in Toronto. Although many of them have lived and worked in Canada for more than a decade, their most important social ties remain with other Calcutta Chinese, either those who have also immigrated and live in Canada, or those who remain in India. In many ways they remain closer to individuals from their own singular community than to neighbors and co-workers in Toronto with whom they might interact more frequently.

It is primarily through familial connections that ties have been forged between Calcutta Chinese immigrants in Toronto and community members back home. As discussed in previous chapters, decisions about emigration are part of an ongoing family dynamic that takes account of both the political and economic pressures faced by individuals and families in the Calcutta Chinese community. Sponsoring the immigration of additional family members, arranging marriages between community members in North America and India, and a continuous flow of familial visitors in both directions create real, and not merely imagined, social connections. As I argued in Chapter 1, in analyzing the nature of immigrant communities, one must have an understanding of the relationship between internal family dynamics and external pressures in the host society or societies.

Thus, I now focus on the microdynamics within sixteen Calcutta Chinese families in Toronto, and relate these microdynamics to larger political and economic forces, to understand the nature of the continuing connections between the families in Toronto and their relatives in Calcutta. In the process I uncover some of the radical discontinuities between the lives of the Hakka in the two cities. Finally, I consider whether such discontinuities will alter their ethnic identity in fundamental ways, or whether their continuing familial links with community members in India, and the conditions that make these possible, will preserve a sense of distinctiveness.

Sixteen Households—A Profile

In the summers of 1986 and 1987, I visited Toronto to learn about Calcutta Chinese immigrants there. I was concerned primarily with emigrants from the Dhapa tanning community. However, there were a number of Calcutta Hakka in Toronto who were not from Dhapa, for example, families who had shoe shops or restaurants in India. When I refer to Calcutta Hakka in Toronto, I refer to all these groups, though of course, I focus primarily on emigrants from the tanning community in Dhapa.

During my visit to Calcutta in 1985, I had collected the names and addresses from my Dhapa Chinese friends and acquaintances who had relatives in Toronto. I telephoned these people when I arrived in Toronto the following year, and attempted to arrange meetings with them. I also made contact with Dhapa Chinese immigrants in Toronto by getting in touch with individuals whom I had known in Calcutta and who had subsequently emigrated.

Attempting to meet with people was an experience that demonstrated the differences between their lives in India and in Canada. In Toronto, most people went to work every weekday, so weekends were usually the only times I could meet with them. Nevertheless, I was

[245]

ultimately able to visit with and interview members of sixteen Calcutta Chinese households in their homes.

In addition to these households, I met a number of other Calcutta Chinese immigrants in Toronto on a more informal basis. In particular, in the summer of 1987 I was invited to K. C. Yan's wedding in Toronto. This turned out to be a splendid opportunity to observe the transplanted Calcutta Chinese community in Toronto. K. C.'s father, Yan Baoxia, as well as K. C.'s two older brothers, flew in from India for the wedding, and more than four hundred guests attended, all but twenty of whom were Calcutta Chinese immigrants.

The sixteen households I visited displayed a number of common characteristics. (Table 6 summarizes household membership, occupational categories, and other key data for these sixteen households.) Every household included a married couple and one or more small children, and almost all households also had other residents. In eight of the sixteen households, a parent or parents lived with a married son or daughter. Interestingly, in three of these cases parents were living with married daughters, a residence pattern that was certainly a change from the strict patrilocality of the Dhapa community. Furthermore, in two more households, the son or daughter had applied and was waiting for an elderly parent to receive an immigrant visa, and in another household, that of Stephen Kong, the parents visited yearly in order to maintain the validity of their immigrant status. Grandparents had also lived in two other households, but for reasons discussed later in this epilogue, they moved out. Members of the senior generation were not the only additional members of these households. In six of the households there also resided an unmarried sibling or a relative or friend of the husband or wife.

Only three of the couples in my sample had immigrated to Canada after getting married. In all the other cases, the men had emigrated from India alone, worked for a few years in Canada, and then married. Their brides usually were Dhapa Chinese whom they knew from home, and who subsequently immigrated in order to marry them, or Dhapa Chinese whom they met in Toronto. Sometimes, however, they returned home for an arranged marriage. All those who emigrated while still unmarried lived with other relatives in Canada when they first arrived. A few of the men, like Stephen Kong, later went on to share apartments with other friends from India. Most of the women emigrated from India precisely for the purpose of marrying a fiancé who was already in Toronto, but in two cases single women came to

[246]

able 6. Characteristics of sixteen Calcutta Chinese households in Toronto, 1986

Name of married couple	No. of children	Other adult residents in household	Occupations of employed members of household	First household member to emigrate, year	Apartment/ house
ᴸlan Chang and ᴜhang ᴜhunhua	1	Chunhua's parents and siblings	Engineer (Alan) Secretary (Chunhua)	Alan, 1975	House
ᴷenneth Fei ᴜnd Fei Maylee	0	Maylee's parents	Transport company worker (Kenneth) Bank teller (Maylee) Plastics factory workers (Maylee's parents)	Kenneth, 1969 (at age 13 with parents)	Apartment
ᴵtephen Kong ᴜnd Kong ᴬifang	1	None, but Stephen's parents visit yearly	Computer programmer (Stephen)	Stephen, 1973	House
ᴸee Yugong ᴜnd Lee Ailing ᴸee Ailing is ᴵietnamese ᴜhinese)	1	Yugong's mother and nephew	Accountant (Yugong)	Yugong, 1973	House
ᴵhomas and ᴵlizabeth Liang	0	Thomas's 2 cousins	Accountant (Thomas) Bank teller (Elizabeth)	Thomas, 1976	House
ᴡilliam and ᴵheila Lin	0	Sheila's sister, and Sheila's brother-in-law's brother (K. C. Yan)	Secretary (Sheila) Auto worker (William) Window factory worker (K. C.) Data entry operator (Sheila's sister)	Sheila and William emigrated together, 1975	House
ᴼiao Songjing ᴜnd Janet Qiao	1	Songjing's mother	Welder (Songjing) Claims processor for insurance company (Janet)	Songjing, 1976 (Janet is French Canadian)	House

(continued)

[247]

Table 6. *(Continued)*

Name of married couple	No. of children	Other adult residents in household	Occupations of employed members of household	First household member to emigrate, year	Apar ho
Thomas and Susan Qin	3	Thomas's mother	Secretary (Susan) Machinist (Thomas)	Thomas, 1972	Hou
Tan Guofei and Lisa Tan	1	Lisa's sister, Guofei's parents	Plastics factory workers (Lisa and Guofei)	Guofei, 1982	Apar
Robert and Mary Xi	2	Mary's sister, applying for Mary's parents	Machinist (Robert) Data entry operator (Mary)	Robert, 1978	Hou
David Xiong and Yuan Meihua	2	David's mother at first, later she moved out	Machinist (David)	David, 1975	Hou
T. F. Xiu and Xiu Suibao	2	None	Owners of family business, mobile catering truck (T. F. and Suibao)	T. F., 1975	Hou
Yeh Lizhang and Theresa Yeh	2	Lizhang's mother	Janitor (Lizhang)	Theresa, 1979	Apar
Yu Hongzhang and Yu Feilin	2	Hongzhang's parents at first, later they moved out	Plastics factory workers (Hongzhang and Feilin)	Hongzhang and Feilin emigrated together, 1982	Apar
Henry and Maria Zhang	2	Maria's mother	Cook (Henry) Office worker (Maria)	Henry, 1979	Hou
Zhang Zhunfang and Zhang Hsuehlan	3	None, have applied for Zhunfang's father	Tannery worker (Zhunfang) Factory worker (Hsuehlan)	Zhunfang and Hsuehlan emigrated together, 1982	Apar

live with their married sisters and subsequently married Calcutta Hakka whom they met in Toronto.

Indeed, of the sixteen households, there were only two in which Hakka Chinese from India had married someone from a different community. In one case, a Calcutta Hakka man married a Vietnamese Chinese woman, and in the other a Calcutta Hakka man married a French Canadian. This low incidence of intermarriage between Calcutta Hakka and other Chinese, not to mention non-Chinese, was characteristic of most of the families, both those I met on a casual basis and those I interviewed.

The economic activities of family members also displayed a number of common characteristics. Among the sixteen married couples, both partners worked outside the home in twelve families, and the women remained at home to care for small children in the other four. Although individuals were employed in a number of different jobs, a few categories predominated. Thirteen individuals (nine men and four women) worked in factories. Six of these people worked in the same plastics factory, which employed almost twenty-five Calcutta Chinese in total. Among the factory workers in my sample, three men worked as machinists, and one man actually worked in a tannery. (Ironically, there are two tanneries in Toronto, and at the time each employed approximately fifteen Calcutta Chinese, most of whom came from families that operated their own tanneries in India.)

After factory work, the clerical/secretarial category, under which I have included such jobs as bank tellers and data entry operators, occupied the next most numerous category of employment. Seven women among the members of these sixteen households were employed in such a capacity. The remainder of the individuals in these households worked in a diversity of occupations, including one welder, one cook, one janitor, two accountants, and one engineer. Only the last two categories can be classified as professional.

The dream of running one's own business, though still held by many Calcutta Chinese immigrants, had been achieved by only one family in my sample, and even so, their business was a small one. This family operated a mobile food stall that sold breakfast and luncheon items outside a large workplace. Only one other Calcutta Chinese family in Toronto has succeeded in starting a business of its own. This family operates a small restaurant on Spadina Street, near the center of Chinatown.

Although most of the Calcutta Chinese immigrants in my sample did not work in lucrative professions or receive extremely high wages, eleven of the sixteen households were paying mortgages on homes rather than renting apartments when I interviewed them in 1986. In part, this was a function of the number of years they had resided in Toronto. All of those who were paying mortgages on their homes arrived in Toronto in the 1970s. Thus, most of them had lived in Canada for at least eight years before buying a home. On the other hand, of the five households in my sample that were renting apartments, three of them had arrived in the early to mid-1980s.

This description is but a thumbnail sketch. Let us now take a closer look at the lives of these Calcutta Chinese immigrants in Toronto.

First Stop: St. Jamestown

St. Jamestown is a public housing project in Toronto. With its well-maintained physical environment—neatly manicured grounds, clean tile-floored hallways, and windows, doors, and stairwells in good condition—plus its low crime rate, it bears little resemblance to such projects in the United States. A brief walk around the grounds reveals that this project is home to a large immigrant population, including East, Southeast, and South Asians.

"Before, most of the Chinese from India lived here, but now [1986] a lot of them have bought homes in Scarborough" [an eastern suburb of Toronto], says Theresa Yeh. Theresa is a Hakka Chinese whose family first migrated from India to Pakistan to run a restaurant, and later, several of her siblings emigrated from Pakistan to both the United States and Canada. She is now married to Yeh Lizhang, a Calcutta Hakka whose family has a very small tannery in Dhapa and who emigrated in the late 1970s.

Yeh Lizhang's sister was my colleague in the Pei Mei School in Dhapa where I taught from 1980 to 1982. By sheer coincidence, Teacher Yeh is visiting her brother in Toronto, and I bumped into her this morning on the subway. Since Teacher Yeh and I are now old acquaintances, she has brought me to her brother's apartment, and so ironically, on my first day of fieldwork in Toronto, I am visiting the housing project, which is often the first residence for many Calcutta Chinese.

The Yeh's apartment consists of a living room with a kitchen space on the side, and a long hallway with three bedrooms. They live here with their two children and Yeh Lizhang's mother; their monthly rent is about four hundred dollars. Teacher Yeh and I are eating a lunch of fried noodles prepared by Theresa and are talking with her about life in Toronto. From the Yeh's apartment, Teacher Yeh and I descend two floors to visit with Lisa Tan, another Pei Mei School teacher whom I knew in Calcutta and who emigrated from Dhapa in 1982. Four floors above the Tan's apartment lives yet another Calcutta Chinese couple, also teachers. The Yus were the principals of another Hakka Chinese school, located in central Calcutta. They have now lived in Toronto for about four years.

With Calcutta Chinese living throughout the project, it might seem that social life in St. Jamestown might partly replicate that of Dhapa, where everybody is aware of people's comings and goings, or, in Stephen Kong's words, "the eyes are always on you." But Principal Yu is quick to point out to me that work schedules in Canada make that kind of life difficult to duplicate. In fact, she says, although they have been in Canada for about four years, Teacher Tan has never come up to her apartment until today! Ironically, they still meet everyday—but not where they live. Teacher Tan and Principal Yu now work in the same factory, a plastics factory that makes such items as plastic flowerpots and chairs.

While most Calcutta Chinese in Toronto do not work in the same place, there are a few factories where a number of Calcutta Chinese are employed. As mentioned, these include the plastics factory with approximately twenty-five Calcutta Chinese employees, as well as two tanneries, each of which employs approximately fifteen Calcutta Chinese out of a total work force of seventy to eighty. Of course, in the case of the two tanneries, it is obvious that Calcutta Hakka, with their intimate knowledge of tanning, would have an advantage in obtaining jobs. Additionally, in both tanneries and the plastics factory, Calcutta Chinese workers introduce their friends and relatives to the plant managers when there are job openings, and Calcutta Hakka have, thereby, gradually been added to their work forces.

"The pay is low and the hours are bad," says Principal Yu of her night shift job in the plastics factory. "But," she adds, "it's secure." Teacher Tan joins in by stating that contrary to what one might assume, it is not really good to work with so many people whom you know, since there tends to be more gossip. Further, she states, the foreman of the factory is a Calcutta Hakka, and when he is angry he tends to use bad language with them.

When I visit the plastics factory a few days later with a middle-aged Hakka couple who had formerly owned a shoe shop in Calcutta, there certainly is no doubt about the gossip. There are two fifteen-minute breaks and a lunch break during their shift. Ten Calcutta Hakka, two Cantonese from Hong Kong, and two Italian women gather around a large table to eat snacks and drink coffee. As the Hakka chatter away, the Cantonese and Italian workers sit quietly and talk among themselves, looking like the outcasts in a junior high school cafeteria.

On this visit to the factory, my hosts, who are older than Teacher Tan and Principal Yu, and who know no English, tell me that far from finding it annoying to work with their acquaintances from India, they like it. Indeed, the wife, who had spent her days in Calcutta working at home or in the shoe shop, says she is much happier now that she goes out to work, because in Calcutta she was always inside the house whereas now she is "working with a lot of co-workers."

Clearly, the nature of the work performed by the Calcutta Chinese when they emigrate to Canada is very different from their work in India. I examine this topic more closely in the next section.

"Time Is Money": Earning a Living in Toronto

Although Toronto has a vibrant immigrant Chinese economy, few Calcutta Chinese are employed within it. Even the three factories with a number of Hakka employees are far from Chinatown and are not owned or operated by Chinese. Why is it that Calcutta Hakka immigrants are not employed within Chinese enterprises? First, the dominant ethnic group among Toronto's Chinese immigrants is the Cantonese, composed primarily of immigrants from either Hong Kong or Guangdong Province in China. There is also a significant population of Southeast Asian Chinese (Johnson 1982b:246). Speaking Hindi and Hakka, and sometimes English and Mandarin, the Calcutta Hakka don't interact easily with the Cantonese. For example, on a visit to a Chinese restaurant with Mr. Kong, he complained energetically about the waiters, none of whom, he said, spoke Mandarin. But because the Calcutta Hakka felt so different from the Cantonese majority in Toronto's Chinese community, I frequently felt they overstated their case. For instance, as a foreigner who could speak Mandarin, I found numerous individuals in Chinese-run businesses in Toronto who could speak with me, but most Calcutta Chinese whom I met in Toronto claimed that Mandarin was useless there.

A second, and more important, reason that Calcutta Hakka stay away from jobs within the Chinese subeconomy is simply that they consider such work to be a dead end, offering neither security nor moderate pay. (In their view, even low-paying factory jobs outside the Chinese subeconomy, such as Principal Yu's, are more secure than those within it.) As Graham Johnson states in a study of the Canadian Chinese, "Immigrant Chinese whose facility in English and educational level is low are trapped in the sub-economy" (Johnson 1982a:261). But he also adds that "the range in occupational profile of the Toronto [Chinese] community is substantial, and its members are no longer confined to a restricted set of occupational choices" (1982a:261).

Indeed, Calcutta Hakka residents in Canada often articulated the opinion that Canada has the advantage over the United States when it comes to securing work outside the Chinese subeconomy. "New York is not a good place for a family," one Calcutta Hakka immigrant in Toronto told me. "It's only okay for a single guy, since you can only work in restaurants and garment factories there." In addition, Canada's social welfare system, including its much-vaunted free medical care, plus its cleanliness and lack of crime were also often cited to me as evidence of its greater desirability as a destination for immigrants.

The Calcutta Hakka in Toronto whom I interviewed found their jobs in a number of different ways. I begin with Susan Qin's experiences, which have elements in common with those of several other Calcutta Hakka women. Susan came to Toronto in 1974 when she was twenty-three years old. She told me that she emigrated in order to marry her fiancé, who had already been residing in Canada for two years. Like many Calcutta Hakka of her generation, who studied in Chinese schools during primary school years but then switched to English medium schools, she was comfortable with English. She had also had some secretarial training while in Calcutta.

When she first arrived in Toronto, however, she could only find a job in a Chinese garment factory cutting strings off the clothes. The pay was minimum wage. But later, one of the managers of the factory saw her résumé, noticed that she was educated and knew English, and that she had clerical skills. So, she said, "when a position opened up in the shipping department, then I was transferred out to that department." Later she applied for a clerical job at a hospital, a job she presently holds.

Women with less fluency in English have not been able to obtain clerical jobs. These women, such as Teacher Tan and Principal Yu, have secured factory jobs.

Men's occupational categories were also influenced in part by their degree of English competency. Susan Qin's husband, for instance, was less fluent in English than she was when he came to Canada. He spent his first few years in Canada jumping from job to job. He ultimately landed at his present factory, where he learned to be a machinist while on the job, and he gradually rose to the level of lead-hand. Several other men whom I met informally, however, studied technical skills while still in Calcutta and later secured jobs as machinists in Toronto. Only one man among the household residents I interviewed was then working at a job within the Chinese subeconomy. This was Henry Zhang, who worked as a cook.

Only a few Calcutta Chinese have secured bureaucratic or professional jobs. These individuals—all male—not only received a good education in India but also were able to live with relatives and continue their education in Canada for a period of time before being forced to look for work. For instance, Stephen Kong lived with an uncle while he studied computer programming during his first year in Canada. He then went on to work in a series of computer-related jobs before being accepted in his present position with a government ministry. Thomas Liang had already studied up to higher secondary in India (the equivalent of the last year of high school and first year of college in the United States) before arriving in Canada in 1976. He lived with relatives and furthered his studies during his first four years in Canada, working only during the summers. He was then able to secure work as an accountant shortly after graduating from a Canadian university. Finally, the brother of another man I interviewed is now studying for a doctorate in a scientific field at a university in Toronto.

No one is completely immune from the fluctuations of the world economy, however. In the early 1990s, some of the Toronto factories in which Calcutta Chinese immigrants worked either were closed or moved their bases of operation. In fact, one of the tanneries that employed Calcutta Chinese immigrants actually moved to the United States as a result of the free trade agreement between the United

States and Canada, an agreement which has already led to the loss of thousands of jobs in Canada. Although most of those affected by the closings have looked for alternative employment in Toronto, and collected unemployment benefits in the meantime, a few individuals have returned to Calcutta to work in their family businesses (see Chapter 7). Thus, while individuals continue to emigrate from India to Toronto, there is also a small flow in the other direction.

But even those who have steady, secure work often indicate that employment in Canada is a mixed blessing when compared to work in India. Take Zhang Zhunfang, for instance, one of those Calcutta Chinese immigrants working in a tannery in Toronto. His family did not have a business of its own in Calcutta; he worked in a relative's tannery there. Since in India he was "working for other people," he told me, he had no qualms about emigrating from India to Canada. Nevertheless, he emphasized that working for a relative in India was less stressful than performing factory work in the West. (The difference between the lot of Chinese workers in Dhapa, who mainly work for relatives and are treated as potential managers or apprentice entrepreneurs, and Indian workers, who have neither ethnic nor kin ties to their Chinese employers, is discussed at length in Chapter 5, and should be kept in mind.) "Here," Zhunfang said, "you work in one machine, and you have to stay there for eight hours. Not like in India, you can sit down and talk for twenty minutes, come back and work a little bit, then walk around."

Susan Qin, who taught in one of the Chinese schools in Calcutta, made a similar point to me when she stated: "Over there, there is no stress. The stress level is very low, very very low. But over here, working in Toronto, people work faster here. You don't take the afternoon nap or anything, you know, you work through, and the stress level is very high. . . . In India, if you don't feel like going to work, or if your friend is sick, or somebody is sick, you can drop your work and then go to visit the friends or consult the person. Over here you can't afford to, except to just pick up the phone and talk on the phone . . . there is no human touch in it." In Canada, Susan told me, "time is money."

Qiao Songjing, who emigrated to Toronto in 1977, now works as a welder, a job he chose because it pays quite well, despite the fact that he had received a bachelor's degree in India and studied business administration in Canada. However, his father was Qiao Tanming, one of the most successful entrepreneurs in Dhapa, and Songjing's brothers have continued to run his highly profitable tanning business. Reflecting on the difference between his present work and the work he would have done in India had he stayed, Songjing told me: "For a person in the business . . . we were pretty okay in India. Over here it's just eight hours of work, probably two more hours of driving and then back home, then cook and do the house chores. . . . I worry about money here and don't worry about money there."

Similarly, the daughter of Yuan Dongtai, another prosperous tanner in Dhapa, asserted that "everytime I go to work, I will just tell my friends, 'Back home, my father has a big business! We hire more people, they work for us. Now I have to work for them!'" She added, "If you have the money back home, that is good, if you work for somebody back home, then it is better over here [in Canada]".

Her brother, who was visiting her in Toronto and listening in on our interview, interjected, "I don't work with my hands [in Calcutta], I work with my mouth." He went on to explain that in Toronto he could at best hope to be a worker in someone else's factory, rather than the boss who gives the orders. This sentiment was commonly expressed by those who chose to remain in business in Dhapa, rather than to emigrate. Indeed, many Dhapa Chinese whom I met while they were visiting in North America, or whom I talked with on visits to Calcutta in 1985 and 1989, expressed the view that despite heat, electricity cuts, and the difficulties of being a minority in Calcutta, they had control over their work in India in a way that their immigrant relatives did not.

The fact that salaried employment and wage labor have replaced family business as their primary means of economic support, however, does not mean that Calcutta Chinese immigrants do not view business as an ultimate goal, even if it is one that may not be realized. Susan Qin and her husband have even taken evening courses to learn about the technicalities of starting a small business in Canada. Many of those I interviewed expressed a fervent desire to start a business of their own. Sentiments like those of Thomas Liang were common: "As long as you work [for a salary] . . . you still are responsible to someone. Mind you, if you have your own business you're responsible for your customers, but it's a different kind of responsibility." Continuing, he told me that he would "love to" start a business of his own if he thought he had any chance of success. K. C. Yan articulated similar feelings when he explained, "Over there you do your own business, no one bothers you. Here . . . you are reliant on the boss's control." But he added that in India there was also a lot of *kunnan,* or turmoil, in selling, watching over workers, and all the other responsibilities of running a tannery.

Most people said that despite their dreams of going into business in their new host society, they thought it would be difficult to do so because their capital does not amount to much when converted from Indian rupees into dollars. In this regard, Calcutta Chinese immigrants in Toronto often compared themselves unfavorably to the wealthiest among the Hong Kong immigrants. Looking around at a large complex of *dim sum* restaurants and other Chinese establishments in Scarborough, Mr. Kong told me, "This is all Hong Kong money, we can't possibly compete on this level."

Although the aspiration of starting one's own business remains unrealized for most Calcutta Chinese immigrants in Toronto, many emphasized to me that despite fairly modest jobs, they were able to save money, in part because they thought they were more frugal than nonimmigrants. Several told me they lived on the salary of one partner in the marriage and saved the salary of the other. And unlike the situation in Calcutta, where women did not always have direct access to business profits (see Chapter Six), most couples with whom I spoke in Toronto told me that they kept joint accounts.

Interestingly, it is now the senior generation that is dependent on the largesse of other family members for funds, though they were precisely the individuals who often controlled the family purse in Calcutta (see Chapter Six). Indeed, as we will now see, the incorporation of the senior generation into the homes of Calcutta Chinese immigrants in Canada is not a mere process of duplicating the arrangements that existed in India. Differences in these two societies, as well as in the abilities of such elderly family members to adjust to their new host culture in Canada, have changed the dynamics and power relationships between young and old Calcutta Chinese immigrants in the Canadian setting.

Guests in Their Children's Homes: Elderly Immigrants

Yan Baoxia's wife is talking about her son K. C. who lives in Canada. It is the summer of 1989, and I am visiting with the Yan family in Calcutta. K. C. was married in 1987, and he and his wife now have a baby. They are thinking of sponsoring his parents' immigration to

Canada, and K. C.'s mother is now assessing the situation as she sees it. "My son wants us to go out there and help look after the baby," she tells me. "But I don't think I want to go there to live. It's different over there. I don't think my daughter-in-law will listen to me or like me."

K. C.'s mother certainly has plenty of evidence on which to base her suspicions. For the past several years, pitiful stories have been traveling back to Dhapa about elders who emigrated abroad to live with their married children, only to find themselves mistreated by these children or even, in extreme cases, tossed out of the children's homes. The story of Mr. and Mrs. Xi is particularly infamous, and serves as a constant reminder to the senior generation in Dhapa that emigration may carry special risks for them.

The Xis left India to live with their son and daughter-in-law in Austria, where their son worked in a Chinese restaurant. After less than a year in Austria, however, at least according to the story as it made its way back to Dhapa, the Xis were cruelly thrown out of the house by their daughter-in-law. (When asked about the son's role in this turn of events, the response was usually that he had come under his wife's negative influence. Thus, an old theme in Chinese culture, that of the conniving daughter-in-law, who enters the family as a stranger and breaks its unity by disturbing the bonds between her husband, his mother, and his brothers, reappears in this story as a new phenomenon—the upsetting of family relationships among those who live abroad.)[1]

Cast out of her son's house, Mrs. Xi left for Sweden to live with her daughter's family. Her husband, perhaps unable to swallow the indignity of living with a married daughter's family, did not join her. Instead, he chose to remain "homeless," passing his nights in a railway station. Fortunately, they had not sold their tannery before leaving Dhapa but had instead decided to lease it. After several more months, they returned to Dhapa to continue their small tanning business as before.

In Toronto, I found no stories to rival that of the Xis, in which an elderly parent actually became temporarily "homeless." But I was not surprised that a story like that made its way back to Dhapa, for whatever the actual truth of the Xis' situation, there is no doubt that in Canada, the country to which the vast majority of Dhapa Chinese

[1] For more on attitudes toward the daughter-in-law in Chinese culture, see Ahern 1975 and Wolf 1972.

immigrate, there are significant shake-ups in the power relationships between the elderly and their married children.

The situation of Susan Qin's family serves as a good example of this phenomenon. When Susan emigrated from India in 1974, she had not been that keen on leaving India, where as the only daughter among five siblings, she received lots of attention. But she felt that her fiancé, Thomas, who had already emigrated in 1972, had no other option. As Susan told me, Thomas came from "a big family, and the tannery is not big enough to house all of them [his nine other brothers]. So, he was smart to branch out."

Within a few years of their marriage, however, both Susan and Thomas found themselves busily occupied with jobs and with the task of raising three small daughters. Thus, when Thomas's mother visited in 1977, they encouraged her to stay and applied for a change in her immigrant status. Thomas's mother now takes care of the children after they come home from school each day, and she also does laundry and cooking on weekdays.

In fact, since both women and men must work in order to get ahead financially in Toronto, the task of finding child care has become a dilemma for most Calcutta Chinese families. Whereas large families are the norm in Calcutta, none of the couples I interviewed in Toronto had more than three children. Indeed, one or two children was the norm, and all of my interviewees mentioned the cost of living, and the fact that both parents must work, as reasons for not having large families in Canada. In the few cases where Dhapa families who already have many children have emigrated to Canada, they are usually roundly criticized by both Toronto-based and Calcutta-based community members, most of whom express the belief that in the West it is not possible to raise many children.

Whatever the number of children, many working parents have solved the problem of child care by sponsoring their parents' immigration, since a grandparent at home can take care of small children while the parents are at work. It is therefore not surprising to find that many Toronto-based Calcutta Chinese immigrants are in the process of applying for their parents' immigration—just as the Qins did in sponsoring Thomas's mother.

But although she makes a substantial contribution to the family in Toronto, her incomplete mastery of the host culture has made Thomas's mother dependent on her children in ways she would not be at home. For instance, because she is over sixty-five, Mrs. Qin receives a monthly social security check from the government. Yet without a knowledge of English, she has difficulty cashing these checks. (Most Calcutta Chinese of her generation do not know English.) Hence, she relies on her son to cash them for her. In addition, whereas in Calcutta a mere walk out the door would put her in contact with acquaintances with whom to talk and gossip, Mrs. Qin now has to do most of her gossiping over the telephone. And although Susan knows she should be grateful for the tremendous help she gets from her mother-in-law, she complains about her, often focusing on seemingly small items (e.g., the amount of time her mother-in-law spends on the phone and the fact that her mother-in-law didn't like some clothes Susan had bought for her and ended up having to return).

In addition to their lack of English skills and difficulty in dealing with the outside society, there are other reasons for the less powerful position of the senior generation among Dhapa Chinese in Toronto. In Toronto, the elders are usually latecomers. That is, they arrive only after their children have been living and making daily decisions on their own in Canada for several years. Unlike in Calcutta, where they continue to exercise their influence by controlling their family businesses, in Toronto seniors have no control over their children's economic activities. Their monthly social security stipends comprise the smallest portion of the income that comes into a household, and as in the case of Susan Qin's mother-in-law, these checks are usually considered merely as the elder's personal spending money.

In Calcutta, sons remain in their parents' homes after marriage. The authority of the parents that began in childhood is continued in an uninterrupted manner, even in an unchanged physical location. But in Toronto, seniors often come to live in a home that these sons, or sometimes daughters, have been living in for several years before their arrival. If these children are not renting an apartment, but have already purchased a home and are paying a mortgage, the children's sense of control over this property is even more pronounced. The married children of these seniors are very clear about the fact that these houses are their own, and that the elders can only look upon their children's financial struggles to secure these homes from the outside. Said Susan Qin, for instance, "the elderly people, they're always on the phone, and they compare, 'Oh, your son bought a house. Oh, how big is it?'. . . They don't *know* how much mortgage we are carrying!"

That parents live in their childrens' homes in Toronto, rather than the reverse, is clearly demonstrated by the story of the Qiaos, an elderly couple who alternated their time between two different married sons, living in two different apartments. When friends who were visiting from Calcutta telephoned Mr. and Mrs. Qiao to say they would be visiting, the Qiaos had to say that they could not put them up. This was a very shameful experience for them, since they had to turn away prominent members of the Dhapa Chinese community with whom they had long-standing relationships. Further, they knew that these people would return to India and report this lack of hospitality, contributing to a great lose of face (*diu lian*) on their part, since they were unable to live up to expected standards of social reciprocity. But they felt they could not reveal to the visiting parties the reason for their lack of hospitality—namely, that their sons and daughters-in-law did not want to host guests at that time, and they were powerless to override this decision since they did not live in their "own" house.

In some cases, therefore, especially when both parents are alive and they run a very successful firm in Calcutta, they may prefer visiting over emigrating. Some, like K. C. Yan's mother, openly articulate their fear of being dependent on the goodwill of their children in a foreign land. Others, like Stephen Kong's father and Ma Hongzhang, are anxious to avoid the kind of catastrophe faced by the Xis. Both Mr. Kong and Mr. Ma are permanent residents of Canada and must therefore return there once every year. Thus, during the uncomfortable and relatively unproductive months of the monsoon in India, they leave their businesses in their sons' hands and visit their children in Canada. Then, when the weather in Canada starts to get cold, they return to Calcutta to oversee their businesses. In this way, they take advantage of the best of both worlds.

Finally, in at least two cases that I know about, elderly members of the households who started out living with their sons and daughters-in-laws later moved out. Principal Yu told me that her mother-in-law used to wait for her to return from work before eating, although this was usually at 1:00 A.M.! She ultimately rented another apartment for her parents-in-law, although this meant that she had to pay two rents. In another case, a woman who lived with her son and daughter-in-law in Toronto actually decided to move out on her own, over the objections of her children. This woman applied for and received an apartment in senior citizen housing, and she was then able to support herself with her monthly social security stipend from the government. Her daughter-in-law, commenting indignantly on this turn of events,

[261]

explained to me that in her view, "in Canada, the money is first. They don't think about the grandchild or the granddaughter or anything. Actually, I need her a lot, you know, because she could look after my daughter, since I have two now, she should help me with the baby. But she doesn't. . . . My mother-in-law, since she came here almost ten years, maybe she learned from the Canadian people. I no longer have a mother-in-law. I have a mother-out-law!"

The elderly Calcutta Chinese in Toronto are therefore caught in the horns of a dilemma. Their married children would like their parents to live with them and take care of the grandchildren. But when the grandparents arrive, they often find that they, as well as the grand-children, are dependent on the generation in the middle. If they remain in Calcutta, however, they can continue to exert considerable control over both family and business.

Despite having decreased power within their families, these elderly immigrants do exercise some influence over the social life of Calcutta Chinese living in Toronto. I consider this social life next.

The Community Regroups in Toronto

When Kenneth Fei planned his wedding in Toronto, in 1980, he called upon some elderly Calcutta Chinese immigrants from his sur-name group for help. These individuals compiled a list of all the mem-bers of their surname group who were living in Toronto at the time, and Kenneth, following the same practice as he would have in Calcut-ta, invited every one of them to his wedding. Although he should have invited all the members of his mother's surname group to the wedding as well, not to mention his wife's relatives, Kenneth drew the line at his own surname. Fortunately for Kenneth, who did not want a "big" wedding, there were not many Feis in Toronto, and he was able to invite a "modest" number of people—sixteen tables, or 160 guests.

As the number of Calcutta Chinese immigrants in Toronto has grown, the community has reconstituted itself in certain ways. Daily contact is still difficult, for most young and middle-aged people are working and besides, those who have left St. Jamestown tend to be dispersed throughout the sprawling suburb of Scarborough. But social occasions, particularly weddings, have become a focal point of commu-nity social life and are gradually becoming larger and more grandiose, now rivaling the large weddings of forty, fifty, and sixty tables that are held in Dhapa. Indeed, had Kenneth Fei been married in 1990 instead of 1980, he probably would have had difficulty limiting the number of guests at the reception.

The size of these gatherings can be partly explained by the sheer increase in the numbers of Chinese immigrants from Calcutta. When one invites all the members of one's surname group now, there are simply many more of them. In addition, according to many members of the community, as the number of Calcutta Chinese immigrants has increased, they have also brought with them all their old rivalries and concerns about status (see Chapter 4). As Kenneth put it, "There are a lot of people that came over here from India, so the tradition is almost starting over." It's just like Dhapa all over again, Kenneth told me, "like over there they say, 'oh the other tannery invited sixty tables then I am going to make sure I invite 100 tables!'" Kenneth's mother-in-law, in the room while I was conducting the interview, chimed in that "they just want 'face'" (*tamen jiu shi yao mianzi*), meaning here that it is a question of prestige.[2] (This quest for prestige takes place simultaneously in both the Calcutta and Toronto communities, since visitors from Calcutta often return home with the latest news about community members living abroad.)

Many younger people, however, tended to distance themselves from this *competition* (a word they frequently used) and explain its resurgence as the result of the influence of the elderly. For instance, Susan Qin complained about how the elderly compare everything from the relative size of the houses that their Toronto-based children buy to the number of guests at various Calcutta Chinese wedding receptions in Toronto. Younger people who work, she went on to emphasize, have *no* time for such gossip! "Everybody is working; everybody is paying a mortgage; there is nothing to compare."

But it is difficult to understand how the elderly immigrants with such diminishing influence at home could wield such overwhelming authority in the social sphere. Rather, it seems more likely that these social events play into a number of different needs. "Face," or status, is certainly one of these, but wedding celebrations also bring together

---

[2] See note 2, Chapter 1, for an explanation of the two meanings of *face* in Chinese society: *lian*, or "moral standing," and *mianzi*, or "prestige." The Qiaos, who could not host their friends from Dhapa because their sons would not cooperate, were losing *lian*, since their actions cast doubt on basic moral values. On the other hand, the question of inviting large numbers of people to a wedding reception is clearly a question of social status, or *mianzi*.

Calcutta Chinese immigrants, who are normally kept apart by work schedules and physical dispersal. For instance, "T. F." Xiu, Susan Qin's brother who runs a mobile food stand in Toronto, told me that weddings "are the only time we meet . . . we were neighbors then, and now we're so far apart." Indeed, most of the community members I spoke with emphasized that lack of time, and infrequent chances to see other people, characterized their life in Canada. Thus, when I asked T. F. who his friends were in Toronto, he answered as follows: "In social life Calcutta is better, here there's no social life at all, it's only work, work, work. . . . I couldn't count too many people here for friends because I don't have time."

Even when there is time for social life, most people indicated that their only really meaningful relationships were with relatives and other Calcutta Chinese. They described their interactions with fellow workers in offices or factories as pleasant but hardly ever mentioned a non-Calcutta Chinese whom they considered a real friend. In fact, most people emphasized that their most frequent social interactions were with other relatives. As Thomas Liang told me, "most of my friends are my relatives." And Yuan Meihua said that "once in awhile we go to a relative's house . . . but most of the time we are busy, and then on Saturday and Sunday we have to clean up the house, do the shopping, and that's it."

Ironically, of the people who did mention friendships outside the Calcutta Chinese community, several of them identified these friends as South Asians, either immigrants from India or ethnic Indians from Uganda. (Despite their differences in India, Calcutta Chinese and Indians at least can draw upon shared knowledge.) Thus, when Yan Baoxia's son, K. C., was married in Toronto in 1987, there was only one table out of approximately forty that was not composed of immigrant Calcutta Chinese. In addition to the owner of the factory in which K. C. worked, who was an Anglo-Canadian, most of the others at this "foreigners" table were South Asians. But even these cases were not very numerous. Most Calcutta Chinese in Toronto still seem tied together by the particularities of their own experience, interacting only on a superficial level with members of other ethnic groups in Toronto.

The exceptions to this general pattern actually accentuate its overall dominance. For instance, when Qiao Songjing married a French Canadian woman, he and his bride had a registry marriage, inviting only two friends as witnesses, and eschewing all the hoopla that normally surrounds such events. In fact, Songjing did not even tell his mother in Calcutta about his marriage until the birth of his first child, although his mother came to live with them later. Similarly, Kenneth Fei, who immigrated to Toronto with his family when he was only thirteen, and therefore attended secondary school in Canada, told me that he had a broader range of friends than most Calcutta Chinese immigrants because he had come at such a young age. But he added that because of his experiences, he felt that there was a distance between himself and his relatives from India.

"One of my friends is Cantonese from Hong Kong, and I have another friend who is half Chinese and half Negro, and he is from Jamaica, and then there are a few other friends also who are Canadian," he told me. Of his relatives, however, he said, "They feel a little bit more prejudiced to Negroes, or whites, or whatever. Because they are brought up that way . . . if they go out to meet friends, they don't really like to associate with a lot of whites, or blacks, usually it's within their own group from India."

Besides Kenneth Fei, the only individuals who indicated to me that they had close friends who were not Calcutta Chinese were the two men who had married outside the community.

Travel between India and Canada serves to reinforce the connections among Calcutta Chinese immigrants with one another and with their home community. Calcutta Chinese in Toronto travel back to India for important family occasions like weddings, funerals, and the birthday celebrations of elders. In a number of cases several young women have returned to India to live for several months, so that their families can arrange marriages for them. Family members in India come to Canada to visit as well. Yuan Meihua's experience may be extreme, but neither is it atypical. Almost every year, one of her four brothers from Dhapa, or her parents, or at the very least a sister-in-law, has come to visit Canada and stayed with her.

In addition to strengthening ties, the continuing influx of Indian Chinese immigrants and visitors has reinforced the separation of immigrant Calcutta Hakka from other groups. But what of the future? The young children of these immigrants go to school with children from many different social backgrounds. They speak Hakka Chinese at home with their parents, but even when playing with one another, they slip into English; of course, many of these children have never been to India. As they pass through the Canadian school system, they will most likely enter a greater variety of occupations than their parents have.

T. F. Xiu acknowledged that the connections that bind Calcutta

Chinese immigrants to one another may be less powerful in the next generation: "When we talk about home we talk about Calcutta, it's still our root, for our father it's China, and for my children, it's Brampton [the area of Toronto where he lives]."

Ethnic Identity in a Transnational World

So long as the "Calcutta" Hakka remained in Calcutta, ethnic identity was not particularly problematic for either themselves or the outside analyst. As explained in Chapter 2, Indian political history, particularly the Sino-Indian Conflict, as well as Calcutta's ethnically differentiated and stratified economy, and a Hindu religious ideology that distinguishes the pure from the impure, all helped to define and separate the Hakka from other ethnic groups in Calcutta, and even from other groups of Chinese.

Orlando Patterson has said of ethnicity that it is a "condition wherein certain members of a society, in a given social context, choose to emphasize as their most meaningful basis of primary, extrafamilial identity certain assumed cultural, national, or somatic traits" (1975:308). But, I would add to Patterson's definition of *ethnicity* an insistence that ethnic identity is not simply a matter of how a group chooses to define itself but also a question of the identity that others ascribe to it. The manner in which others view an ethnic group may play into its own self-perceptions in a variety of ways. Group members may incorporate, reject, invert, or ignore the images that others have of them. And the images that others have of an ethnic group will in turn color the attitudes that ethnic group members hold toward these others.

Ethnic identity is therefore dialogic or reflexive, in the sense that it is created, maintained, and reaffirmed through a continuous set of oppositions between one's own group and others.[3] To use Fredrik Barth's language, ethnic interaction creates ethnic boundaries, but the "stuff" that these boundaries enclose, the particular diacritica that are utilized as ethnic boundary markers can be discovered only by looking at particular contexts of interaction (1969).

---

[3] Where one of these "others" is the state, as Harrell has so trenchantly demonstrated in an article on Yi communities in southwest China (1990), the process by which groups create self-definitions is exceedingly complex.

However, while ethnic identity is created through interaction, the process of its creation is also historical, and changes in social conditions over time may create the need for either investing ethnic identities with new meanings or for dissolving certain ethnic categories altogether. Says G. Carter Bentley, "As individuals develop new ways of dealing with a changing world, old truths erode; as what was formerly inconceivable becomes commonplace, degrees of sharing and affinity, hence ethnic identities, become problematic. At the least, under these conditions ethnic symbolism is likely to take on different meanings for differentially adapted segments of a population" (1987:43).

But Bentley also points out that ethnic identities have great affective power and are not shed lightly. He utilizes Bourdieu's notion of the *habitus* to explain this affective power. The habitus, for Bourdieu, comprises the conscious and unconscious inclinations and outlooks inculcated and internalized from the earliest years of a person's life, and ethnic identity is integral to these. It is *because* they have such power, because they are a part of one's most strongly internalized behaviors, outlooks, and obligations, that ethnic bonds are so profound a force in the reproduction of differentiated social formations, says Bentley (1987:42).

Since ethnic identity is so fundamental in the formation of people's conscious and unconscious understandings of the world, Bentley asserts, individuals may experience "crises of ethnic identity" (1987:43) when they undergo changed social circumstances. In such cases, they may respond with new formulations of ethnic identity, or they may reinvigorate already existing notions (Bentley 1987:43). For instance, in making sense of their situation, the Calcutta Hakka often draw upon the label that was originally applied to them by the Cantonese in Guangdong—that of *guest people*. "You know, we are the guest people, and we keep moving from place to place, we even did that in China," one friend in Calcutta told me. It was a refrain I heard frequently among residents of the Calcutta Chinese tanning community.

This term has continued potency for the Calcutta Chinese not because of some instinctive "primordial" (see Isaacs 1975) identification with past experiences, but because it still has power to describe their present situation, in which they are an ethnic minority and still on the move. Indeed, in their new environment of Toronto, Calcutta Hakka immigrants once again find distinctions between both Chinese and non-Chinese others to be socially significant, and they still find relevance in the notion of themselves as guests. As noted earlier, they distinguish themselves not only from the multitude of non-Chinese groups but also from the dominant Chinese group, the Cantonese, particularly the wealthy Hong Kong immigrants whose presence is a constant reminder of their still unfulfilled aspirations to establish themselves in business in Canada.

But will a sense of themselves as guest people, or even the Hakka language itself, take root among the children of Calcutta Hakka immigrants who are born and brought up in Canada? If not, will constant immigration continue to refurbish the ranks of the Calcutta Hakka in Toronto and help to maintain a self-conscious community, even while others assimilate into a larger Chinese-Canadian or Canadian population? And will the search for profit and the dream of running one's own business continue to fuel both harmonious and contending relationships among and within families?

While we cannot answer these questions with certainty, to understand the changes that do occur in the future, we must continue to analyze the relations between internal family dynamics and political and economic conditions and transformations on local, national, and even global levels. For the moment, there are a number of countervailing tendencies. On the one hand, "time-space compression" and the relative ease of travel and communication have made it easier for community members to maintain links, despite the vast physical distances that separate them. And the increasing numbers of immigrants from Calcutta have also enabled community members to reconstitute a corporate social life that revolves mainly around weddings, and in which surname groups and surname group elders still play a significant role.

Furthermore, the flow of individuals is not solely in one direction. As we have seen, some Calcutta Chinese immigrants to Toronto have returned to India because they must attend to their family businesses there, or because they have lost their jobs in Canada. These developments themselves are often the result of larger political and economic changes. As mentioned earlier, the U.S.-Canada free trade agreement led to the loss of many Canadian jobs, including some held by Calcutta Chinese.[4]

---

[4] This agreement itself is both a symptom and a symbol of even more global economic transformations. The agreement makes it easier for capital to cross the U.S.-Canada border, and such movement is symptomatic of what David Harvey terms a *regime of*

At the same time, the demands of the local economy also create forces that conspire to dissolve a distinct Calcutta Hakka identity in Toronto. Unlike their relatives in Calcutta, this group does not inhabit a specific economic niche. And as Eric Wolf points out in his analysis of labor immigration under capitalism, "ethnicities rarely coincided with the initial self-identification of the industrial recruits, who first thought of themselves as Hanoverians or Bavarians rather than as Germans, as members of their village or parish . . . rather than as Poles, as Tonga or Yao rather than as 'Nyasalanders.' The more comprehensive categories emerged only as particular cohorts of workers gained access to different segments of the labor market and began to treat their access as a resource to be defended both socially and politically. Such ethnicities are therefore not 'primordial' social relationships. They are historical products of labor market segmentation" (1982:381).

Thus, the fact that Calcutta Chinese immigrants in Toronto do not inhabit a particular economic niche, and the fact that the conditions of wage labor and salaried employment in Toronto create new demands on time, inhibiting the unscheduled daily social interactions characteristic of life in Calcutta, may also work against the continued solidarity of the community in the future.

It is also possible that class differences among Calcutta Chinese immigrants in Toronto will become more pronounced over time. In a 1979 article on Toronto's Chinatown, Richard Thompson indicated that the Chinese community included economic groups as divergent as entrepreneurs who had invested millions of dollars in new enterprises, and low-paid workers who labored in ethnic Chinese businesses. Moreover, within this community, the classes had clearly split over a number of community issues (Thompson 1979). In a subsequent article Thompson proposed that social class, rather than the traditional categories of surname group or home district in China, was now the

---

flexible accumulation, the most recent form of global capitalism, in which the emphasis is on a rapid turnover time in production and consumption, and on quick and easy movements of capital and financial reserves. Flexible accumulation involves a changed emphasis in labor practices as well, and a shift from reliance on a fairly immobile work force with secure, steady employment to an increased emphasis on subcontracting, temporary employment, and small business (Harvey 1989). Impediments to such flexibility, including protectionism on the national level, have come under attack during this most recent era.

most important basis of urban overseas Chinese social organization (1980). But as noted in this chapter, surname groups still play an important role in the social life of Calcutta Hakka immigrants. Furthermore, variations in economic status among Calcutta Hakka immigrants in Toronto are not nearly as great as Thompson found within the Toronto Chinese community in general. Indeed, most Calcutta Chinese work in factories or do clerical work; only a few hold professional positions; and none can possibly be compared with the wealthy Chinese investors now coming to Canada from Hong Kong. So even though most individuals are not employed in the same workplace or industry, community members are not dealing with widely divergent economic situations.

Whatever the ultimate outcome, family members will continue to be constrained by certain of these realities as well as to contrive new responses to them. And as with their predecessors in Calcutta, these responses will entail strategies that will be played out over both time and space. Despite this continuous flux and movement, some Calcutta Chinese in Toronto have found, at least for the moment, a sense of stability. "We are the guest people," said Stephen Kong during his son's birthday party on that August morning of 1986, "but maybe Canada will be the last stop."

References

Abu-Lughod, Lila. 1985. A Community of Secrets: The Separate World of Bedouin Women. *Signs* 10(4):637–657.

Acts of Parliament, 1962. 1963. New Delhi: Goverment of India Press.

Ahern, Emily. 1973. *The Cult of the Dead in a Chinese Village.* Stanford: Stanford University Press.

———. 1975. The Power and Pollution of Chinese Women. In *Women in Chinese Society*, ed. Margery Wolf and Roxane Witke, 193–214. Stanford: Stanford University Press.

Alabaster, C. 1975 [1858]. The Chinese Colony in Calcutta. In *Calcutta: People and Empire, Gleanings from Old Journals*, ed. Pradip Chaudhury and Abhijit Mukhopadhyay. Calcutta: India Book Exchange.

All India Leather Directory, 1960–1961. 1960–1961. Calcutta: Indian Leather Technologists Association.

All India Leather Directory, 1965–1966. 1965–1966. Calcutta: Indian Leather Technologists Association.

Althusser, Louis. 1971. *Lenin and Philosophy.* New York: Monthly Review Press.

Appadurai, Arjun. 1986. Is Homo Hierachicus? *American Ethnologist* 13(4):745–761.

———. 1991. Global Ethnoscapes: Notes and Queries for a Transnational Anthropology. In *Recapturing Anthropology: Working in the Present*, ed. Richard Fox, 191–210. Santa Fe: School of American Research Press.

Baker, Hugh D. R. 1968. *A Chinese Lineage Village: Sheung Shui.* London: Cass.

———. 1979. *Chinese Family and Kinship.* New York: Columbia University Press.

Bakhtin, M. M. 1981. Discourse in the Novel. Trans. Caryl Emerson and Michael Holquist. In *The Dialogic Imagination: Four Essays by M. M. Bakhtin*, ed. Michael Holquist, 259–422. Austin: University of Texas Press.

———. 1986. The Problem of Speech Genres. Trans. Vern W. McGee. In *Speech Genres and Other Late Essays*, ed. Caryl Emerson and Michael Holquist, 60–102. Austin: University of Texas Press.

References

Bandyopadhyay, Raghbab. 1990. The Inheritors: Slum and Pavement Life in Calcutta. In *Calcutta: The Living City*, ed. Sukanta Chaudhuri, 78–87. Calcutta: Oxford University Press.

Barth, Fredrik. 1969. Introduction. In *Ethnic Groups and Boundaries*, ed. Fredrik Barth, 1–38. Boston: Little, Brown.

Basu, Ellen Oxfeld. 1991a. Profit, Loss, and Fate: The Entrepreneurial Ethic and the Practice of Gambling in an Overseas Chinese Community. *Modern China* 17(2):227–259.

———. 1991b. The Sexual Division of Labor and the Organization of Family and Firm in an Overseas Chinese Community. *American Ethnologist* 18(4):700–718.

Bayly, C. A. 1983. *Rulers, Townsmen, and Bazaars*. Cambridge: Cambridge University Press.

Bengal Past and Present, Journal of the Calcutta Historical Society. 1907. Some Transactions of the C. H. S. July/December.

Bengal Past and Present, Journal of the Calcutta Historical Society. 1909. Some Leaves from the Editor's Notebook. January–April.

Bentley, G. Carter. 1987. Ethnicity and Practice. *Comparative Studies in Society and History* 29(1):24–55.

Berry, Brian J. L., and Philip H. Rees. 1969. The Factoral Ecology of Calcutta. *American Journal of Sociology* 74(5):445–491.

Blake, C. Fred. 1981. *Ethnic Groups and Social Change in a Chinese Market Town*. Honolulu: University of Hawaii Press.

Bonacich, Edna. 1973. A Theory of Middleman Minorities. *American Sociological Review* 38(October):583–594.

Bonacich, Edna, and John Modell. 1980. *The Economic Basis of Ethnic Solidarity*. Berkeley: University of California Press.

Bose, Nirmal Kumar. 1965. Calcutta: A Premature Metropolis. *Scientific American* 213(September):91–102.

———. 1968. *Calcutta: 1964, A Social Survey*. Bombay: Lalvani Publishing House.

Boserup, Esther. 1970. *Women's Role in Economic Development*. London: George Allen and Unwin.

Bourdieu, Pierre. 1977. *Outline of a Theory of Practice*. Cambridge: Cambridge University Press.

———. 1984. *Distinction: A Social Critique of the Judgement of Taste*. Cambridge, Mass.: Harvard University Press.

Calcutta Statesman [correspondent]. 1982. Tanneries in the City Face Decline. 19 July.

Cator, W. L. 1936. *Economic Position of the Chinese in the Netherlands Indies*. Chicago: University of Chicago Press.

Census of India, 1911. 1913. *Bengal, Bihar, Orissa and Sikkim*. Volume 5. Part 1. Report by L. S. S. O'Malley. Calcutta: Bengal Secretariat Book Depot.

Census of India, 1921. 1923. *City of Calcutta*. Volume 6. Part 1. Report by W. H. Thompson. Calcutta: Bengal Secretariat Book Depot.

Census of India, 1931. 1933. *West Bengal, Sikkim, and Chandernagore*. Volume 6. Delhi: Manager of Publications.

Census of India, 1951. 1953. *Language Tables.* Volume 1. Delhi: Manager of Publications.

Census of India, 1961. 1964. *Language Tables.* Volume 1. Part 2C(ii). Civil Lines, Delhi: Manager of Publications.

Census of India, 1971. 1975. *West Bengal, Social and Cultural Tables.* Series 1. Part 2C(ii). Calcutta: Government of West Bengal Publications.

Census of India, 1971. 1977. *Social and Cultural Tables.* Part 2C(i). New Delhi: Controller of Publications.

Chakraborty, Satyesh. 1990. The Growth of Calcutta in the Twentieth Century. In *Calcutta, The Living City,* ed. Sukanta Chaudhuri, 1–14. Calcutta: Oxford University Press.

Chaliha, Jaya, and Bunny Gupta. 1990. The Armenians of Calcutta. In *Calcutta: The Living City,* ed. Sukanta Chaudhuri, 54–55. Calcutta: Oxford University Press.

Chatterjee, Nilanjana. 1990. The East Bengal Refugees, A Lesson in Survival. In *Calcutta: The Living City,* ed. Sukanta Chaudhuri, 70–77. Calcutta: Oxford University Press.

Chayanov, A. V. 1966 [1925]. Peasant Farm Organization. In *The Theory of Peasant Economy,* ed. Daniel Thorner, Basile Kerblay, and R. E. F. Smith, 29–269. Homewood, Ill.: Richard D. Irwin.

Chen, Jack. 1980. *The Chinese of America.* San Francisco: Harper and Row.

Chin, Frank. 1972. Confessions of the Chinatown Cowboy. *Bulletin of Concerned Asian Scholars* 4(Fall):58–70.

Choong, Ket Che. 1983. Chinese Divination. *Contributions to Southeast Asian Ethnography* (2/August):49–97.

Chowdhury, Pritha, and Joyoti Chaliha. 1990. The Jews of Calcutta. In *Calcutta: The Living City,* ed. Sukanta Chaudhur, 52–53. Calcutta: Oxford University Press.

Cohen, Abner. 1969. *Custom and Politics in Urban Africa.* Berkeley: University of California Press.

———. 1974. Introduction: The Lessons of Ethnicity. In *Urban Ethnicity,* ix–xxiv. London: Tavistock.

Cohen, Myron. 1968. The Hakka or 'Guest People': Dialect as a Sociocultural Variable in Southeastern China. *Ethnohistory* 15(3):237–292.

———.1970. Developmental Process in the Chinese Domestic Group. In *Family and Kinship in Chinese Society,* ed. Maurice Freedman, 21–36. Stanford: Stanford University Press.

———. 1976. *House United, House Divided.* New York: Columbia University Press.

Coppel, Charles. 1976. Patterns of Chinese Political Activity in Indonesia. In *The Chinese in Indonesia,* ed. J. A. C. Mackie, 19–76. Honolulu: University of Hawaii Press.

Coughlin, Richard J. 1960. *Double Identity: The Chinese in Modern Thailand.* Hong Kong: Hong Kong University Press.

Crapanzano, Vincent. 1990. On Self Characterization. In *Cultural Psychology: Essays on Comparative Human Development,* ed. James Stigler, Richard Shweder, and Gilbert Herdt, 401–426. Cambridge: Cambridge University Press.

Crissman, Lawrence. 1967. The Segmentary Structure of Urban Overseas Chinese Communities. *Man* 2(2):185–204.

Curtin, Philip. 1984. *Cross-Cultural Trade in World History*. Cambridge: Cambridge University Press.

D'Andrade, Roy. 1986. Cultural Schemas as Motives. Paper presented at invited session, "The Directive Force of Cultural Models," at the 85th Annual Meeting of the American Anthropological Association, Philadelphia, December.

De, J. K. 1972. A Brief History of the Leather Industry of Bengal in Pre-Partition Days. *Journal of the Indian Leather Technologists Association* 20(1):233–240.

DeGlopper, Donald. 1972. Doing Business in Lukang. In *Economic Organization in Chinese Society*, ed. W. E. Willmott, 297–326. Stanford: Stanford University Press.

Devereux, Edward. 1949. Gambling and Social Structure: A Sociological Study of Lotteries and Horseracing in Contemporary America. Ph.D. diss., Harvard University.

di Leonardo, Micaela. 1984. *The Varieties of Ethnic Experience*. Ithaca: Cornell University Press.

Downes, David, et al. 1976. *Gambling, Work, and Leisure*. London: Routledge and Kegan Paul.

Dumont, Louis. 1970. *Homo Hierarchicus*. Chicago: University of Chicago Press.

——. 1985. A Modified View of Our Origins: The Christian Beginnings of Modern Individualism. In *The Category of the Person*, ed. Michael Carrithers, Steven Collins, and Steven Lukes, 93–122. Cambridge: Cambridge University Press.

Eadington, William R. 1976. *Gambling and Society*. Springfield, Ill.: Charles C. Thomas.

Economic Review, 1979–1980. Alipore, West Bengal: Government of West Bengal Press.

Economic Times, The (Bombay). 1972. Leather Growth Prospects Dim. January.

Eitzen, D. Stanley. 1968. Two Minorities: The Jews of Poland and the Chinese of the Philippines. *Jewish Journal of Sociology* 10:221–240.

Elvin, Mark. 1973. *The Pattern of the Chinese Past*. Stanford: Stanford University Press.

——. 1985. Between the Earth and Heaven: Conceptions of the Self in China. In *The Category of the Person*, ed. Michael Carrithers, Steven Collins, and Steven Lukes, 153–189. Cambridge: Cambridge University Press.

Fei, Hsiao-t'ung. 1939. *Peasant Life in China*. London: Routledge.

Firey, Walter. 1980 [1947]. *Land Use in Central Boston*. Cambridge, Mass.: Harvard University Press.

Fischer, Michael. 1973. Zorastrian Iran between Myth and Praxis. Ph.D. diss., University of Chicago.

Fortes, Meyer. 1958. Introduction. In *The Developmental Cycle in Domestic Groups*, ed. Jack Goody, 1–14. Cambridge: Cambridge University Press.

Freedman, Maurice. 1959. The Handling of Money: A Note on the Background to the Economic Sophistication of Overseas Chinese. *Man* 59:64–65.

——. 1960. Immigrants and Associations: Chinese in Nineteenth-Century Singapore. *Comparative Studies in Society and History* 3(1):25–48.

——. 1966. *Chinese Lineage and Society: Fukien and Kwangtung.* London: Athlone Press.

——. 1970. Ritual Aspects of Chinese Kinship and Marriage. In *Family and Kinship in Chinese Society*, ed. Maurice Freedman, 163–187. Stanford: Stanford University Press.

Furnivall, J. S. 1944. *Netherlands India: A Study of Plural Economy.* New York: Macmillan.

Gallin, Bernard. 1960. Matrilateral and Affinal Relationships of a Taiwanese Village. *American Ethnologist* 62:632–642.

——. 1966. *Hsin Hsing, Taiwan: A Chinese Village in Change.* Berkeley: University of California Press.

Gallin, Bernard, and Rita Gallin. 1988. Daughters Cry at Your Funeral. Paper presented at the annual meeting of the Association for Asian Studies, San Francisco, March.

Ganguli, Amulya. 1973. Treading Softly in Calcutta. *The Statesman*, 2 July:sec. 6, col. 4.

Gates, Hill. 1987. Money for the Gods. *Modern China* 13(3):259–277.

Geertz, Clifford, 1973. Deep Play: Notes on the Balinese Cockfight. In *The Interpretation of Cultures*, 412–454. New York: Basic Books.

Geib, Margaret, and Ashok Dutt. 1987. *Atlas of South Asia.* Boulder: Westview Press.

Gilligan, Carol. 1982. *In a Different Voice: Psychological Theory and Women's Development.* Cambridge, Mass.: Harvard University Press.

Glazer, Nathan, and Daniel Moynihan. 1975. *Ethnicity: Theory and Experience.* Cambridge, Mass.: Harvard University Press.

Goffman, Erving. 1961. *Encounters: Two Studies in the Sociology of Interaction.* Indianapolis: Bobbs-Merrill.

——. 1967. *Interaction Ritual: Essays in Face to Face Behavior.* Garden City, N.Y.: Anchor Books.

Goswami, Omkar. 1990. Calcutta's Economy, 1918–1970: The Fall from Grace. In *Calcutta: The Living City*, ed. Sukanta Chaudhuri, 88–96. Calcutta: Oxford University Press.

Greenhalgh, Susan. 1985a. Is Inequality Demographically Induced? The Family Cycle and the Distribution of Income in Taiwan. *American Anthropologist* 87(3):571–594.

——. 1985b. Sexual Stratification: The Other Side of 'Growth with Equity' in East Asia. *Population and Development Review* 11(2):265–314.

——. 1988. Families and Networks in Taiwan's Economic Development. In *Contending Approaches to the Political Economy of Taiwan*, ed. Susan Greenhalgh and Edwin Winckler, 224–248. Armonk, N.Y.: M. E. Sharpe.

Gupta, Akhil. 1992. The Song of the Nonaligned World: Transnational Identities and the Reinscription of Space in Late Capitalism. *Cultural Anthropology* 7(1):63–80.

Gupta, Akhil, and James Ferguson. 1992. Beyond 'Culture': Space, Identity, and the Politics of Difference. *Cultural Anthropology* 7(1):6–23.

Hamilton, Gary. 1978. Pariah Capitalism: A Paradox of Power and Dependence. *Ethnic Groups* 2:1–15.

References

Hammel, E. A. 1972. The Zadruga as Process. In *Household and Family in Past Time*, ed. Peter Laslett and Richard Wall, 335–374. Cambridge: Cambridge University Press.

Hansen, Chad. 1985. Individualism in Chinese Thought. In *Individualism and Holism: Studies in Confucian and Taoist Values*, ed. Donald Munro, 35–56. Ann Arbor: University of Michigan, Center for Chinese Studies.

Harrell, Stevan. 1981. Normal and Deviant Drinking in Rural Taiwan. In *Normal and Abnormal Behavior in Chinese Culture*, ed. Arthur Kleinman and Tsung-yi Lin, 49–59. Dordrecht, Holland: D. Reidel.

———. 1982. *Ploughshare Village: Culture and Context in Taiwan*. Seattle: University of Washington Press.

———. 1985. Why Do the Chinese Work So Hard? Reflections on an Entrepreneurial Ethic. *Modern China* 11(2):203–226.

———. 1987. The Concept of Fate in Chinese Folk Ideology. *Modern China* 13(1):90–109.

———. 1990. Ethnicity, Local Interests, and the State: Yi Communities in Southwest China. *Comparative Studies in Society and History* 32(3):515–548.

Harris, Grace Gredys. 1989. Concepts of Individual, Self, and Person in Description and Analysis. *American Anthropologist* 91(3):599–612.

Harvey, David. 1989. *The Condition of Postmodernity: An Enquiry into the Origins of Cultural Change*. New York: Basil Blackwell.

Hazarika, Sanjoy. 1987. India Shoes Gaining in the West. *The New York Times*, 3 August.

Honig, Emily. 1985. Burning Incense, Pledging Sisterhood: Communities of Women Workers in the Shanghai Cotton Mills, 1919–1949. *Signs* 10(4):700–714.

Hsu, Francis. 1948. *Under the Ancestors' Shadow*. New York: Columbia University Press.

———. 1968. Chinese Kinship and Chinese Behavior. In *China's Heritage and the Communist Political System System*, ed. Ping-ti Ho and Tsuo Tang, 579–608. Chicago: University of Chicago Press.

———. 1971. Eros, Affect, and Pao. In *Kinship and Culture*, ed. Hsu, 439–476. Chicago: Aldine Press.

———. 1973. Kinship Is the Key. *Center Magazine* 6:4–14.

———. 1981. *Americans and Chinese: Passage to Differences*. Honolulu: University Press of Hawaii.

———. 1983. *Rugged Individualism Reconsidered*. Knoxville: University of Tennessee Press.

Hu, Hsien Chin. 1944. The Chinese Concepts of "Face." *American Anthropologist* 46:45–64.

Hwang, Kwang-kuo. 1987. Face and Favor: The Chinese Power Game. *American Journal of Sociology* 92(4):944–974.

Irons, Peter. 1983. *Justice at War*. Oxford: Oxford University Press.

Isaacs, Harold R. 1975. Basic Group Identity: The Idols of the Tribe. In *Ethnicity: Theory and Experience*, ed. Nathan Glazer and Daniel P. Moynihan, 29–52. Cambridge, Mass.: Harvard University Press.

Ito-Adler, James P. 1982. Japanese Family Enterprises in Brazil. Paper presented at the annual meeting of the American Anthropological Association, Washington, D.C., December.

Jiang, Joseph P. L. 1968. Toward a Theory of Pariah Entrepreneurship. In *Leadership and Authority: A Symposium*, ed. Gehan Wijeyewarndene, 147–162. Singapore: University of Malaya Press.

Johnson, Graham. 1982a. The Chinese Ethnic Community in the 1970s. In *From China to Canada: A History of Chinese Communities in Canada*, ed. Edgar Wickberg, 254–267. Toronto: McClelland and Stewart.

——. 1982b. A New Kind of Chinese. In *From China to Canada: A History of Chinese Communities in Canada*, ed. Edgar Wickberg, 244–253. Toronto: McClelland and Stewart.

Kelly, John D. 1989. The Methodicality of Fiji Gujarati Businessmen and the Ontological Basis of Economic Rationality. Paper presented at the 41st Annual Meeting of the Association for Asian Studies, Washington, D.C., 17 March.

Khare, R. S. 1984. *The Untouchable as Himself: Ideology, Identity, and Pragmatism among the Lucknow Chamars*. Cambridge: Cambridge University Press.

King, Ambrose Y. C. 1985. The Individual and Group in Confucianism: A Relational Perspective. In *Individualism and Holism: Studies in Confucian and Taoist Values*, ed. Donald Munro, 57–72. Ann Arbor: University of Michigan Center for Chinese Studies.

Kingston, Maxine Hong. 1975. *The Woman Warrior*. New York: Random House.

Kleinman, Arthur. 1986. *Social Origins of Distress and Disease: Depression, Neurasthenia, and Pain in Modern China*. New Haven: Yale University Press.

——. 1990. Personal correspondence.

Kleinman, Arthur, and Joan Kleinman. 1989. Suffering and Its Professional Transformation; Toward an Ethnography of Experience. Paper presented at the First Conference of the Society for Psychological Anthropology, San Diego, 6–8 October.

Kolenda, Pauline. 1985. *Caste in Contemporary India*. Prospect Heights, Ill.: Waveland Press.

Kondo, Dorinne. 1990. *Crafting Selves*. Chicago: University of Chicago Press.

Kung, Lydia. 1984. Taiwan Garment Workers. In *Lives: Chinese Working Women*, ed. Mary Sheridan and Janet Salaff, 109–122. Bloomington: Indiana University Press.

Lang, Olga. 1946. *Chinese Family and Society*. New Haven: Yale University Press.

Lelyveld, Joseph. 1967. Curbs on Chinese Retained in India. *New York Times*, 4 September, A12.

——. 1975. *Calcutta*. Hong Kong: Perennial Press.

Leng, Shao-chuan, and Jerome Alan Cohen. 1972. The Sino-Indian Dispute over the Internment and Detention of Chinese in India. In *China's Practice of International Law*, ed. Jerome Cohen, 268–320. Cambridge, Mass.: Harvard University Press.

Leong, S. T. 1980. The Hakka Chinese: Ethnicity and Migrations in Late Imperial

China. Paper presented at the annual meeting of the Association of Asian Studies, Washington, D.C.

Levy, Marion. 1963 [1949]. *The Family Revolution in Modern China*. New York: Octagon Books.

Light, Ivan. 1972. *Ethnic Enterprise in America*. Berkeley: University of California Press.

——. 1977. Numbers Gambling among Blacks: A Financial Institution. *American Sociological Review* 42:892–904.

Lin, Nan. 1988. Chinese Family Structure and Chinese Society. *Bulletin of the Institute of Ethnology* 65(Spring):59–129. Academia Sinica.

Lin Yutang. 1950. *Widow, Nun, and Courtesan*. New York: John Day.

Loewen, James W. 1971. *Mississippi Chinese: Between Black and White*. Cambridge, Mass.: Harvard University Press.

Lubell, Harold. 1974. *Calcutta: Its Urban Development and Economic Prospects*. Geneva: International Labour Office.

Lyman, Stanford. 1982. Foreword. In Robert Seto Quan, *Lotus among the Magnolias*, ix–xiv. Jackson: University Press of Mississippi.

McCreery, John L. 1976. Women's Property Rights and Dowry in China and South Asia. *Ethnology* 15(2):163–175.

Mandelbaum, David G. 1939. The Jewish Way of Life in Cochin. *Jewish Social Studies* 1:423–460.

Mark, Lindy Li. 1972. Taiwanese Lineage Enterprises: A Study in Familial Entrepreneurship. Ph.D. diss., University of California, Berkeley.

Marriott, McKim. 1968. Caste Ranking and Food Transactions: A Matrix Analysis. In *Structure and Change in Indian Society*, ed. Milton Singer and Bernard S. Cohn, 133–171. Chicago: Aldine.

Mauss, Marcel. 1985 [1938]. A Category of the Human Mind: The Notion of Person; the Notion of Self. In *The Category of the Person*, ed. Michael Carrithers, Steven Collins, and Steven Lukes, 1–25. Cambridge: Cambridge University Press.

Mayer, Adrian C. 1960. *Caste and Kinship in Central India*. Berkeley: University of California Press.

Mencher, Joan. 1974. The Caste System Upside Down, or the Not-So-Mysterious East. *Current Anthropology* 15:469–478.

Mines, Mattison. 1988. Conceptualizing the Person: Hierarchical Society and Individual Autonomy in India. *American Anthropologist* 90(3):568–579.

Morris, Colin. 1972. *The Discovery of the Individual, 1050–1200*. London: S. P. C. K. for the Church Historical Society.

Munro, Donald J. 1985. Introduction. In *Individualism and Holism: Studies in Confucian and Taoist Values*, ed. Donald Munro, 1–34. Ann Arbor: University of Michigan Center for Chinese Studies.

Murray, Alexander. 1978. *Reason and Society in the Middle Ages*. New York: Clarendon Press.

Netting, Robert, Richard Wilk, and Eric Arnould. 1984. *Households: Comparative and Historical Studies of the Domestic Group*. Berkeley: University of California Press.

New Encyclopaedia Britannica, The. 1982. Leather and Hides. Encyclopaedia Britannica.

Niehoff, Justin. 1987. The Villager as Industrialist: Ideologies of Household Manufacturing in Rural Taiwan. *Modern China* 13:278–309.

Nonini, Donald. 1979. The Mysteries of Capital Accumulation: Honoring the Gods and Gambling among Chinese in a Malaysian Market Town. In *Southeast Asia.* Vol. 3, *Proceedings of the First International Symposium on Asian Studies.* Hong Kong: Asian Research Service.

Noricks, Jay Smith, L. Helen Agler, Margaret Bartholomew, Susan Howarth-Smith, David Martin, Steve Pyles, and William Shapiro. 1987. Age, Abstract Thinking, and the American Concept of Person. *American Anthropologist* 89(3):667–675.

Olsen, Stephen. 1972. The Inculcation of Economic Values in Taipei Business Families. In *Economic Organization in Chinese Society,* ed. W. E. Willmott, 261–296. Stanford: Stanford University Press.

Omohundro, John T. 1981. *Chinese Merchant Families of Iloilo.* Athens: Ohio University Press.

Ortner, Sherry B., and Harriet Whitehead. 1981. Introduction. In *Sexual Meanings, The Cultural Construction of Gender and Sexuality,* ed. Sherry Ortner and Harriet Whitehead, 1–27. Cambridge: Cambridge University Press.

Owens, Ray. 1973. Peasant Entrepreneurs in a North Indian Industrial City. In *Entrepreneurship and Modernization of Occupational Cultures in South Asia,* Monograph No. 12, ed. Milton Singer. Monograph and Occasional Papers Series. Duke University Program in Comparative Studies in South Asia.

Oxfeld, Ellen. 1992. Individualism, Holism, and the Market Mentality: Notes on the Recollections of a Chinese Entrepreneur. *Cultural Anthropology* 7(2). (Also see Ellen Oxfeld Basu.)

Parkin, David. 1974. Congregational and Interpersonal Ideologies in Political Ethnicity. In *Urban Ethnicity,* ed. Abner Cohen, 119–157. London: Tavistock.

Parry, Jonathan, and Maurice Bloch. 1989. Introduction: Money and the Morality of Exchange. In *Money and the Morality of Exchange,* ed. Jonathan Parry and Maurice Bloch, 1–32. Cambridge: Cambridge University Press.

Pasternak, Burton. 1972. *Kinship and Community in Two Chinese Villages.* Stanford: Stanford University Press.

Patterson, Orlando. 1975. Context and Choice in Ethnic Allegiance: A Theoretical Framework and Caribbean Case Study. In *Ethnicity: Theory and Experience,* ed. Nathan Glazer and Daniel P. Moynihan, 305–349. Cambridge, Mass.: Harvard University Press.

Plattner, Stuart. 1983. Economic Custom in a Competitive Marketplace. *American Anthropologist* 85(4):848–858.

Polanyi, Karl. 1957. The Economy as Instituted Process. In *Trade and Market in the Early Empires,* ed. Karl Polanyi, Conrad Arensberg, and Harry Pearson, 243–270. Chicago: Henry Regnery.

Potter, Jack. 1970. Land and Lineage in Traditional China. In *Family and Kinship in Chinese Society,* ed. Maurice Freedman, 121–138. Stanford: Stanford University Press.

References

Potter, Sulamith Heins. 1988. The Cultural Construction of Emotion in Rural Chinese Social Life. *Cultural Anthropology* 16(2):181–208.
Potter, Sulamith Heins, and Jack M. Potter. 1990. *China's Peasants*. Cambridge: Cambridge University Press.
Purcell, Victor. 1965. *The Chinese in Southeast Asia*. London: Oxford University Press.
Pusey, Anne Wang, and Richard W. Wilson. 1982. Achievement Motivation and Small-Business Relationship Patterns in Chinese Society. In *Social Interaction in Chinese Society*, ed. Sidney Greenblatt, Richard Wilson, and Amy Auerbacher Wilson, 195–208. New York: Praeger.
Quinn, Naomi. 1986. The Directive Force of Self-Understanding: Evidence from Wives' Inner Conflicts. Paper prepared for presentation at the session "The Directive Force of Cultural Models" at the 85th Annual Meeting of the American Anthropological Association, Philadelphia, December.
Report on the Census of the Town of Calcutta. 1876. Taken on 6 April 1876 by H. Beverley. Calcutta: Bengal Secretariat Press.
Roland, Alan. 1988. *In Search of Self in India and Japan*. Princeton: Princeton University Press.
Rosaldo, Michelle Zimbalist. 1974. Woman, Culture, and Society: A Theoretical Overview. In *Woman, Culture, and Society*, ed. Michelle Zimbalist Rosaldo and Louise Lamphere, 17–42. Stanford: Stanford University Press.
——. 1980. The Use and Abuse of Anthropology: Reflections on Feminism and Cross-Cultural Understanding. *Signs* 5(Spring):389–417.
Rosaldo, Renato. 1986. From the Door of His Tent: The Fieldworker and the Inquisitor. In *Writing Culture*, ed. James Clifford and George Marcus, 77–97. Berkeley: University of California Press.
Rudner, David. 1989. Banker's Trust and the Culture of Banking among the Nattukottai Chettiars of Colonial South India. *Modern Asian Studies* 23(3):417–458.
Ryan, Edward J. 1961. *The Value System of a Chinese Community in Java*. Ph.D. diss., Harvard University.
Sahlins, Marshall. 1972. *Stone Age Economics*. Chicago: Aldine.
——. 1976. *Culture and Practical Reason*. Chicago: University of Chicago Press.
Said, Edward. 1978. *Orientalism*. New York: Pantheon.
Salaff, Janet W. 1981. *Working Daughters of Hong Kong: Filial Piety or Power in the Family?* Cambridge: Cambridge University Press.
Sartre, Jean-Paul. 1963. *Search for a Method*. New York: Vintage.
Schermerhorn, R. A. 1978. *Ethnic Plurality in India*. Tucson: University of Arizona Press.
Schneider, David. 1968. *American Kinship: A Cultural Account*. Englewood Cliffs, N.J.: Prentice-Hall.
Seldon, Mark. 1985. Income Inequality and the State. In *Chinese Rural Development*, ed. William Parish, 193–218. Armonk, N.Y.: M. E. Sharpe.
Seton-Karr, W. S. 1864. *Selections from Calcutta Gazettes of the Years 1784, 1785, 1786, 1787, & 1788, Showing the Political and Social Conditions of the*

English in India Eighty Years Ago. Calcutta: O. T. Cutter, Military Orphan Press.

Shweder, Richard, and Edmund J. Bourne. 1984. Does the Concept of Person Vary Cross-Culturally? In *Culture Theory: Essays on Mind, Self, and Emotion*, ed. Richard Shweder and Edmund Bourne, 158–199. Cambridge: Cambridge University Press.

Singer, Milton. 1968. The Indian Joint Family in Modern Industry. In *Structure and Change in Indian Society*, ed. Milton Singer and Bernard Cohn, 423–452. Chicago: Aldine.

Sinha, Pradip. 1978. *Calcutta in Urban History*. Calcutta: Firma, KLM.

Sircar, Jawhar. 1990. The Chinese of Calcutta. In *Calcutta: The Living City*, ed. Sukanta Chaudhuri, 64–66. Calcutta: Oxford University Press.

Skinner, G. William. 1957. *Chinese Society in Thailand: An Analytical History*. Ithaca: Cornell University Press.

———. 1958. *Leadership and Power in the Chinese Community in Thailand*. Ithaca: Cornell University Press.

———. 1968. Overseas Chinese Leadership: Paradigm for a Paradox. In *Leadership and Authority*, ed. Gehan Wijeyewardene, 191–207. Singapore: University of Malaya Press.

———. 1973a. Change and Persistence in Chinese Culture Overseas: A Comparison of Thailand and Java. In *Southeast Asia, the Politics of National Integration*, ed. John T. McAlister, 399–415. New York: Random House.

———. 1973b. Chinese Assimilation and Thai Politics. In *Southeast Asia, The Politics of National Integration*, ed. John T. McAlister, 383–396. New York: Random House.

Somers, Mary. 1964. *Peranakan Chinese Politics in Indonesia*. Interim Reports Series. Ithaca: Cornell University, Southeast Asia Program.

Sorensen, Clark. 1981. Women, Men, Inside, Outside: The Division of Labor in Rural Central Korea. In *Korean Women: View from the Inner Room*, ed. Laurel Kendall and Mark Peterson, 63–79. New Haven: East Rock Press.

Spence, Jonathan. 1978. *The Death of Woman Wang*. New York: Penguin.

Srinivas, M. N. 1966. *Social Change in Modern India*. Berkeley: University of California Press.

Stack, Carol. 1974. *All Our Kin*. New York: Harper and Row.

Stevens, William K. 1983. Calcutta, Symbol of Urban Misery, Won't Give Up. *The New York Times*, 5 June, sec. 1, p. 10.

Stites, Richard. 1985. Industrial Work as an Entrepreneurial Strategy. *Modern China* 11(2):227–246.

Strauch, Judith. 1981. Multiple Ethnicities in Malaysia: The Shifting Relevance of Alternative Chinese Categories. *Modern Asian Studies* 15(2):235–260.

———. 1983. Changing Village Life in Hong Kong: Immigrants in an Emigrant Community. Paper presented at symposium "Chinese Mobility" at the 82d Annual Meeting of the American Anthropological Association, Chicago, November.

Strauss, Claudia. 1987. Culture, Cognition, and Motives: The Directive Force of Beliefs about Work and Success. Unpublished draft.

References

——. 1990. Who Gets Ahead? Cognitive Responses to Heteroglossia in American Political Culture. *American Ethnologist* 17(2):312–328.

Strizower, Schifra. 1962. *Exotic Jewish Communities*. London: Tomas Yoseloff.

Su Zhiliang. 1988. A Summary of the History of the Secret Societies in Shanghai. Paper presented at "International Symposium on Modern Shanghai," 7–14 September.

Sung, Lung-sheng. 1981. Property and Family Division. In *The Anthropology of Taiwanese Society*, ed. Hill Gates and Emily Martin Ahern, 361–378. Stanford: Stanford University Press.

Thompson, Richard. 1979. Ethnicity vs. Class. *Ethnicity* 6(4):306–326.

——. 1980. From Kinship to Class: A New Model of Urban Overseas Chinese Social Organization. *Urban Anthropology* 9(3):265–293.

Times of India. 1963a. Internees Go Aboard China's Ships. 14 April:sec. 1, pg. 1.

——. 1963b. Another Batch Goes to Madras. 22 May:sec. 1, pg. 5.

——. 1963c. Second Batch to Leave Today. 25 May:sec. 1, pg. 5.

Traube, Elizabeth G. 1989. Secrets of Success in Postmodern Society. *Cultural Anthropology* 4(3):273–300.

Tu, Wei-ming. 1985. *Confucian Thought: Selfhood as Creative Transformation.* Albany: State University of New York Press.

Tysen, Frank. 1971. Interest Groups in Calcutta. In *Bengal: Change and Continuity*, Occasional Paper No. 16, ed. Robert Paul and Mary Beech, 227–237. South Asia Series. East Lansing: Michigan State University.

Ullman, Walter. 1966. *The Individual and Society in the Middle Ages*. Baltimore: Johns Hopkins University Press.

United Nations Council on Trade and Development (UNCTAD). 1971. *Leather and Leather Products*. New York: United Nations.

Voloshinov, V. N. [M. M. Bakhtin]. 1983. The Construction of the Utterance. Trans. Noel Owen. In *Bakhtin School Papers*. In *Russian Poetics in Translation*, no. 10, ed. Ann Shukman, 114–138. Oxford: RPT Publications.

Wakeman, Frederic. 1985. *The Great Enterprise: The Manchu Reconstruction of Imperial Order in Seventeenth-Century China*. Berkeley: University of California Press.

Wang Gungwu. 1981. *Community and Nation*. Singapore: Heineman Educational Books.

Wasserstrom, Jeffrey. 1984. Resistance to the One-Child Family. *Modern China* 10(3):345–374.

Watson, James L. 1975. *Emigration and the Chinese Lineage*. Berkeley: University of California Press.

Watson, Rubie. 1981. Class Differences and Affinal Relations in South China. *Man* 16:593–596.

——. 1984. Women's Property in Republican China: Rights and Practice. *Republican China* 10(November):1–12.

——. 1985. *Inequality among Brothers*. Cambridge: Cambridge University Press.

Weber, Max. 1978. *Max Weber: Selections in Translation*. Ed. W. G. Runciman. Trans. E. Matthews. Cambridge: Cambridge University Press.

——.1983 [1920–21]. *Max Weber on Capitalism, Bureaucracy, and Religion*. Ed. Stanislav Andreski. London: Allen and Unwin.

Wertheim, Willem Frederik. 1964. The Trading Minorities of Southeast Asia. In *East-West Parallels*, ed. W. F. Wertheim, 39–82. The Hague: W. Van Hoeve.

Willmott, Donald Earl. 1960. *The Chinese of Semarang*. Ithaca: Cornell University Press.

Wiser, Charlotte V., and William H. Wiser. 1971. *Behind Mud Walls*. Berkeley: University of California Press.

Wolf, Arthur. 1968. Adopt a Daughter-in-Law, Marry a Sister. *American Anthropologist* 70(5):864–874.

——. 1970. Chinese Kinship and Mourning Dress. In *Family and Kinship in Chinese Society*, ed. Maurice Freedman, 163–188. Stanford: Stanford University Press.

——. 1974. Gods, Ghosts, and Ancestors. In *Religion and Ritual in Chinese Society*, ed. Arthur Wolf, 131–182. Stanford: Stanford University Press.

——. 1981. Domestic Organization. In *The Anthropology of Taiwanese Society*, ed. Hill Gates and Emily Martin Ahern, 341–360. Stanford: Stanford University Press.

Wolf, Arthur, and Chieh-shan Huang. 1980. *Marriage and Adoption in China, 1845- 1945*. Stanford: Stanford University Press.

Wolf, Eric. 1982. *Europe and the People without History*. Cambridge: Cambridge University Press.

Wolf, Margery. 1970. Child Training and the Chinese Family. In *Family and Kinship in Chinese Society*, ed. Maurice Freedman, 37–62. Stanford: Stanford University Press.

——. 1972. *Women and the Family in Rural Taiwan*. Stanford: Stanford University Press.

——. 1974. Chinese Women: Old Skills in a New Context. In *Woman, Culture, and Society*, ed. Michelle Zimbalist Rosaldo and Louise Lamphere, 157–172. Stanford: Stanford University Press.

Wong, Bernard. 1982. *Chinatown: Economic Adaptation and Ethnic Identity of the Chinese*. New York: Holt, Rinehart, and Winston.

Wong, Siu-lun. 1988. *Emigrant Entrepreneurs: Shanghai Industrialists in Hong Kong*. Hong Kong: Oxford University Press.

Yanagisako, Sylvia Junko. 1979. Family and Household: The Analysis of Domestic Groups. *Annual Review of Anthropology* 8:161–205.

——. 1985. *Transforming the Past: Tradition and Kinship among Japanese Americans*. Stanford: Stanford University Press.

Yang, Martin. 1945. *A Chinese Village*. New York: Columbia University Press.

Index

Anthropology of Contemporary Issues

A SERIES EDITED BY

ROGER SANJEK